Lecture Notes in Computer Science 2820

Edited by G. Goos, J. Hartmanis, and J. van Leeuwen

Springer
Berlin
Heidelberg
New York
Hong Kong
London
Milan
Paris
Tokyo

Giovanni Vigna   Erland Jonsson
Christopher Kruegel (Eds.)

Recent Advances in Intrusion Detection

6th International Symposium, RAID 2003
Pittsburgh, PA, USA, September 8-10, 2003
Proceedings

Springer

Series Editors

Gerhard Goos, Karlsruhe University, Germany
Juris Hartmanis, Cornell University, NY, USA
Jan van Leeuwen, Utrecht University, The Netherlands

Volume Editors

Giovanni Vigna
Christopher Kruegel
University of California, Santa Barbara, Department of Computer Science
Santa Barbara, CA 93106, USA
E-mail: {vigna, chris}@cs.ucsb.edu

Erland Jonsson
Chalmers University of Technology, Department of Computer Engineering
41296 Goteborg, Sweden
E-mail: erland.jonsson@ce.chalmers.se

Cataloging-in-Publication Data applied for

A catalog record for this book is available from the Library of Congress

Bibliographic information published by Die Deutsche Bibliothek
Die Deutsche Bibliothek lists this publication in the Deutsche Nationalbibliographie;
detailed bibliographic data is available in the Internet at <http://dnb.ddb.de>.

CR Subject Classification (1998): K.6.5, K.4, E.3, C.2, D.4.6

ISSN 0302-9743
ISBN 3-540-40878-9 Springer-Verlag Berlin Heidelberg New York

Springer-Verlag Berlin Heidelberg New York
a member of BertelsmannSpringer Science+Business Media GmbH

http://www.springer.de

© Springer-Verlag Berlin Heidelberg 2003
Printed in Germany

Typesetting: Camera-ready by author, data conversion by Olgun Computergrafik
Printed on acid-free paper   SPIN: 10953587   06/3142   5 4 3 2 1 0

Preface

On behalf of the Program Committee, it is our pleasure to present to you the proceedings of the Sixth Symposium on Recent Advances in Intrusion Detection (RAID 2003).

The program committee received 44 full paper submissions from 10 countries. All submissions were carefully reviewed by at least three program committee members or additional intrusion detection experts according to the criteria of scientific novelty, importance to the field, and technical quality. The program committee meeting was held in Berkeley, USA on May 14–15. Thirteen papers were selected for presentation and publication in the conference proceedings.

The conference technical program included both fundamental research and practical issues, and was shaped around the following topics: network infrastructure, anomaly detection, correlation, modeling and specification, and sensor technologies.

The slides presented by the authors are available on the RAID 2003 web site, http://www.raid-symposium.org/raid2003.

We would like to thank the authors that submitted papers as well as the program committee members and the additional reviewers who volunteered their time to create a quality program. In addition, we want to thank the Conference General Chair, John McHugh, for organizing the conference in Pittsburgh, Joshua Haines for publicizing the conference, Don McGillen for finding support from our sponsors, and Christopher Kruegel for maintaining the RAID web site and preparing the conference proceedings.

Special thanks go to our sponsors Cisco Systems and Symantec, who provided financial support for student participation to the symposium, and to CERT/CMU for hosting the conference.

September 2003   Giovanni Vigna
                                                                 Erland Jonsson

Organization

RAID 2003 was organized by and gratefully acknowledges the support of the Center for Computer and Communications Security at Carnegie Mellon University and the CERT Coordination Center.

Conference Chairs

General Chair: John McHugh (CERT/SEI, Carnegie Mellon University, USA)

Program Chairs: Giovanni Vigna (UC Santa Barbara, USA)
Erland Jonsson (Chalmers University of Technology, Sweden)

Publication Chair: Christopher Kruegel (UC Santa Barbara, USA)

Publicity Chair: Joshua Haines (MIT Lincoln Laboratory, USA)

Sponsor Chair: Don McGillen (Carnegie Mellon University, USA)

Program Committee

Marc Dacier	Eurecom, France
Hervé Debar	France Telecom R&D, France
Joshua Haines	MIT Lincoln Laboratory, USA
Dick Kemmerer	UC Santa Barbara, USA
Calvin Ko	Network Associates Inc., USA
Christopher Kruegel	UC Santa Barbara, USA
Wenke Lee	Georgia Institute of Technology, USA
Ulf Lindqvist	SRI, USA
Roy Maxion	Carnegie Mellon University, USA
Ludovic Mé	Supélec, France
Vern Paxson	ACIRI/LBNL, USA
Phil Porras	SRI, USA
Rama Sekar	SUNY Stony Brook, USA
Stuart Staniford	Silicon Defense, USA
Kymie Tan	Melbourne University, Australia
Al Valdes	SRI, USA
Andreas Wespi	IBM Research, Switzerland
S. Felix Wu	UC Davis, USA
Diego Zamboni	IBM Research, Switzerland

Steering Committee

Marc Dacier (Chair)	Eurecom, France
Hervé Debar	France Telecom R&D, France
Deborah Frincke	University of Idaho, USA
Ming-Yuh Huang	The Boeing Company, USA
Wenke Lee	Georgia Institute of Technology, USA
Ludovic Mé	Supélec, France
S. Felix Wu	UC Davis, USA
Andreas Wespi	IBM Research, Switzerland
Giovanni Vigna	UC Santa Barbara, USA

Additional Reviewers

Dominique Alessandri	IBM Zurich Research Laboratory, Switzerland
Magnus Almgren	Chalmers University of Technology, Sweden
Sandeep Bhatkar	SUNY Stony Brook, USA
Ramesh Govindan	University of Southern California, USA
Jeffery Hansen	Carnegie Mellon University, USA
Klaus Julisch	IBM Zurich Research Laboratory, Switzerland
Kevin Killourhy	Carnegie Mellon University, USA
Zhenkai Liang	SUNY Stony Brook, USA
Emilie Lundin	Chalmers University of Technology, Sweden
Darren Mutz	UC Santa Barbara, USA
Fabien Pouget	Eurecom, France
William Robertson	UC Santa Barbara, USA
Umesh Shankar	University of California, Berkeley, USA
Prem Uppuluri	SUNY Stony Brook, USA
Fredrik Valeur	UC Santa Barbara, USA
V. Venkatakrishnan	SUNY Stony Brook, USA
Wei Xu	SUNY Stony Brook, USA

Table of Contents

Anomaly Detection II

Mitigating Distributed Denial of Service Attacks Using a Proportional-Integral-Derivative Controller

Marcus Tylutki and Karl Levitt

Security Laboratory
Department of Computer Science
University of California, Davis
{tylutki,levitt}@cs.ucdavis.edu

Abstract. Distributed Denial of Service (DDoS) attacks exploit the availability of servers and routers, resulting in the severe loss of their connectivity. We present a distributed, automated response model that utilizes a Proportional-Integral-Derivative (PID) controller to aid in handling traffic flow management. PID control law has been used in electrical and chemical engineering applications since 1934 and has proven extremely useful in stabilizing relatively unpredictable flows. This model is designed to prevent incoming traffic from exceeding a given threshold, while allowing as much incoming, legitimate traffic as possible. In addition, this model focuses on requiring less demanding modifications to external routers and networks than other published distributed response models that impact the effect of DDoS attacks.

Keywords: Distributed Attacks, PID control law, Distributed Denial of Service, DDoS, Denial of Service, DoS, Control Theory, Automated Response.

1 Introduction

Distributed Denial of Service (DDoS) attacks originate from multiple slave machines, each previously compromised by a worm or worm-like behavior [1]. DDoS attacks such as Stacheldraht, Trinoo, and Tribal Flood Network [1, 2] have become an increasing threat since the CERT advisory [3] released on January 10, 2001. This is due, in part, to the increasing number of novel worms (e.g., Nimda [4]) and Denial of Service (DoS) attacks. Newer versions of well-known DDoS attacks generally use newer vulnerabilities to propagate, creating more slaves, and use new DoS vulnerabilities to increase the effectiveness of each slave's attack [2].

Previously, there have been two main components used in approaches that alleviate the effects of DDoS attacks: IP traceback [5, 6] and bandwidth pushback [7–9]. Each of these approaches requires a significant amount of cooperation from external networks. IP traceback is initiated from the local network and expands to external networks to localize the sources of the attack. As the traceback occurs, bandwidth pushback filters DDoS traffic within the routers closest to the attack. These approaches require all pushback routers to be directly connected to at least one additional pushback router. Extending this pushback network to include most backbone routers is expected to be difficult, if not impossible. Although distinct remote pushback router networks can exist to mitigate the effects of an attack, if the attack is

G. Vigna, E. Jonsson, and C. Kruegel (Eds.): RAID 2003, LNCS 2820, pp. 1–16, 2003.

sufficiently distributed, the effects will be minimized, since foreign pushback networks may not identify the attack traffic.

We present a bandwidth pushback model that only affects one router per external network, and does not require modifications of backbone routers, but does require a multilateral trust model and authentication via a public key infrastructure (PKI). The focus of this paper is to describe how a control theoretic model typically used in vastly different applications, can be integrated into aspects of computer security. This assumes all external hosts must pass through one of these border routers. This approach requires much less router communication and cooperation within an external network since this approach does not require IP traceback within an external network, and only requires the use of one border router per external network capable of dropping packets destined for the local network. This model uses a filtering method based on Proportional-Integral-Derivative (PID) control theory to predict traffic flow[1] changes in each border router. This information, along with the ratio of legitimate to DDoS packets, determines how much traffic that is destined for the local network each router should drop. Traditional traffic models [10–13] predict aggregate traffic flows of various types (e.g., wireless, DSL, ISDN), or are used to generate traffic [14, 15]. PID control theory gives immediate, real-time predictions of highly erratic flows, and how best to respond to maintain preset conditions. Similarly, PID control theory can account for hidden patterns in traffic flow, and has been widely used in many engineering disciplines [16]. Traditional traffic models, on the other hand, do not account for these additional unknown attack patterns. According to recent surveys [17], 90% of control loops in process industries use PID control.

2   PID Control Law Background

Many new intrusion detection and response research projects use control theory to aid in reasoning from unpredictable events. One widely used application of control theory is PID control theory [16], which has proven extremely useful in controlling variables exhibiting unpredictable behavior. We examine three key types of parameters to aid in controlling such a variable:

- y_o : the observed value of the parameter we wish to control
- y_d : the desired value of the parameter we wish to control
- x : the value of a directly controllable variable which effects y_o

The parameter y_o is prone to disturbances that are impossible to definitively predict, thus making y_o impossible to predict. However, the value of y_o can be influenced by a directly controlled parameter, x. Suppose a vehicle heating system is activated and warm air is circulated inside the vehicle, making the passengers more comfortable. As time passes, the temperature inside the vehicle becomes too warm, causing the passengers to lower the heat. Perhaps they lower the heat too much and become cold again. The variable x in this example represents the heating system control setting. The parameter y_d represents the temperature at which the passengers are comfortable, and the parameter y_o represents the temperature that the passengers experience.

---

[1] Traffic flows analyzed are those that are only destined for the local network, as opposed to total traffic passing through the external border router.

PID control law helps predict and stabilize of the value of y_o so that it converges to the desired value y_d. As the name states, there are three main components (Proportional, Integral, and Derivative) that shall be discussed separately to explain each of their roles.

Proportional Mode. This mode yields a control signal that is proportional to the disturbance affecting the observed parameter:

$$c(t) = K_c e(t) + c_b \qquad (1)$$

The value of $e(t)$ represents the error at time t, which is usually y_o - y_d. K_c is the proportionality constant between x and y_o. The value of c_b represents an offset between the theoretical and actual value of $c(t)$ and typically refers to mechanical abnormalities, such as poorly calibrated measuring instruments. This method is usually utilized alone in systems with highly unpredictable disturbances.

Integral Mode. This mode yields a control signal that responds to errors that build up over time:

$$c(t) = \frac{K_c}{\tau_I} \int e(t)dt + c_b \qquad (2)$$

Here τ_I represents the reset time or aging constant. This effectively controls how fast or slow errors build up over time. The drawback with this mode is that misconfigurations can cause *integral windup* which is caused by lasting errors and control signal boundaries and results in the signal remaining at a maximum (or minimum) value indefinitely (unless particular counter-measures are employed).

Derivative Mode. This mode yields a control signal that predicts future changes by examining the rate of change in the error signal, and is represented by:

$$c(t) = K_c \tau_D \frac{de(t)}{dt} + c_b \qquad (3)$$

This mode anticipates future errors by examining the rates of error change. τ_D represents how much influence the rates of error change have on the control signal.

All of these modes can be combined to yield the final overall form of PID control law:

$$c(t) = K_c \left[e(t) + \frac{1}{\tau_I} \int e(t)dt + \tau_D \frac{de(t)}{dt} \right] + c_b \qquad (4)$$

The values of K_c, τ_I, and τ_D, are generally learned from training data or empirically derived in specific cases.

3   Response Model

Fig. 1 depicts how this response model can be used to mitigate the effects of DDoS attacks originating from Networks A and B that target Network C. The term border router used in this case represents both the actual border router, and additional systems required to implement certain actions, such a firewall for dropping packets. Each border router in Fig. 1 is the only access point between the network and the rest of the Internet. Border router C notifies all other border routers how much traffic destined for Network C they should drop. Since attack packets primarily come from Network B, a majority of traffic from Network B is dropped at Network B's border router. Since Network A's traffic has many fewer attacks, nearly all of their traffic is accepted by Network C.

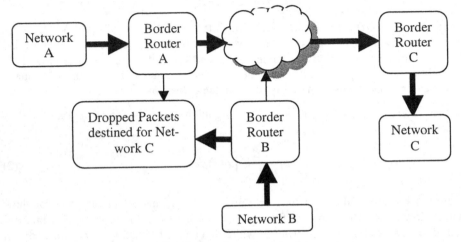

Fig. 1. Overall response model

3.1 Assumptions

For this model to function properly, a few assumptions must be made:

- There is a sensor available that can determine if a packet is part of a DDoS attack.
- The flow of packets destined for the protected network from any border router can be detected.
- There is a technique that can be employed that will drop a percentage of packets destined for the protected network at the source's border router.
- The border router that forwarded a particular DDoS attack packet can be accurately identified.

Now we shall rationalize the feasibility of each of our assumptions. The first assumption may be satisfied with work previously done in this area by attempting to use heuristics and attack signatures to identify DDoS packets [18]. Most response approaches towards DDoS attacks either treat the attack as a congestion problem [8, 9], or allude to heuristics that may be used to detect such attacks with significant uncertainty [7, 8]. It is important to note that using this detection tool on every incoming packet is infeasible. However, using it probabilistically gives a rough estimate of attack and non-attack packets coming from a particular network. This assumption does not require a perfect detector, merely one that has reasonable performance, as described later in Section 4.1. If no such detector is available, this model can resort to categorizing attack traffic from non-attack traffic based off of traffic flow analysis, as previous response approaches have done [7–9].

The itrace protocol [19] is a possible candidate to satisfy the second assumption. The itrace protocol must be in place on all border routers. This protocol probabilistically sends itrace packets from the border router to the destination and source in an attempt to trace back the actual sources of the DDoS attack. In addition, the protocol can be used simply for flow measurement, to quantify the flow of traffic headed towards the target network that is passing through that border router. If our fourth assumption is valid, itrace packets need only to be sent to the destination.

Authentication of itrace messages could be implemented with HMAC [28], as suggested in a previous itrace draft [29]. Additionally, filtering requests sent from one border router to another can be authenticated with SSL. SSL requires a PKI, although HMAC uses a single secret shared key. Both of these authentication mechanisms require a PKI. Since each filtering request only involves traffic destined for the sender of the request, then provided the sender is authenticated, the filtering request should be processed. The discovery of new border routers could be done at a centralized location, although it will serve as an attack magnet, and present difficulties such as scaling issues, and conflicts of commercial interests. Alternatively, it may be assumed for the purposes of this paper that all border routers are participating, and the mechanism is in a form of steady state (i.e., the list of participating border routers remains constant). If this assumption is used, filtering requests would only be initiated from participating border routers (or from compromised backbone routers), since filtering requests initiated behind a particular border router could be easily blocked.

Running a secure server on each border router is a simple implementation that satisfies the third assumption. The server then modifies the appropriate outgoing firewall rule based on packets that are destined for the border router that is sending the update. Similarly, one or more firewalls could be placed before reaching the border router that could run a secure server. Most DDoS response approaches require this assumption as well, and utilize similar implementations [7–9].

The fourth assumption can be upheld with the cooperation of foreign networks. If each foreign network drops outgoing packets that have source addresses not within their domain, the attacks are forced to spoof only addresses within the network of the actual source. Cisco Express Forwarding [20] is an example of a technology that may be used to accomplish this with virtually no effect on throughput. Since each border router drops packets not originating from within their network, it may be easy to share this information with cooperating border routers along the same channel as filtering requests. Additionally, a traceroute may be initiated to determine the corresponding border router closest to the particular foreign address, or traceroute may be used to verify that certain addresses lie behind the border router that claims to be closest to it. By examining the list of hops between the local border router and a particular foreign address, depicted explicitly in traceroute output, the foreign border router address, taken from the list of authenticated participating border routers, that is located closest to the particular foreign address is the closest border router in front of the particular foreign address, given the assumption that all border routers each provide the only connection from the network behind them to backbone routers and all other foreign addresses. Thus, the source address of all packets that the protected network receives can be used with a hash table to determine which border router forwarded the packet.

Unlike some pushback models [8][9], this model does not identify attack prefixes in order to prevent spoofed packets. If attack prefixes were identified, attacking hosts behind the border router could spoof attacks appearing to originate from a distributed set of addresses, making prefix identification difficult. Similarly, at a leaf pushback router, attackers may initiate spoofed attacks from a distributed set of addresses, foiling any attempts at attack prefix identification. Since border routers used in the model we present are similar to these leaf pushback routers, attack prefixes are not identified.

3.2 Application of PID Control

There are three main goals of this model:

- Maximize the percentage of legitimate packets in the flow reaching the protected network.
- Bound the total amount of traffic passing through to the protected network.
- Minimize the overall impact of the overhead produced by this model.

In order for a PID controller to optimize these goals, we define $c(t)$, y_o, y_d, and x_i as follows:

$c_i(t)$ = the change in the filter ratio of border router i.
y_o = the observed value of incoming traffic.
y_d = the desired value of incoming traffic.
x_i = the filter ratio of border router i, which effects y_o.

For example, a value of .60 for $c_i(t)$ would translate to border router i dropping an additional 60% of all packets destined for the protected network. If border router i was already blocking 15% of the packets destined for the protected network, it would now block 75% of these packets.

3.3 Border Router Reconfiguration Details

The response model first sorts each border router by the percentage of legitimate packets in their flow destined for the protected network. The border router with the most legitimate traffic percentage is unblocked and added to a running sum until adding the traffic of the next border router in the list would violate the limit of the total amount of traffic set by the protected network. For example, suppose the protected network depicted in Fig. 1 has a traffic limit of 1000. Suppose Network A has a traffic flow of 400, and Network B has a traffic flow of 3,000, each destined for Network C. First, all of Network A's traffic would be allowed since it has relatively fewer attacks. Network B's traffic would not be added yet, since adding it would violate the limit of 1000. PID control law would then be used to determine the percentage of traffic that should be allowed from Network B in order to obtain a total traffic flow close to the limit. If Network D was added to Fig. 1, where Network D has an even higher percentage of attack traffic than Network B, all of Network D's traffic would be blocked.

One disadvantage of this model is its bias against "smaller" routers. Although these border routers are significantly close to backbone routers and handle a significant amount of traffic, the traffic one border router sends to another particular border router may be much smaller than those of other border routers. If the system still requires to service as many legitimate packets as possible within the constraints of this model, then this must be accepted. Alternatively, if this activity is undesirable, smaller routers could occasionally be unblocked for brief periods, sacrificing a few legitimate packets in order to give smaller routers a chance at successfully transmitting.

Additionally, new multi-lateral trust issues inherent in this model introduce new problems, not present in pushback. Although it is assumed that it can be determined if a border router is indeed a border router, their trustworthiness towards the execution of received filtering requests may be uncertain. If a border router is asked to block 100% of traffic destined for a protected network, and traffic still persists after a significant time period, it is obvious that particular border router is untrustworthy. In the more complex case, where a border router is asked to block a percentage of traffic between 0 and 100%, the results may be tested by the observation of the success of TCP replies from machines within the protected network, although this is notably difficult. Another possible solution may include the examination of flow rates from the particular border router. If the border router's flow appears to raise or remain constant, despite numerous filtering requests with continually increasing block percentages, then it may be requested to block 100% of such traffic, and the border router with the next highest percentage of legitimate traffic may switch places with the erratic border router.

Additional trust issues can arise on the opposite side. If a border router receives a throttling request, ISP service level agreements (SLAs) may prevent them from executing a valid request. Additionally, there may be an issue with attacks on the throttling request channel. These issues are very challenging, and generally beyond the scope of this paper. However, in order to address these issues, the assumption mentioned earlier can be applied, in which all border routers are authenticated and participating, and the list of border routers is in a form of steady state. As a result, attacks initiated from behind border routers are prevented, provided border routers are not compromised. This significantly reduces the likelihood of attacks on this communication channel. Another assumption, required in order to satisfy these secondary trust issues, is that SLAs of ISP border routers must be in agreement with throttling requests produced by the model. This heavily depends on the wording of SLAs, as well as other legal issues. From a technical point of view, however, if a border router decides not to comply with a throttling request from a foreign border router, they may experience a more extreme form of "throttling" at the requesting foreign border router, resulting in a much lower amount of end-to-end service than if the throttling request was honored.

Similar trust issues are present for the acquisition of information regarding foreign address to border router translations. It is possible the border router may send false information, or perhaps the border router is an internal gateway rather than a border router. These complex trust issues are difficult to resolve, and beyond the scope of this paper.

4   Experiment

This section will discuss the details of an experiment carried out to determine the effectiveness of this response model in comparison to a pushback model and the baseline case. Fig. 2 depicts the overall setup of our experiment. Host *xeno* represents the target border router of the DDoS attack, where hosts *baruntse* and *izzy* represent border routers that are relaying traffic that includes attack and non-attack packets. However, for this experiment, the attack and non-attack traffic is generated by hosts *baruntse* and *izzy* and is received by host *xeno*.

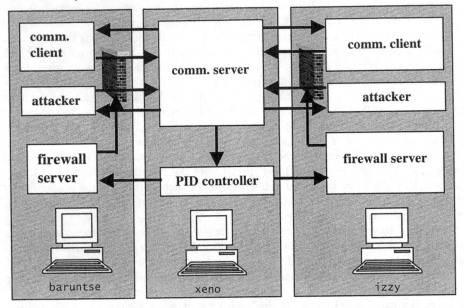

Fig. 2. Experiment setup

4.1 Assumptions

We shall now discuss a few assumptions that were made during this experiment:

Uniform packet weights. DDoS attack packets and non-attack packets are assumed to have an equal impact on the protected services.

Only one DDoS target. It is assumed that only one network, *xeno*, is experiencing a DDoS attack.

Firewall servers in place. It is assumed that each border router is running a firewall server.

Limited types of spoofed packets. The border router that forwarded a particular attack can be identified. This assumption was described in detail within Section 3.1.

DDoS traffic protocol. This experiment assumes that all DDoS traffic is over TCP/IP. Although this model can handle attacks over UDP, UDP tests were not included in this experiment. In the event UDP traffic is included, a partially blocked router may have the effect of a fully blocked router, since a significantly lossy voice or video link is useless[2]. One known solution to this problem includes the use of incorporating Quality of Service (QoS) guarantees towards DoS attacks [21].

---

[2] However, periodic status updates sent over UDP may be relatively unaffected.

Table 1. Example with an inaccurate packet analyzer

Border Router (BR)	Actual LT% (ALT%)	OLT% Range w/ DA=90%	Result on BR Ordering (DA=90%)	OLT% w/ FP=30%, FN=40%
1	100%	90%-100%	remains same	70%
2	75%	65%-85%	remains same	62.5%
3	50%	40%-60%	remains same	55%
4	25%	15%-35%	may swap with 5	47.5%
5	10%	0%-20%	may swap with 4	43%

Attack packets must be detected consistently. The initial assumption used for this experiment held that attack packets are assumed to be distinguishable from non-attack packets with 100% accuracy and every packet is analyzed. However, with some analysis, this assumption was lessened due to the properties and assumptions of this model. A less accurate detector could potentially modify the order in which border routers are sorted. Table 1 depicts an example comparing results of inaccurate detectors with a flawless detector. The percentage of legitimate traffic (LT%) sent from the corresponding border router measured by a flawless detector is shown in the second column. The variance of the observed LT% (OLT%) is inversely proportional to the detector's accuracy. If the detection accuracy (DA) is 90%, the only result (on average) would be the possible swap of border router 4 with border router 5, since the observed LT% of border router 4 may be 15%, and the observed value of border router 5 may be 20%. If traffic is only accepted from border routers 1, 2, and 3, then the possible swap of border router 4 and 5 is insignificant, since their traffic will be fully blocked in either case. In the second case, the detector has a constant false positive percentage, and a false negative percentage. If the detector maintains constant false positive and false negative percentages for each traffic flow from different border routers, the border router order remains unchanged for almost any accuracy, as long as the false positive percentage (FP) plus the false negative percentage (FN) is no larger than 100%. This statement is based on the following facts. The equation for determining the average observed LT% is:

$$ALT\% + (1 - ALT\%) \cdot FN - ALT\% \cdot FP = ALT\% \cdot (1 - (FP + FN)) + FN$$

where ALT% represents the actual legitimate traffic percentage. This equation for observed LT% increases as ALT% increases, as long as FP + FN is no greater than 100%. Thus, this assumption was modified to hold that the detector must have a false positive and false negative rate such that their sum does not exceed 100% and each packet must be analyzed. As long as multiple DDoS attacks are not in progress, it may be reasonable to assume that the FP and FN performance of a detector will remain constant across traffic flows from different networks. All other DDoS response approaches [7–9] only identify DDoS attacks based on traffic flow analysis. This model can support large, but consistent errors in a detector. If such a detector meets these constraints, this model may be used to evaluate traffic flows in a way that is superior to previous response approaches. Similarly, if the sensor used in pushback, which categorizes attack traffic based on traffic flow rates, satisfies these properties, it may be used within an implementation of this model to classify attack traffic as well as a sensor with 100% accuracy.

Attacks do not originate from within the protected network. Attack packets are assumed to not originate from within the protected network.

PID mode and parameters are static. Once the PID controller is started, the mode of control (Proportional, Proportional-Derivative, or Proportional-Integral-Derivative) cannot be changed, nor can the corresponding constants K_c, τ_I, and τ_D, which are used for both *izzy* and *baruntse*.

Attacks do not bypass the TCP stack. Attack packets are assumed to not violate the TCP stack. If attacks bypassed the TCP stack (e.g., a syn flood [22]), they would presumably be easier to detect with TCP header analysis. Such attacks could be represented by a different packet weight.

4.2 Technical Details

Each host was installed with FreeBSD 4.5-stable, and hosts *baruntse* and *izzy* were configured with dummynet [23] and ipfw. Ipfw can simulate a lossy network by dropping a random percentage of packets with a plr argument (e.g., ipfw pipe 1, config plr .50 would simulate a network that drops 50% of the packets for traffic matching the characteristics described in pipe 1).

The program comm. server on *xeno* accepts multiple simultaneous connections created from the non-attack client (comm. client) and the attack client (attacker) on each border router. Each of these connections sends a single character via TCP/IP to comm. server, with a non-attack connection sending the character 'B' and an attack sending the character 'A'. A Poisson probability distribution function was used to determine when the next "event" (i.e., connection and transmission) should occur to generate psuedo-random legitimate and attack traffic [24]. Attack traffic is crafted to have smaller delays than legitimate traffic. The comm. server program then sends a report every 20 seconds to the PID controller program, which includes the total traffic received and the portion of non-attack traffic received within that interval. The PID controller program then uses PID control theory to predict the percentage each border router should block to maintain the two major overall constraints: bound the incoming traffic to *xeno* to a predetermined limit and maximize the incoming traffic flow to contain the highest percentage of non-attack traffic as possible. Many of the calculations require information of traffic that *xeno* and *baruntse* would send if they were unblocked. This was estimated from the traffic received by *xeno* and the percentage that the corresponding router was blocking. For example, if 100 transmissions were received from *baruntse* within the 20-second interval, and *baruntse* is blocking 50% of packets destined for *xeno*, then roughly 200 transmissions could have been sent if *baruntse* was not blocking outgoing packets to *xeno*. This becomes extremely difficult to predict if *baruntse* was blocking 100% of packets destined for *xeno*. As a result, the highest block percentage is set to 99%, always allowing some transmissions to be received from *baruntse* and *izzy*.

Blocking a percentage of packets does not necessarily translate into blocking the same percentage of successful transmissions over TCP/IP. TCP uses exponential backoff for retransmissions [25], essentially doubling the timeout timer for each retransmission. This translation of blocking percentages was incorporated into the PID controller before sending corresponding UDP blocking messages to the appropriate firewall server. Once received, the firewall server updates the appropriate rule with the ipfw command.

5 Results and Interpretation

In this section, we shall discuss the results of our experiment and how they may be applied. In each case, PID control law constants (K_c, τ_I, and τ_D) were manually tuned by trial and error. Numerous other standard tuning techniques exist [16], although each tends to make varying assumptions in order to use them (i.e., they are applicable only for certain well-defined chemical or electrical systems). Most approaches tend to utilize a seesaw approach comparable to Newton's Method for obtaining the root of an equation. Due to the dependencies between control parameters, this tuning approach becomes more complex as a more advanced form of PID control is used. Since PID control law has not yet been applied towards computer security or network flows to create useful simplifications, a trial and error approach was used.

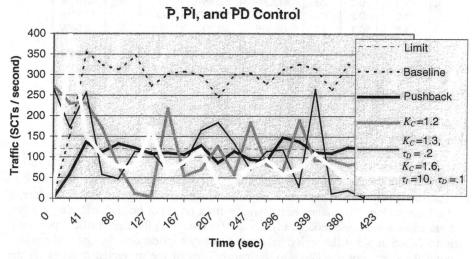

Fig. 3. Results of Proportional, Proportional Integral, and Proportional Derivative Control

Fig. 3 depicts the effects of this model under the effects of a DDoS attack from hosts *izzy* and *baruntse* using P, PD, and PID modes of control. Traffic is measured in successful single character TCP/IP transmissions (SCTs). The limit of total permissible traffic for this experiment was set to 120 SCTs/second. Baseline represents the traffic experienced if no responses are initiated to the DDoS attack *and* the system is capable of handling the increased flow resulting from the attack. Given that the limit is set to 120 SCTs/second, the protected system will likely continually halt and restart, resulting in an average traffic flow that is serviced to be as low as 20 SCTs/second. The pushback line in Fig. 3 depicts the effects if an optimal pushback model was used, in which attack packets were detected instantaneously with 100% accuracy, and all responses to block every source of the attack occur instantaneously. An actual pushback approach generally attempts to cache and/or throttle bandwidth as soon as an attack is detected, while it traces back attacks to block as close to the sources as possible. This would result in a higher traffic rate at the beginning of the attack, as well as a lower percentage of legitimate traffic serviced if their cache is not large enough. Additionally, since all pushback approaches categorize attack traffic from traffic flow analysis, it is highly likely the percentage of legitimate traffic in the flow entering their protected network will be significantly less than 100%. The oscillations present in Fig. 3 are primarily due to the impact of Poisson probability distribution on transmission delays described in Section 4.2. The three modes of PID control (P, PD, PID) shown performed best in their respective modes. Although the performance of optimal pushback is clearly superior, the performance of the various modes of PID control perform significantly well, considering their more realistic assumptions.

Table 2. Statistical results

K_c	τ_D	τ_I	Average Traffic Flow (SCTs/sec)	Standard Deviation	Max	Min	LT%
1.3	0.2	20	113.316	82.8875	325	15	49.65%
1.3	0.2	50	100.421	86.1300	306	5	53.11%
1.6	0.1	10	96.316	40.1072	165	36	52.64%
1.3	0.1	---	90.684	59.3240	248	21	50.63%
1.3	0.2	---	103.211	74.5509	265	3	50.94%
1.5	0.1	---	104.579	87.6263	282	10	55.91%
1	---	---	76.368	70.0216	288	3	50.96%
1.2	---	---	107.158	65.1001	231	4	51.13%
1.4	---	---	112.211	97.1811	423	4	49.88%
1.6	---	---	119.158	72.9926	282	6	51.37%
Pushback	---	---	117.368	17.0366	148	86	100%
Baseline	---	---	290.962963	26.4217	356	246	38.59%

Results with different values of K_c, τ_I, and τ_D have been summarized in Table 2 on the following page. The values in each column are taken after the second update of traffic information, since some runs started with a report of no traffic during the first update, and the response model only starts after receiving the first traffic report indicating a DDoS attack. Like with most control theory applications, the optimal solution of control parameters is relative to the capabilities of the protected network. If the protected servers have a very large queue, then perhaps a solution with a large standard deviation is acceptable as long as the average is close to the acceptable limit. An example in the table satisfying these conditions is $K_c = 1.6$, since it has the closest average to the traffic limit. If they have a very small queue, standard deviation would become much more important, even if the total traffic received is significantly lower than other approaches that are closer to the limit. These conditions may be satisfied with the PID mode of control, with $K_c = 1.6$, $\tau_I = 10$, and $\tau_D = .1$, since this has a much lower standard deviation than other modes of control, while providing a moderate average traffic flow. Another consideration is the percentage of legitimate packets (LT%) serviced within the incoming traffic flow, although in this experiment it is believed the differences in LT% are mostly due to randomness from the Poisson traffic generation.

Additionally, the percentage of legitimate traffic that was serviced is relatively low due to the limited number of border routers used in the experiment, and the fact that the two border routers had attack rates that were designed to be within 10% of each other (i.e., *baruntse* was designed to produce 10% more attack traffic than *izzy* on average). If a relatively low LT% border router, *pinatubo*, was added to this experiment, the baseline case's LT% would decrease. However, the LT% of an implementation using our model would not decrease, since it would be dropped in favor of traffic from border routers *izzy* and *baruntse*, which both have a higher LT%. Similarly, if a relatively high LT% border router, *halfdome*, is added, the Baseline LT% increases. However, the LT% of an implementation using our model increases more significantly than the baseline case, since the new higher LT% traffic would be substituted for lower LT% traffic from border router *baruntse*[3]. The total traffic limit also impacts the difference between the LT% of the baseline and the LT% of an implementation using this model. Suppose we have border routers *baruntse*, *izzy*, and *halfdome*, as described previously. If the limit were decreased to the point where we can only accept traffic from border router *halfdome*, then the LT% of our implementation would be much greater than the baseline case, since all traffic from lower LT% border routers is completely dropped by our implementation, yet completely accepted by the baseline case. Increasing the total traffic with respect to the limit has a similar effect. Thus, the larger the DDoS attack is compared to the limit, the larger the difference between the Baseline LT% and the LT% of an implementation using our model.

Going by the criteria of an average close to our limit of 120, and a relatively small standard deviation, the optimal solution appears to be proportional integral derivative mode with $K_c = 1.6$, $\tau_I = 10$, and $\tau_D = .1$, due to the fact that it has a much lower standard deviation than other modes of control, and has the lowest maximum traffic rate, with an acceptable average traffic flow. If standard deviations and large spikes are permissible, proportional mode with K_c equal to 1.6 may be acceptable as well. Additionally, if the traffic generation were to introduce more subtle patterns (e.g., a non-instantaneous DDoS attack), PID control should perform even better.

Once a set of optimal parameters has been determined, they may be used in the event of a DDoS attack of this type. If desired, various flows, network settings, etc. could be used to store multiple sets of PID control law parameters. In the simplest case, parameters could be determined and stored for DDoS attacks of varying severities. In the event of an attack, an external system could determine the severity of the attack, and use the corresponding set of PID control law parameters to defend against the attack.

Additionally, a few modifications can be made to this implementation to handle more complex attacks, such as syn floods. A stateless syn flood detector, such as one described in [30], could provide input to a component between comm. server and the PID controller in Fig. 2, where the presented implementation has attack flow information delivered directly from comm. server.

6 Conclusion

We have presented a model for mitigating the effects of DDoS attacks, currently limited to particular types (i.e., uniform resource consumption per packet) and other

---

[3] This assumes that the limit does not change, nor does the total flow per border router.

assumptions listed in Section 4.1. This model requires considerably less cooperation from foreign networks than other current approaches and has been proven to be effective against such attacks. Current approaches can have difficulties with spoofed packets, whereas the impact of spoofed packets with this model is eliminated if the fourth assumption of Section 3.1 is valid. Similarly, current models require a technique for perfectly accurate identification of the true source of the attack. This model provides graceful or no degradation of effectiveness, as described in Section 4.1, when used with a lower accuracy attack detector. Additionally, as long as the attack packet detector performs consistently across each traffic flow, relatively poor detectors can still be used to achieve identical results to those of a flawless detector, as described in detail in the 6th assumption of Section 4.1. Current approaches [7–9] rely solely on traffic flow information and categorize abnormally high traffic flows as attack traffic. Although some of the assumptions of the model presented are demanding, they may be lessened with relatively little impact on its effectiveness.

While the model has not yet proven itself against a popular DDoS attack such as Stacheldraht, we believe modifications to the implementation can be made to handle such attacks. Although the experiment was limited to TCP/IP traffic, alternative attack types such as ICMP floods, UDP floods, and syn floods could be tested with relatively minimal changes, as briefly discussed in the end of Section 5. The main weakness of the model lies with the multi-lateral trust issues between border routers. Although some suggestions on how to deal with these issues were presented, they would still pose tremendous problems in an actual implementation on currently existing border routers. Another weakness of the model lies in the case where all foreign networks have nearly identical percentages of attack traffic. Worms such as Nimda [4] tend to infect machines within the same network more quickly than machines outside their local network. Clearly some networks are traditionally more secure than others. University networks tend to be less secure than a Fortune 500 corporate virtual private network (VPN). Similarly, it is typically easier for an attacker to compromise machines on the same network than on a remote network. Thus, it is likely that a few networks will have a very high percentage of attack traffic, and other networks will have no attack traffic. It should be extremely rare that all networks contain nearly identical percentages of attack traffic, which is the worst-case scenario for this model. Although this model does not provide the optimal protection from a DDoS attack by blocking as close to the source as physically possible, we believe it shows an effective, less intrusive, rapid response for mitigating the effects of DDoS attacks. More importantly, this paper shows how control theoretic approaches widely used in other disciplines can be applied to aspects of computer security.

7 Future Work

Given the numerous assumptions made throughout this paper, there are many ways to improve upon this model. Some venues for future improvements include:

More dynamic attacks. Currently the attack and non-attack traffic are relatively static, despite using a Poisson distribution. Attacks that produce a more dynamic traffic flow would help exhibit the usefulness of PID control law in this context. Similarly, chaotic maps [14, 15] could be used to provide a more accurate representation of traffic than Poisson.

Multidimensional PID control. PID control could be made multidimensional, predicting streams of legitimate traffic flow and attack traffic flow as opposed to total traffic flow. Similarly, PID control could be used to predict HTTP traffic flow or SMTP traffic flow. It may be likely that only traffic destined for specific ports or services are causing the DDoS. This would allow all traffic going to different ports to remain unblocked. Much of the previous work [8] can be used to achieve this.

Apply weights to attack flow. Attack packets typically consume more resources than non-attack packets. These weights could vary on the type of DoS used in the attack. This enables the model to be tested against more popular DDoS attacks [1, 2]. Similarly, these weights could be used to slow attacks that require multiple attempts, such as TCP sequence number guessing. This could also be used to model CPU and/or memory usage to slow potential attack processes.

Support for non-border routers. Add support for routers where hosts can pass through various border routers to reach the protected network.

Use of commercial PID controllers. Several commercial controllers exist which automatically determine the optimal PID parameters of K_C, τ_I, and τ_D and prevent many situations that would otherwise cause the controller to go out of control.

Faster, more accurate PID parameter tuning. Additional research needs to be done into assumptions that can possibly be made about network flow in these circumstances to aid in faster, more accurate tuning of K_C, τ_I, and τ_D. One potential solution [26] uses unfalsified control theory [27] to automatically tune PID controllers without any knowledge of the underlying processes, and is derived from aspects in machine learning.

References

1. J. Howard, "An Analysis of Security Incidents on the Internet," Ph.D. thesis, Carnegie Mellon University, 1998.
2. D. Dittrich, "Distributed denial of service (DDoS) attacks/tools resource page," http://staff.washington.edu/dittrich/misc/ddos/, 2000.
3. Computer Emergency Response Team (CERT), Carnegie Mellon University, "Denial-of-Service Developments," 2000. CA-2001:01.
4. Computer Emergency Response Team (CERT), Carnegie Mellon University, "Nimda Worm," Sept. 2001. CA-2001:26.
5. D. Song and A. Perrig, "Advanced and authenticated marking schemes for IP traceback," *Proceedings of IEEE INFOCOM 2001*, March 2001.
6. J. Li, J. Mirkovic, M. Wang, P. Reiher, and L. Zhang, "SAVE: source address validity enforcement," *Proceedings of IEEE INFOCOM 2002*, June 2002, http://www.cs.ucla.edu/adas/ucla_tech_report_010004.ps.
7. D. Sterne, K. Djahandari, B. Wilson, B. Babson, D. Schnackenberg, H. Holliday, and T. Reid, "Autonomic response to distributed denial of service attacks," *Recent Advances in Intrusion Detection, 2001*, October 2001.

8. J. Ioannidis and S. M. Bellovin, "Implementing pushback: router-based defense against DDoS attacks," in *Proceedings of the Network and Distributed System Security Symposium*, February 2002.
9. R. Mahajan, S. Bellovin, S. Floyd, J. Ioannidis, V. Paxson, and S. Shenker, "Controlling High Bandwidth Aggregates in the Network," in *Computer Communications Review* 32:3, July 2002, pp. 62-73.
10. K.S. Meier-Hellstern, P.E. Wirth, Y.L. Yan, and D.A. Hoeflin, "Traffic models for ISDN data users: office automation application," *Teletraffic and Data Traffic in a Period of Change, ITC 13*, A. Jensen and B. Iversen (eds.), Elsevier, Amsterdam, pp. 167-172.
11. X. Hong, M. Gerla, G. Pei, and C.-C. Chiang, "A group mobility model for ad hoc wireless networks," in *ACM International Workshop on Modeling Analysis and Simulation of Wireless and Mobile Systems*, Aug. 1999, pp. 53-60.
12. K.K. Leung, W.A. Massey, and W. Whitt, "Traffic models for wireless communication networks," *IEEE Journal on Selected Areas in Communications*, 12(8):1353-1364, October 1994.
13. W.S. Cleveland, D. Lin, and D. Sun, "IP packet generation: statistical models for TCP start times based on connection-rate superposition," *Proceedings of ACM SIGMETRICS 2000*, June 2000.
14. A. Erramilli, E.P. Singh, and P. Pruthi, "Chaotic maps as models of packet traffic," in *Proceedings of the 14th ITC, June 1994*, pp. 329-338.
15. Erramilli and R.P. Singh, "Application of deterministic chaotic maps to model packet traffic in broadband networks," in *Proceedings of the 7th ITC Specialist Seminar, Morristown, NJ*, 8.1.1-8.1.3, 1990.
16. K.J. Astrom and T. Hagglund, *PID Controllers: Theory, Design, and Tuning*, Jan-uary 1995.
17. C.-C. Yu, *Autotuning of PID Controllers*, pp. 1, 1999.
18. http://www.sandfordtechnology.com/pdfs/ws_whitepaper.pdf
19. A. Mankin, D. Massey, C.L. Wu, S.F. Wu, L. Zhang, "On Design and Evaluation of Intention-Driven ICMP Traceback," in *IEEE International Conference on Computer Communication and Networks,* October 2001.
20. http://www.isel.ipl.pt/~pribeiro/RC2/DocCisco/QOS/cef_wp.pdf
21. E. Fulp, Z. Fu, D. Reeves, S.F. Wu, and X. Zhang, "Preventing Denial of Service Attacks on Network Quality of Service," in *2001 DARPA Information Survivability Conference and Exposition (DISCEX 2001)*, June 2001.
22. Computer Emergency Response Team (CERT), Carnegie Mellon University, "TCP Syn Flooding and IP Spoofing Attacks," Sept. 1996. CA-96:21.
23. L. Rizzo, "Dummynet: a simple approach to the evaluation of network protocols," *ACM Computing Communication Review*, January 1997.
24. http://www.neas-seminars.com/Samples/j3/MSG-5B-S6.htm
25. W.R. Stevens, "TCP timeout and retransmission," in *TCP/IP Illustrated, Volume 1*, pp. 297-322.
26. M. Jun, and M. Safonov, "Automatic PID Tuning: An Application of Unfalsified Control," http://citeseer.nj.nec.com/jun99automatic.html.
27. M. Safonov, and T. Tsao, "The Unfalsified Control Concept and Learning," in *IEEE Transactions on Automatic Control*, vol. 42, no. 6, June 1997, pp. 843-847.
28. M. Bellare, R. Canetti, and H. Krawczyk, "Keying Hash Functions for Message Authentication," *Advances in Cryptography – CRYPTO '96*, Lecture Notes in Computer Science, vol. 1109, pp. 1-15, 1996.
29. S. Bellovin, "ICMP Traceback Messages," Internet Draft, March 2001.
30. H. Wang, D. Zhang, and K. Shin, "Detecting SYN Flooding Attacks," in *Proceedings of IEEE Infocom 2002*, June 2002.

Topology-Based Detection
of Anomalous BGP Messages

Christopher Kruegel, Darren Mutz, William Robertson, and Fredrik Valeur

Reliable Software Group
University of California, Santa Barbara
{chris,dhm,wkr,fredrik}@cs.ucsb.edu

Abstract. The Border Gateway Protocol (BGP) is a fundamental component of the current Internet infrastructure. Due to the inherent trust relationship between peers, control of a BGP router could enable an attacker to redirect traffic allowing man-in-the-middle attacks or to launch a large-scale denial of service. It is known that BGP has weaknesses that are fundamental to the protocol design. Many solutions to these weaknesses have been proposed, but most require resource intensive cryptographic operations and modifications to the existing protocol and router software. For this reason, none of them have been widely adopted. However, the threat necessitates an effective, immediate solution.
We propose a system that is capable of detecting malicious inter-domain routing update messages through passive monitoring of BGP traffic. This approach requires no protocol modifications and utilizes existing monitoring infrastructure. The technique relies on a model of the autonomous system connectivity to verify that route advertisements are consistent with the network topology. By identifying anomalous update messages, we prevent routers from accepting invalid routes. Utilizing data provided by the Route Views project, we demonstrate the ability of our system to distinguish between legitimate and potentially malicious traffic.

Keywords: Routing Security, BGP, Network Security

1   Introduction

Research in network security is mainly focused on the security of end hosts. Little attention has been paid to the underlying devices and protocols of the network itself. This has changed with the emergence of successful attacks against the infrastructure of the global Internet that resulted in major service interruptions. The services to handle the translation between domain names and IP addresses (such as the Domain Name System) and protocols to facilitate the exchange of reachability information (such as routing protocols) have been recognized as essential to correct network operation.

The Internet can be described as an interconnected collection of autonomous domains or local networks, each of which is subject to the administrative and technical policy of a single organization. There exist two types of routing protocols: *intra-domain* and *inter-domain* routing protocols. The task of intra-domain

G. Vigna, E. Jonsson, and C. Kruegel (Eds.): RAID 2003, LNCS 2820, pp. 17–35, 2003.

routing protocols is to ensure that hosts inside a single domain or local network can exchange traffic. The goal of inter-domain routing protocols, on the other hand, is to exchange reachability information between such domains. This enables hosts to communicate with peers that are located in different networks.

There are several different intra-domain protocols used today (e.g., RIP [19], OSPF [22]), while the Border Gateway Protocol (BGP) is the de facto standard for inter-domain routing.

Version 4 of the Border Gateway Protocol was introduced in RFC 1771 [28]. It specifies an inter-autonomous system routing protocol for IP networks. The definition given for an *autonomous system* (AS) is *"a set of routers under a single technical administration, using an interior gateway protocol and common metrics to route packets within the AS, and using an exterior gateway protocol to route packets to other ASes"*.

The basic function of BGP is to enable autonomous systems to exchange reachability information that allows so-called BGP speakers to build an internal model of AS connectivity. This model is used to forward IP packets that are destined for receivers located in other ASes. The protocol includes information with each reachability message that specifies the autonomous systems along each advertised path, allowing implementations to prune routing loops. In addition, BGP supports the aggregation of path information (or routes) and utilizes CIDR (classless inter-domain routing) to decrease the size of the routing tables.

The protocol operates by having BGP speakers, usually routers, in different ASes exchange routing information with their *BGP peers* in the neighboring ASes. In addition to announcing its own routes, a BGP speaker also relays routing information received from its peers. By doing this, routing information is propagated to all BGP speakers throughout the Internet. The two basic operations of the BGP protocol are the announcement and the withdrawal of a route. The routing data itself is exchanged in UPDATE messages. Although BGP defines three other message types, none of these are directly related to the routing process. A route consists of a set of IP prefixes (stored in the NLRI – *network layer reachability information* – field of an UPDATE message), together with a set of attributes. When a route is announced, the sending BGP speaker informs the receiver that the IP prefixes specified in the NLRI field are reachable through the sending AS. The withdrawal process revokes a previous announcement and declares certain IP prefixes as no longer reachable via the AS. The most important attribute of an announcement is the AS_PATH. It specifies the path (i.e., the sequence of autonomous systems) that the route announcement has previously traversed before reaching that AS. Other attributes give information about the origin of a route or indicate whether routes have been aggregated at a previous AS.

Recently, a security analysis of BGP [23] and related threat models [5] pointed out two major areas of vulnerabilities of the inter-domain routing process.

One area includes threats that emanate from outsiders. Outsiders can disrupt established BGP peer connections and thereby launch denial of service attacks. They do not have privileges to influence the routing infrastructure directly, but can attempt to gain access to (break into) a legitimate router or impersonate a trusted BGP peer. Threats at this level usually do not aim at the routing protocol design but at the implementation level, in which bugs or vulnerabilities in routing software can be exploited to crash a machine or to elevate one's privileges. It might also be possible to bypass the authentication scheme to impersonate a legitimate BGP peer.

When an outsider is successful in compromising a trusted machine or an attacker already is in legitimate control of such a router, the focus shifts to direct threats from BGP peers. This area includes problems that occur when routers that legitimately participate in the routing infrastructure maliciously (or by accident) insert incorrect routing information. This can be the announcement of false IP address origins or invalid AS paths. Attacks at this level primarily focus on vulnerabilities in the routing protocol design and exploit the fact that there exists a significant level of trust between BGP peering partners. Invalid updates can propagate despite message filtering performed by many ASes, because it is often impossible to evaluate the validity of an update message given only local information. This might lead to worst-case scenarios where a single malicious or misconfigured router influences the routing state of the whole Internet.

We propose a technique that is capable of detecting malicious BGP updates utilizing geographical location data from the whois database and the topological information of an AS connectivity graph. By passively monitoring UPDATE messages, the connectivity graph is constructed by connecting two autonomous systems if traffic can be directly exchanged between them. Using this graph, we classify all autonomous system nodes as either *core* or *periphery* nodes. In general, core nodes represent the autonomous systems of the Internet backbone (such as large ISPs) while periphery nodes correspond to local providers, companies or universities. An important observation is that periphery AS nodes that are directly connected to each other are also close in terms of geographic distance. In most cases, peripheral autonomous systems have at most a few links to core nodes to obtain connectivity to distant networks and additionally peer only with partners in their geographic neighborhood. This observation leads to the determination that a valid AS_PATH contains at most a single sequence of core nodes, which must appear consecutively. That is, a path that has traversed core nodes and enters a periphery node never returns to the core of the graph. By checking the AS_PATH attribute of update messages, we can determine if the sequence of autonomous systems satisfies the constraints dictated by our observations and detect violations.

The structure of the paper is as follows. Section 2 presents related research in the area of routing security. Section 3 introduces the underlying threat model and discusses the attacks the system is designed to detect. Section 4 and Section 5 explain our proposed detection techniques. Section 6 provides experimental validation of important assumptions and reports on the results of our system. Section 7 outlines future work and Section 8 briefly concludes.

2   Related Work

Much research effort has focused on the security issues of intra-domain routing protocols [4, 24, 27, 30] and systems that perform intrusion detection for RIP [12, 21] as well as for OSPF [12, 26] have been proposed.

In contrast to intra-domain protocols, research on inter-domain protocols has concentrated on BGP, and its apparent weaknesses. Several authors have proposed extensions to the BGP protocol [14, 30] that attempt to authenticate routing information by means of cryptography. These modifications aim at countering threats from BGP peers that inject bogus information into the routing process, exploiting the fact that this information cannot be verified and, therefore, has to be trusted.

The most well-known approach is called the Secure Border Gateway Protocol (S-BGP) [13, 14] and operates as follows. During the propagation of an UPDATE message from AS to AS, each member on the path appends its information to the message and cryptographically signs the result before passing it along. This allows everyone in the chain to verify that the NLRI information is correct and that the update has actually traversed the autonomous systems that appear in the AS_PATH attribute. Unfortunately, this solution requires a public key infrastructure in place that assigns public keys to all participating autonomous systems. Because it cannot be expected that S-BGP will be adopted by all ASes simultaneously, it is necessary to be backward compatible with BGP. Hence, during the transition phase, an attacker might send information using the old protocol. In case of plain BGP updates, the level of trust in the included routing information is set by the site policy. The obvious risk is that such policies will often default to accepting the normal BGP update, especially in the beginning of the change-over.

A major drawback of S-BGP and related schemes is the requirement to apply changes to the existing protocol. Such changes not only imply a huge cost as hardware devices need to be upgraded, but there is also a reluctance to switch to designs that are not proven to work effectively on a large scale. Currently, it is not clear whether S-BGP will eventually take hold or how long the necessary transition phase will last. In [9], Goodell et al. highlight the fact that existing BGP security approaches have not been widely deployed. The authors consider the protocols' limited ability to be incrementally deployed, the high computational costs and the infeasibility of modifying the vast installed base of BGP software as the main contributors to the slow rate of adoption. Recognizing these limits, a protocol (ASRAP – autonomous system routing authority protocol) that can be incrementally deployed in parallel to the existing routing infrastructure is proposed. Similar to S-BGP, this protocol allows autonomous systems to verify routing updates. Unlike S-BGP, however, the UPDATE messages themselves are not modified. Instead, each participating AS has to provide an ASRAP service that can be queried by others to verify transmitted routing updates. The authors themselves realize that the success of their solution requires AS administrators to install such services and maintain an additional database, initially without receiving any obvious benefit. Even if such a solution is eventually realized, it would take a considerable amount of time until a majority of ASes support ASRAP. In the meantime, however, there is a need to provide a mechanism that can help routers to decide whether information received in update messages appears suspicious or not. This functionality is provided by our techniques to verify route updates.

3   Threats from BGP Peers

Threats from BGP peers have their origin in the trust a router has to place in the information it receives from its peers. The protocol standard does not include or suggest any mechanism to verify this information – that is, the routing data. Therefore, a malicious or misconfigured router can propagate invalid route advertisements or route withdrawals virtually without restrictions.

The most important information in a routing UPDATE message consists of the reachability information in the NLRI field and the AS_PATH attribute. The NLRI field specifies the IP address blocks that are either announced as reachable through a route or that are withdrawn as unreachable at this point in time. The AS_PATH attribute enumerates the autonomous systems that have to be traversed to reach the announced address blocks. This is needed to prevent routing loops but can also be used to make routing decisions based on policy or performance metrics. For example, when receiving a route to the same target IP address via multiple routes, the shorter one (as represented by less intermediate entries in the AS_PATH attribute) can be chosen.

As neither the reachability information nor the path attribute can be validated by a BGP peer receiving an UPDATE message, a malicious router is able to

1. specify an invalid AS path to an IP block so that the path includes the malicious AS itself (i.e., invalid AS path announcement).

2. announce that it controls an IP block that it has no authority over (i.e., IP Address ownership violation).

Such malicious injections can cause traffic to be routed to the malicious AS while legitimate sites become unreachable. This enables the attacker to perform man-in-the-middle attacks or to launch a large-scale denial of service.

Although many ISPs employ filters to discard invalid route updates, these mechanisms do not provide sufficient protection. This is confirmed by the continuous occurrences of incidents [7, 15, 16, 18] where invalid BGP updates are accepted, leading to large scale loss of connectivity. The following two sections describe detection techniques that are capable of identifying updates that are suspicious in the two ways enumerated above.

4   Detection of Invalid AS Path Announcements

An invalid AS path is an AS_PATH entry in an UPDATE message that announces a potential route to a certain IP address range, although the route does not exist. The AS path specifies the sequence of autonomous systems that a route announcement has previously traversed and describes a potential route to the destination IP addresses in the NLRI field. When a malicious AS crafts an update message with an invalid AS path, it offers a route to the advertised IP destinations that does not exist. Such update messages mislead other ASes, causing them to send traffic to the malicious AS and enabling the aforementioned man-in-the-middle and denial of service attacks.

It is infeasible to determine the validity of an AS path that has not been observed before by solely analyzing single BGP update messages. Consider a malicious AS that advertises a direct route through itself to the address block that it intends to hijack. The update message is crafted such that it appears to originate from the victim AS and an AS that receives such a message cannot tell whether a new, legitimate connection has been established or whether the route is invalid.

4.1   AS Connectivity Graph

The required additional information that enables us to analyze AS_PATH entries is obtained from the topology of the AS connectivity graph. This graph is only based on autonomous systems and the links between them. We do not consider single routers. We observe that each AS, in addition to having authority over a set of IP address blocks, is connected to a set of neighboring autonomous systems. The idea is that these inter-AS connections can be extracted or, to be more precise, sufficiently well approximated from processing UPDATE messages.

The AS connectivity graph is a graph G that consists of a set of n vertices $\{v_1, v_2, \ldots, v_n\}$, each representing a different autonomous system. Each vertex is labeled with a unique identifier that represents the 16-bit autonomous system number that is assigned to organizations by their responsible Internet number registry (e.g., American Registry for Internet Numbers – ARIN [2]). Each node v_i can be connected to zero or more other vertices $\{v_j, \ldots, v_k\}$ by undirected edges $\{e_{ij}, \ldots, e_{ik}\}$. An edge (or link) e_{ij} represents a direct network connection between the autonomous systems represented by v_i and v_j such that routers located in those systems can exchange traffic without having to traverse another autonomous system. Connections between ASes manifest themselves as adjacent AS numbers in the AS_PATH attributes of UPDATE messages. More precisely, they can be retrieved from sequence segments of AS_PATH attributes.

In addition to sequence segments that show the exact trail of a route update, an AS_PATH attribute can also contain AS sets. AS set segments store autonomous systems in an arbitrary fashion and commonly appear in the announcement of aggregated routes. Aggregated routes are utilized to decrease the size of routing tables and are created by an AS that does not forward BGP update messages from its peers immediately. Instead, it collects these messages and merges their address sets into a single block. The AS then announces the resulting block, essentially claiming that it owns the aggregated address space. In most cases, however, there is no single AS path that leads to all the aggregated IP address destinations and the AS_PATH attributes have to be merged as well. This is done by combining all autonomous systems into the unordered collection of AS numbers called AS set. This AS set is then used as new AS_PATH attribute.

The AS set is needed to prevent routing loops. If the sets were omitted and the aggregating router announced a path originating at the local AS, the route might be propagated back to one of the autonomous systems that originally announced parts of the aggregated route. This AS would be unable to determine that it has previously announced parts of that aggregated route itself and might install or forward the update instead of discarding it. Although the omission of the AS sets when propagating aggregated routes is bad practice and might lead to routing loops, it is the default setting in Cisco's BGP implementation. When an AS set is encountered in the AS_PATH attribute, no connectivity information can be retrieved from it.

Several previous studies of the BGP topology [11, 20, 32] have utilized data extracted from BGP routing tables or BGP update messages. The resulting graphs have proven to be useful in determining correspondence between IP addresses, prefixes and ASes. A common classification in this research distinguishes between *core* and *periphery* nodes of the connectivity graph. According to [10], the core consists of international, national and North American regional providers while the periphery corresponds to metropolitan area providers, companies and universities. In [33], the core and the periphery nodes are called *transfer* and *stub* nodes, respectively. The authors state that the connectivity graph is hierarchical with transfer nodes being highly interconnected while stub nodes attach to at most a few other stub nodes and have one or two links to transfer nodes.

Both studies utilize the node degree (i.e., the number of neighbors or links to other nodes) as a distinguishing criteria to classify ASes as either core or periphery systems. Following this observation, we adapted a technique described in [6] to determine the core nodes of the AS graph. The algorithm operates by successively pruning nodes from the graph that have a degree of two or less (i.e., nodes that have at most two connections to the remaining nodes in the graph). The pruning is continued until no more nodes can be removed, and each removed node is classified as periphery. Note that each node of the graph can be evaluated multiple times as the pruning progresses. It is possible that the number of links of a node with a degree greater than two is reduced due to other nodes that are removed from the connectivity graph. When the algorithm terminates, all remaining nodes are classified as core nodes. This process labels between 10% an 15% of all autonomous systems as core nodes, a finding that is in agreement with the two studies mentioned above [10, 33] as well as results reported in [8]. For exact results obtained for a selection of data sets, see Section 6.

Other methods [8, 31] to classify autonomous systems are possible and might improve our detection results. In our work, however, we have chosen the straightforward approach presented in [6] and leave the assessment of alternative classification algorithms for future work.

When the core and periphery nodes of the connectivity graph have been determined, the complete AS connectivity graph can be decomposed into *clusters* of periphery nodes. This decomposition is achieved by removing all core nodes from the graph. The resulting graph is no longer connected – instead it consists of many small groups of interconnected periphery nodes. These groups no longer have paths between them. This can be expected, as the core nodes represent the backbone of the Internet that provides the links between collections of smaller networks. A set (or group) of periphery nodes where each node is reachable from every other node in the set via at least one path is called a cluster. Note that the path between nodes in a cluster may contain intermediate nodes. It is not necessary that each node in a cluster has a direct link to every other node. One exemplary cluster of six ASes located around Toronto in Ontario, Canada is shown in Figure 1. The distances between individual autonomous systems range from 0 kilometers, when two ASes are in the same town (here Toronto), to 238 kilometers. The figure also shows four uplinks that connect ASes to core nodes (such as the link from AS 2767 – AT&T Canada to AS 7018 – AT&T WorldNet).

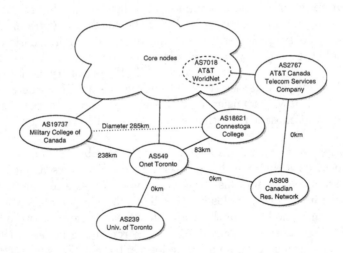

Fig. 1. AS Cluster around Toronto, Canada

We claim that the *geographical distances* between autonomous systems that are represented by the nodes of a single cluster are small. To capture the geographical distances of a cluster more precisely, we define the *cluster diameter* as the maximum geographical distance between any two of its ASes. In Figure 1, the maximum distance is 285 kilometers between AS 18621 and AS 19737. For the calculation of the cluster diameter, it is not necessary that a direct link exists between the most distant ASes. The idea is to confine a geographic area or region in which all ASes are located. The validity of our claim can be intuitively understood by the fact that periphery nodes represent small networks that are connected to large providers to obtain Internet connectivity (represented by core nodes) and to other small networks that are located in close vicinity. It is neither economically nor technically reasonable for a periphery network to install a direct link to another periphery network that is far away (from a geographical point of view). Our hypothesis is verified by deriving the cluster diameters for AS connectivity graphs (containing several thousand ASes) constructed from update messages collected at different points in time over the last two years. For a description of the test methodology and the exact results, consult Section 6.

4.2   Detection Techniques and Limitations

Based on the partition of the AS connectivity graph into core and periphery nodes and the observation that the cluster diameter is small, we define the following two constraints that a valid AS_PATH must satisfy.

1. The sequence of autonomous systems in an AS_PATH may only contain a single subsequence of core ASes. That is, a path that has traversed and left the core may never enter the core again.
2. All consecutive pairs of periphery ASes in an AS_PATH must either be part of the same cluster or, when they establish a link between two previously unconnected clusters, must be in close geographical vicinity.

The first constraint ensures that valid routes between two periphery ASes only traverse the core once and do not detour through a different periphery system before reaching the destination. As the core represents the backbone of the Internet, it is capable of delivering packets between any two periphery clusters directly. This constraint is also discussed in [33] and [8]. Both authors observe that valid paths traverse the core only once and do not have any intermediate periphery nodes.

The second constraint refers to direct connections between periphery systems. As shown in Section 6, periphery ASes that are directly connected are in a close geographical vicinity. When two periphery ASes are consecutively listed in an AS path, a direct link between these two is indicated. When a link between the two ASes already exists or when both belong to the same cluster, the connection is considered legitimate. When the link connects two previously unconnected clusters, the geographical distance between the two ASes has to be calculated. To be a valid update message, this distance has to be below a certain, adjustable threshold that can also depend on the diameter of the two clusters involved. For our experiments, this threshold is set to the maximum between the sum of the two cluster diameters and 300 kilometers[1].

The two aforementioned constraints allow us to validate certain properties of the AS paths in BGP update messages. For example, a malicious periphery AS that attempts to craft an invalid path to a victim usually cannot simply announce a direct route to the victim's AS. This is because such a direct link would violate the second constraint (assuming that the malicious AS and the victim are far enough away). In case the malicious nodes attempts to evade detection and

---

[1] 300 kilometers was chosen as a reasonable low value to capture the notion of close proximity. The threshold was selected prior to the evaluation and was not tuned to improve the experimental results afterwards.

inserts a core AS between itself and the victim's AS, the advertisement of this new route to any core AS would result in a sequence of core nodes that is interrupted by the offending AS. Such an update message would then violate the first constraint.

An obvious restriction of the topology-based approach is that only connections between periphery ASes can be validated using the geographical distance measurement. When a core node installs a new, direct route to another node (which may be either periphery or core), there is no reason why this announcement should be distrusted. It is perfectly reasonable to conclude that simply another direct link has been established. This limitation, however, only affects updates sent by large providers. Since these organizations usually employ network monitoring and implement high security standards, the threat that emanates from them is small compared to local providers or companies. Also note that this limitation does not affect updates that providers receive from their peers. They can still be checked and potential problems detected.

Another limitation prevents the detection of invalid updates when an AS claims that is has a direct connection to another autonomous system that is in a close geographical vicinity. In this case, the distance between the nodes representing the attacker and the victim AS is short and the model assumes that a valid, direct route has been installed. This allows a malicious AS to affect routing to other ASes that are located nearby. However, only a limited number of periphery ASes are located close to any specific autonomous system. This puts a limit on the number of potential targets and the freedom that the attacker has in choosing the victim. When an attacker attempts to forge a route to a distant AS, our system is capable of detecting the invalid path update.

The problem of dynamically updating the network model is left for future work. In our current design, it is necessary to rebuild the network model when the underlying topology changes in an extent that causes a significant raise in the number of false alarms. Note, however, that the network topology model can be built very fast. The model creation process required, for our experiments, update messages collected in a period of less than a day before it converged. Convergences was reached when new update messages did not result in any new information inserted into the graph for more than six hours. The detection process also exhibits a certain robustness against invalid updates during the model creation phase. Although invalid information is entered into the topology graph, the defect remains confined locally.

5   Detection of IP Address Ownership Violation

An IP address ownership violation occurs when an AS announces an IP block that it is not entitled to. This announcement is done by setting the NLRI field of the update message to the illegitimate IP range and transmitting it using an AS_PATH that starts with the malicious AS. An AS that receives such a message considers the originating malicious AS authoritative for the announced IP block and will forward corresponding packets there (given that it has not received a more preferable path to that IP block from the legitimate owner).

This problem, also called Multiple Origin AS (MOAS) conflict, was extensively studied by Zhao et al. [34]. The authors point out that MOAS conflicts occur relatively frequently, and also provide several non-malicious explanations for this phenomenon.

One possibility to distinguish between malicious and legitimate MOAS conflicts are BGP protocol enhancements, either using cryptographic solutions such as S-BGP [14] or protocol extensions such as MOAS lists [35]. A MOAS list contains a list of all ASes that are entitled to announce a certain IP block, and is attached to BGP route announcements. Although individual MOAS lists can be altered or forged, the solution relies on the rich connectivity of the Internet. It is assumed that a router will, in addition to a malicious MOAS list sent by an attacker, also receive a valid MOAS list from a legitimate source, thus being able to detect the inconsistency and raise an alarm.

In contrast to that, we pursue a more naïve strategy and attempt to prevent as many MOAS conflicts as possible that originate from probably legitimate configurations. This is done by ignoring BGP updates with aggregated NLRI fields or set COMMUNITIES attributes, as described in more detail below. Also, updates that announce large IP ranges (in our case, network masks with 8 or less bits) are excluded from our model. This approach aims to reduce the number of false positives, with the downside of an increased false negative rate. Future work will investigate improvements of this technique.

In our current approach, we build a model that stores a mapping between IP address blocks and their respective, authoritative ASes to detect address ownership violations. This mapping is constructed from BGP update messages during the model building phase. In the simplest case, the IP address block that a particular AS owns can be extracted directly from update messages. An IP range is announced by its owner by creating a suitable BGP UPDATE message and sending it to the peering partners of the particular autonomous system. As each AS forwards such updates, it is required to prepend its own number to the already existing AS_PATH attribute. Thus the originating AS appears as the last entry in the path list. Whenever our system observes a BGP message announcing an address block, the mapping between the IP range and its owner is inserted into our model.

It is not a requirement that an AS actually owns an IP block to be entitled to announce it. In fact, it is possible (and quite common) that an autonomous system would be granted the right to announce a block for a related AS. All IP packets that are forwarded to that AS are then correctly relayed to the actual target. In such a case, however, the actual owner is not supposed to announce the address block itself. For an external observer, it appears as if the address block is owned by the AS that announces it.

Unfortunately, there are situations when the owner of an IP block cannot be identified easily. The most common reason is the aggregation of IP address ranges. As previously stated, when an AS performs aggregation it claims that it is the origin of the aggregated address space, effectively masking the true owners of the aggregated IP subranges. An autonomous system that performs this step is required to tag this announcement with a special flag. This enables an external observer to identify aggregated update messages as such. A mechanism similar to aggregation is used with communities. The COMMUNITIES attribute was introduced in RFC 1997 [3] and is used to describe a group of autonomous systems with common properties. It is used to control the propagation of routing information based on communities instead of IP prefixes and AS paths alone in an attempt to simplify routing policies. When routes from different ASes that belong to the same community are aggregated, the aggregation tag is not set. Nevertheless, the original source of an update can no longer be determined with certainty.

The straightforward solution to the problem of aggregated routes[2] is to simply exclude them from the analysis. Unfortunately, a malicious AS could then evade detection by marking a route update as aggregated. Therefore, update messages that announce aggregated routes cannot be discarded immediately. Instead, we only discard these updates when the originating AS is a core node. In this case, it is very probable that the NLRI field contains IP ranges of many different destinations and the information cannot be reliably utilized. In the case of a periphery node, however, a mapping between the aggregated IP block and the corresponding AS is installed. When a periphery AS aggregates routes, we assume that the aggregated IP blocks are unlikely to be announced independently by the actual owner (that is a periphery AS as well). This assumption is confirmed by the low false alert rate that our system produces (as shown in Section 6).

The knowledge of IP address ownership helps to detect attacks or misconfigurations where an AS announces an address block that is not under its authority. UPDATE messages that contain addresses in their NLRI field that are already owned by someone else are classified as malicious. For similar reasons as outlined above, we discard all aggregated routes that originate at core nodes.

In general, the ownership of an address is relatively stable. Although flapping connections or broken links may cause a specific route to certain target addresses to be withdrawn, we cannot delete the address binding from our database as the ownership of the respective block has not changed. The problem of changes in the ownership of IP blocks can be solved in two ways. One approach involves a human operator that notices the increase of alleged attacks caused by clashing IP blocks and removes the old binding after making sure that the alerts are incorrect. Then, the new owner of the now vacant address can be entered into the model and normal operation continues. A more sophisticated automated mechanism determines whether the previous owner has recently announced the disputed IP blocks. When a sufficient amount of time has elapsed since the last announcement, the new owner is considered to be legitimate and ownership is transferred.

---

[2] In the following discussion, the term aggregated routes applies to update messages with community attributes as well.

6   Experiments

We have developed several criteria that help to assess the validity of routing data using an underlying model of the global routing infrastructure. Our model, consisting of the mapping of IP prefixes to ASes and the AS connectivity graph, is built by processing routing updates collected at *Looking Glass* sites such as the one run by the University of Oregon [32]. Looking Glass sites are passive BGP peers that maintain connections to a number of major BGP routers throughout the Internet and obtain the routers' forwarding tables as well as any UPDATE messages the routers receive. This allows one to get BGP data from multiple vantage points in different locations. The data is archived and made publicly available.

The techniques described in the previous sections have been implemented to detect potentially invalid route messages sent by BGP peers. Note that the detection system does not have to be installed at the actual BGP routers. Instead, in a setup that is similar to the one used by Looking Glass sites, UPDATE messages can be forwarded by routers to a regular desktop machine where the analysis can be performed.

The empirical evaluation of our approach uses BGP data collected during four different weeks over the last two years. The first data set contains BGP update messages collected during the week starting from April 5th, 2001, the second set starting from January 10th, 2002, the third set starting from September 15th, 2002, and the fourth starting from March 3rd, 2003. The first day of each week was used to build the IP address to AS mapping and the AS connectivity graph. The subsequent six days were then used as an input for the detection process. We assume that the day utilized for the model creation phase is free of any major incidents. However, minor misconfigurations are likely to occur. This results in a slightly imprecise topology graph, and thereby, might result in incorrect detections. We claim that the effect of these misconfigurations is small; a claim that is supported by the evaluation of the quality of the model and the detection process in the following two sections.

6.1   Model Validation

Our detection mechanisms depend upon both reliable classification of *core* and *periphery* ASes, as well as the validity of the assumption that ASes making up each cluster in the periphery are geographically close. Prior to investigating the detection performance of the system, this section explores these requirements in more detail.

Table 1 provides statistical data for each AS connectivity graph constructed from the BGP update messages of the first day of the respective four data sets. The iterative algorithm for partitioning the AS connectivity graph into core and periphery nodes (described in Section 4.1) performs well. Upon removing the core, the remaining nodes in the graph fall into disjoint clusters. The total number of core AS nodes represent, on average, 12.6% of the total number of

Table 1. AS Connectivity Graph Statistics

Date	Periphery	Core	Clusters	Max. Size	Avg. Size
Apr. 5th, 2001	5831 (89.5%)	686 (10.5%)	4437	64	1.31
Jan. 10th, 2002	10592 (85.1%)	1860 (14.9%)	8692	72	1.20
Sep. 15th, 2002	12006 (87.1%)	1773 (12.9%)	9762	63	1.23
Mar. 3rd, 2003	8422 (87.9%)	1162 (12.1%)	6418	68	1.31

nodes in the graph. This is in close agreement with [10] and [33], which find about 10% of ASes that constitute the core of the Internet. The number of nodes in each cluster is small, usually one, but there are also large clusters with a few tens of nodes. Table 1 shows, for each data set, the number of clusters (*Clusters*) as well as the maximum (*Max. Size*) and average number of nodes per cluster (*Avg. Size*).

For each cluster, we calculate the cluster diameter as defined in Section 4.1. This requires determining the maximum geographical distance between any two of its ASes. To obtain the distance between two autonomous systems, it is necessary to determine the locations for both ASes and to calculate the great circle geographic distance between them. The location for an AS is extracted from the whois database entry of the appropriate local registry (ARIN [2] for the US and Canada, RIPE for Europe, LACNIC [17] for Latin America and APNIC [1] for Asia and the Pacific). The whois entries in the ARIN database list the city, state and country for the autonomous system location in explicitly marked fields. This makes it straightforward to extract the required data. The other three databases, however, do not follow a standardized method of specifying locations. Therefore, we have developed a parser that retrieves the provided organizational description and contact information for each AS and attempts to determine a probable geographical position. Manual inspection of a few hundred locations indicate that the extraction of geographical data is successful. Additionally, our results show that connected periphery ASes are in close proximity (see Figure 2 below). Note, however, that the location information is only useful for periphery nodes. Although core nodes have a specific geographic location as well, their corresponding networks usually span a large geographical area and, thus, this information has less value. Only for peripheral ASes, the location information is meaningful.

Figure 2 is a log-scale histogram plot that shows the distribution of cluster diameters for the four datasets considered in this evaluation. In all cases, the fraction of clusters whose diameter is greater than 300 kilometers is less than 2.4%. There is a relatively small number of high-diameter (i.e., $\geq$ 4000 km) outliers in each plot. These are due to obviously incorrect or stale entries in the whois database or are caused by special purpose links operated by ASes that are not classified as core nodes. For example, NASA operates a branch office in Moscow with its own AS number and this AS has a direct connection to a location in the US. However, the special links are expected to be stable and the

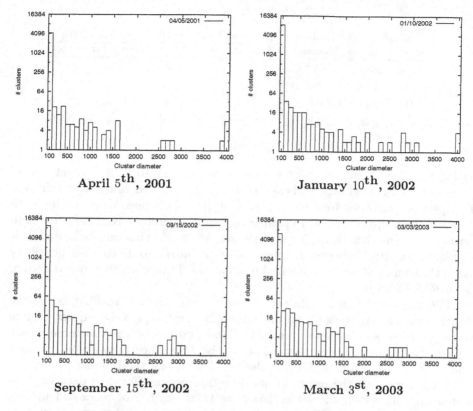

Fig. 2. Cluster Diameter Distribution (logarithmic scale)

installation of such a connections is a relatively infrequent event. Therefore, we do not expect a noticeable influence on the number of false alerts; an assessment that was confirmed by our measurements shown in Section 6.2. Note that we did not manually change any of these 'anomalies' for the evaluation of the detection process, but we expect them to contribute to the observed false alarms.

6.2   Detection Evaluation

The detection approach was evaluated on BGP data collected during four different weeks over the last two years. We used the first day of each week to build our models and the subsequent six days as an input to the detection algorithms.

The first two data sets are important to assess the detection capability of our system as both hold traces of significant misconfiguration problems. The first data set (that starts on April 5th, 2001) contains an incident where Cable and Wireless (AS3561) propagated more than 5000 improper route announcements from one of its downstream customers [7, 18] that illegitimately claimed large IP ranges. This lead to global connectivity problems for about 90 minutes. Clearly, the corresponding messages should be identified as IP address ownership

Table 2. Alert Overview

Week starting at	Update Messages	Address Violation		Invalid AS Path	
		Correct	Incorrect	Correct	Incorrect
Apr. 5th, 2001	1,507,673	2148	18	0	0
Jan. 10th, 2002	5,918,085	0	23	76	0
Sep. 15th, 2002	7,065,598	0	23	0	0
Mar. 3rd, 2003	5,499,401	0	14	0	0

violations. The second data set (that begins on January 10th, 2002) contains evidence of a misconfiguration where a customer propagated routes received from its upstream provider to a peering partner [18]. This peer then continued to forward the routes to its own upstream provider, thereby advertising routes to parts of the Internet through the customer AS itself. This misconfiguration is similar to an attack where a periphery AS announces a route to other periphery ASes through itself and the involved updates should be classified by our system as invalid AS paths.

The third and fourth data set are, after reviewing the mailing list of the North American Network Operators' Group [25] for the periods in question, free of major attacks or misconfigurations. These two weeks serve as more recent data to verify that our assumptions about the AS connectivity graph are valid and to provide an estimate for the false positive rate for the Internet at present.

Table 2 provides the results of our detection system. For each data set (collected over six days), the table shows the total number of processed update messages, the number of IP address ownership violations and the number of invalid AS paths that were reported. All alerts are classified as either correct or incorrect. An alert is classified as correct when it is obviously related to one of the two incidents in the first two data sets as described above. All other alerts are classified as incorrect. Closer examination of the incorrect alerts reveals that a large percentage is due to the misclassification of periphery nodes that are in fact part of the core. Such misclassifications occur mainly for autonomous systems located in Asia or Eastern Europe. The update messages collected from Route View mostly contain traffic sent between ASes in Europe and the US, resulting in an AS connectivity graph that is sparse for other regions. As the node classification relies on the degree of connectivity, core nodes in those regions may not have enough neighbors in our graph and are thus labeled as periphery. To obtain more precise data from these regions, we would require BGP data from routers located in there. Other incorrect alerts might have been the result of actual misconfigurations, but no supporting evidence was found for the relevant dates on the network operator mailing list [25] and the alerts had to be classified as incorrect. Another possible cause are invalid data utilized to create the network topology model.

Note that the numbers in Table 2 reflect unique violations. That is, when multiple invalid update messages with identical routing information are observed, only one alert is produced. This shows the potential tremendous impact of a single misconfiguration on the global infrastructure. For example, the 2148 different address ownership violations detected during one day of the first test week were the result of a single incident.

It is interesting to observe that the properties of the network graph as well as the behavior of the system do not change noticeably for the test sets that reflect samples from a period of over two years. This indicates that our assumptions are stable and that detection can be performed reliably.

7   Future Work

This section gives an overview of our plans to extend the security model as well as our presented technique.

A useful extension of the proposed approach to BGP security is the inclusion of BGP policies. BGP speakers usually define policies that restrict the information exchange with their respective neighbors and influence routing decisions. This allows us to determine whether the current network graph conforms to the specified policies and raise an alarm in case a deviation is detected. Such deviations could either result from misconfigurations or malicious behavior.

The presented design does not automatically take into account changes of IP address ownership and the removal of connections between autonomous systems. It would be desirable to determine when IP address blocks have been transferred between ASes without the intervention of an operator that has to remove the binding from the database. This could be done by including information from the Route Arbiter Project [29] or from miscellaneous network information centers. Also, the information in withdrawal messages is not utilized. This is because it is not straightforward to extract topology information from such updates.

8   Conclusion

The Border Gateway Protocol is the de facto standard for inter-domain routing in today's Internet. Although protocol design weaknesses and implementation flaws in many devices running BGP are well-known, it is difficult to overcome them. The huge base of installed equipment and the fact that, despite several successful attacks, global routing seems to work satisfactorily create an enormous reluctance to the adoption of newer protocols. Although approaches such as S-BGP seem appealing at first glance, they have not been widely deployed. In the meantime, the concept of "security by obscurity" is the only protection against potentially devastating attacks.

We have developed a technique to validate routing data in BGP UPDATE messages to protect routers from installing falsified routes. The mechanism is based on topology information of the autonomous systems connectivity graph and geographical data from whois databases. It is capable of identifying updates where a malicious or misconfigured router announces illegitimate IP address blocks or invalid routes that do not exist. Our system can be applied immediately and does not interfere with the existing infrastructure.

Acknowledgments

This research was supported by the Army Research Office, under agreement DAAD19-01-1-0484. The U.S. Government is authorized to reproduce and distribute reprints for Governmental purposes notwithstanding any copyright annotation thereon.

The views and conclusions contained herein are those of the author and should not be interpreted as necessarily representing the official policies or endorsements, either expressed or implied, of the Army Research Office, or the U.S. Government.

References

1. Asia Pacific Network Information Centre. http://http://www.apnic.net.
2. American Registry for Internet Numbers. http://http://www.arin.net.
3. R. Chandra, P. Traina, and T. Li. BGP Communities Attribute. IETF-RFC 1997, Aug 1996.
4. S. Cheung. An Efficient Message Authentication Scheme for Link State Routing. In *13th Annual Computer Security Applications Conference*, December 1997.
5. S. Convey, D. Cook, and M. Franz. An Attack Tree for the Border Gateway Protocol. IETF Internet Draft, Oct 2002.
6. M. Faloutsos, P. Faloutsos, and C. Faloutsos. On Power-Law Relationships of the Internet Topology. In *Proceedings of ACM SIGCOMM*, 1999.
7. J. Farrar. Cable and Wireless Routing Instability. http://www.merit.edu/mail.archives/nanog/2001-04/msg00209.html.
8. L. Gao. On Inferring Autonomous System Relationships in the Internet. In *Proceedings of IEEE Global Internet*, November 2000.
9. Geoffrey Goodell, William Aiello, Timothy Griffin, John Ioannidis, Patrick McDaniel, and Aviel Rubin. Working Around BGP: An Incremental Approach to Improving Security and Accuracy of Interdomain Routing. In *Network and Distributed Systems Security*, 2003.
10. R. Govindan and A. Reddy. An Analysis of Internet Inter-Domain Topology and Route Stability. In *IEEE InfoCom*, 1997.
11. B. Huffaker, A. Broido, k. claffy, M. Fomenkov, K. Keys, E. Lagache, and D. Moore. Skitter AS Internet Graph. CAIDA, Oct 2000.
12. Y.F. Jou, F. Gong, C. Sargor, X. Wu, F. Wu, H.C. Chang, and F. Wang. Design and Implementation of a Scalable Intrusion Detection System for the Protection of Network Infrastructure. In *DARPA Information Survivability Conference and Exposition*, January 2000.
13. S. Kent, C. Lynn, J. Mikkelson, and K. Seo. Secure Border Gateway Protocol (Secure-BGP) - Real World Performance and Deployment Issues. In *Proceedings of the Symposium on Network and Distributed System Security*, February 2000.
14. S. Kent, C. Lynn, and K. Seo. Secure Border Gateway Protocol (Secure-BGP). *IEEE Journal on Selected Areas in Communications*, 18(4):582–592, April 2000.
15. C. Labovitz, A. Ahuja, and F. Jahanian. Experimental Study of Internet Stability and Wide-Area Network Failures. In *Fault-Tolerant Computing Symposium*, June 1999.
16. C. Labovitz, G. R. Malan, and F. Jahanian. Origins of Internet Routing Instability. In *IEEE INFOCOM*, March 1998.

17. The Latin American and Caribbean Internet Addresses Registry. `http://http://www.lacnic.net`.
18. R. Mahajan, D. Wetherall, and T. Anderson. Understanding BGP Misconfiguration. In *Proceedings of ACM SIGCOMM*, August 2002.
19. G. Malkin. RIP Version 2. IETF-RFC 2453, Nov 1998.
20. Sean McCreary and Bill Woodcook. PCH RouteViews archive. `http://www.pch.net/resources/data/routing-tables`.
21. V. Mittal and G. Vigna. Sensor-Based Intrusion Detection for Intra-Domain Distance-Vector Routing. In *Proceedings of the ACM Conference on Computer and Communication Security (CCS'02)*, Washington, DC, November 2002. ACM Press.
22. J. Moy. OSPF Version 2. IETF-RFC 2328, Apr 1998.
23. Sandra Murphy. Border Gateway Protocol Security Analysis. IETF Internet Draft, Nov 2001.
24. S.L. Murphy and M.R. Badger. Digital Signature Protection of the OSPF Routing Protocol. In *Proceedings of the Symposium on Network and Distributed System Security*, February 1996.
25. The North American Network Operators' Group. `http://www.nanog.org`.
26. D. Qu, B.M. Vetter, F. Wang, R. Narayan, F. Wu, F. Jou, F. Gong, and C. Sargor. Statistical Anomaly Detection for Link-State Routing Protocols. In *In Proceedings of the 1998 International Conference on Network Protocols*, October 1998.
27. A. Przygienda R. Hauser and G. Tsudik. Reducing the cost of security in link state routing. In *ISOC Symposium on Network and Distributed System Security*, February 1997.
28. Y. Rekhter and T. Li. A Border Gateway Protocol 4 (BGP-4). IETF-RFC 1654, Mar 1995.
29. Routing Arbiter Project. `http://www.ra.net`.
30. B.R. Smith, S. Murthy, and J.J. Garcia-Luna-Aceves. Securing Distance-Vector Routing Protocols. In *Proceedings of the Symposium on Network and Distributed System Security*, February 1997.
31. L. Subramanian, S. Agarwal, J. Rexford, and R. H. Katz. Characterizing the Internet Hierarchy From Multiple Vantage Points. In *IEEE INFOCOM*, 2002.
32. University of Oregon - Looking Glass. `http://antc.uoregon.edu/route-views`.
33. E. Zegura, K. Calvert, and M. Donahoo. A quantitative comparison of graph-based models for internetworks. *IEEE/ACM Transactions on Networking*, 5(6):770–783, December 1997.
34. X. Zhao, D. Pei, L. Wang, D. Massey, A. Mankin, S. F. Wu, and L. Zhang. An Analysis of BGP Multiple Origin AS (MOAS) Conflict. In *ACM SIGCOMM Internet Measurement Workshop*, San Francisco, USA, November 2001.
35. X. Zhao, D. Pei, L. Wang, L. Zhang, D. Massey, A. Mankin, and S. F. Wu. Detection of Invalid Route Announcement in the Internet. In *International Conference on Dependable Systems and Networks*, 2002.

Detecting Anomalous Network Traffic with Self-organizing Maps*

Manikantan Ramadas[1], Shawn Ostermann[1], and Brett Tjaden[2]

[1] Ohio University
{mramadas,ostermann}@cs.ohiou.edu
[2] James Madison University
tjadenbc@jmu.edu

Abstract. Integrated Network-Based Ohio University Network Detective Service (INBOUNDS) is a network based intrusion detection system being developed at Ohio University. The Anomalous Network-Traffic Detection with Self Organizing Maps (ANDSOM) module for INBOUNDS detects anomalous network traffic based on the Self-Organizing Map algorithm. Each network connection is characterized by six parameters and specified as a six-dimensional vector. The ANDSOM module creates a Self-Organizing Map (SOM) having a two-dimensional lattice of neurons for each network service. During the training phase, normal network traffic is fed to the ANDSOM module, and the neurons in the SOM are trained to capture its characteristic patterns. During real-time operation, a network connection is fed to its respective SOM, and a "winner" is selected by finding the neuron that is closest in distance to it. The network connection is then classified as an intrusion if this distance is more than a pre-set threshold.

Keywords: Intrusion Detection, Anomaly Detection, Self-Organizing Maps

1   Introduction

We have seen an explosive growth of the Internet in the past two decades. As of January 2003, the Internet connected over 171 million hosts [12]. With this tremendous growth has come our dependence on the Internet for more and more activities of our lives. Hence, it has become critical to protect the integrity and availability of our computer resources connected to the Internet. We have to protect our computer resources from malicious users on the Internet who try to steal, corrupt, or otherwise abuse them. Towards this goal, intrusion detection systems are being actively developed and increasingly deployed.

Intrusion detection systems have commonly used two detection approaches, namely, misuse detection and anomaly detection. The misuse detection approach uses a database of "signature"s of well known intrusions and uses a pattern matching scheme to detect intrusions in real-time. The anomaly detection approach, on the other hand, tries to quantify the normal operation of the host, or

---

* This work was funded by the National Science Foundation under grant ANI-0086642

G. Vigna, E. Jonsson, and C. Kruegel (Eds.): RAID 2003, LNCS 2820, pp. 36–54, 2003.

the network as a whole, with various parameters and looks for anomalous values for those parameters in real-time.

Integrated Network Based Ohio University Network Detective Service (IN-BOUNDS) is an intrusion detection system being developed at Ohio University. INBOUNDS uses the anomaly detection approach to detect intrusions, and is network-based i.e., it can be used to passively monitor the network as a whole. In this paper, we present the Self-Organizing Map based approach for detecting anomalous network behavior developed for INBOUNDS.

We organize this paper as follows. In Section 2, we give a brief description of Self-Organizing Maps and follow up in Section 3 with details of related work in the intrusion detection domain based on Self-Organizing Maps. In Section 4, we describe the INBOUNDS system and the design of the Self-Organizing Map based module for detecting intrusions. In Section 5, we present some of our experimental results, and in Section 6 we conclude and give some recommendations for future work.

2   Self-organizing Maps

The concept, design, and implementation techniques of Self-Organizing Maps are described in detail in [25]. The Self-Organizing Map algorithm performs a non-linear, ordered, smooth mapping of high-dimensional input data manifolds onto the elements of a regular, low-dimensional array [25]. The algorithm converts non-linear statistical relationships between data points in a high-dimensional space into geometrical relationships between points in a two-dimensional map, called the Self-Organizing Map (SOM). A SOM can then be used to visualize the abstractions (clustering) of data points in the input space.

The points in the SOM are called neurons, and are represented as multi-dimensional vectors. If the data points in the input space are characterized using k parameters and represented by k-dimensional vectors, the neurons in the SOM are also specified as k-dimensional vectors.

2.1   Learning

In the SOM Learning phase, the neurons in the SOM are trained to model the input space. This phase has the following two important characteristics:

- **Competitive.** Each sample data point from the input data space is shown in parallel to all the neurons in the SOM, and the "winner" is chosen to be the neuron that responds best. The k-dimensional values of the winner are adjusted so that it responds even better to similar input.
- **Cooperative.** A neighborhood is defined for the winner to include all neurons in its near vicinity in the SOM. The k-dimensional values of neurons in the neighborhood are also adjusted so that they too respond better to a similar input.

The SOM learning principle, illustrated in Figure 1, shows the SOM, with the circles representing neurons. The input data point is fed in parallel to all the

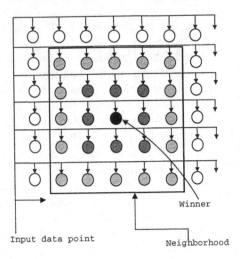

Fig. 1. SOM Learning

neurons in the SOM. The winner neuron is colored black, and a square of length 5 centered around it represents the neighborhood.

During the learning phase, samples of data are collected from the input space and "shown" to the SOM. For this purpose, sample vectors representing input data covering the range of operational behavior are collected. The neurons in the SOM are initialized to values chosen from the range of sample data. The neurons can be assigned values linearly in the range (linear initialization), or assigned random values within the range (random initialization).

Distance Measure. For the purpose of locating the winner neuron given the data sample, a suitable measure of distance has to be defined. The commonly used distance measures are the Euclidean and the Dot-product measures. In the Euclidean measure, given two points X $(x_1, x_2, \ldots, x_k)$ and Y $(y_1, y_2, \ldots, y_k)$ in k-dimensional space, the Euclidean distance is given by

$$\sqrt{(x_1 - y_1)^2 + (x_2 - y_2)^2 + \ldots + (x_k - y_k)^2}$$

If the Dot-product measure is to be used, the input data points and the neurons in the SOM have to be normalized. Normalization of a vector V $(v_1, v_2, \ldots, v_k)$ is a process of transforming its components into

$$\left(\frac{v_1}{\sqrt{v_1^2 + v_2^2 + \ldots + v_k^2}}, \frac{v_2}{\sqrt{v_1^2 + v_2^2 + \ldots + v_k^2}}, \ldots, \frac{v_k}{\sqrt{v_1^2 + v_2^2 + \ldots + v_k^2}} \right)$$

so that the modulus of the normalized vector is unity. The dot-product of the input data point is calculated individually with each of the neurons, where the dot-product of two normalized vectors X $(x_1, x_2, \ldots, x_k)$, and Y $(y_1, y_2, \ldots y_k)$ is defined to be

$$x_1.y_1 + x_2.y_2 + \ldots + x_k.y_k$$

The winner is selected to be the neuron that gives the maximum dot product.

Neighborhood Function. The neighborhood function determines the size and nature of the neighborhood around the winner neuron. The commonly used neighborhood functions are Bubble and Gaussian. In the Bubble function, the neighborhood radius is specified by a variable σ, and all neurons within the neighborhood are adjusted by the same factor α towards the winner. The parameter α, called the learning rate factor, and the neighborhood size σ, are generally chosen to be monotonically decreasing functions of time t, where t is a discrete time measure incremented with every iteration of the training process. The Bubble neighborhood function $h_{ci}(t)$ is specified as:

$$h_{ci}(t) = \begin{cases} \alpha(t) & ||r_c, r_i|| < \sigma(t) \\ 0 & \text{otherwise} \end{cases}$$

where r_c and r_i represent the positions of the winner c and neuron i in the SOM, and $||r_c, r_i||$ is the distance between them.

The Gaussian neighborhood function adjusts the winner neuron the most towards the sample data, and adjusts the remaining neurons within the neighborhood lesser and lesser as their distance from the winner increases, based on a bell shaped Gaussian function. It is specified as:

$$h_{ci}(t) = \begin{cases} \alpha(t)exp\left(-\frac{||r_c, r_i||^2}{2\sigma^2(t)}\right) & ||r_c, r_i|| < \sigma(t) \\ 0 & \text{otherwise} \end{cases}$$

The Gaussian neighborhood function is illustrated in Figure 1. The winner shown in black is moved the most towards the sample data, while the neurons in the neighborhood are moved lesser and lesser as shown in the gray-shades.

Learning Function. After the winner is found and the neighborhood is determined, the k-dimensional values of the neurons are adjusted based on the learning function. The learning function is specified as:

$$m_i(t + 1) = m_i(t) + h_{ci}(t)[x(t) - m_i(t)]$$

where $m_i(t)$, $m_i(t+1)$ represent k-dimensional values of neuron i, at time t and $t + 1$ respectively; $x(t)$ represents the k-dimensional values of the sample data.

To summarize, for every neuron in the SOM, the learning function calculates its distance from the sample data, and adjusts its k-dimensional values towards the sample data by a factor specified by the neighborhood function $h_{ci}(t)$.

2.2   Algorithm

The choice of the factors described in the previous section affect the nature of the SOM generated. Once these factors are decided upon, the following algorithm can be used to train the SOM.

After the SOM is initialized, the learning process is carried out in two phases. In the initial phase, a relatively large neighborhood radius is chosen. The learning rate factor $\alpha(t)$ is also chosen to have a high value, close to unity. This phase is carried out for relatively lesser number of iterations. Most of the map organization happens in this phase. In the final fine-tuning phase, a smaller neighborhood radius and smaller learning rate factor are chosen. This phase is carried out for relatively larger number of iterations. The adjustment done to the neurons are much smaller in this phase.

2.3   Operation

In a k-dimensional space, the sample data and the SOM neurons appear as points. During the course of the learning algorithm described above, the neurons "move" in the k-dimensional space to characterize the sample data as closely as possible. While clusters of neurons would form at spaces where the sample data points are concentrated, fewer neurons would represent the space where sample data occur sparsely.

During operation, a real-time sample can be fed to the SOM, and its winner located. It can be flagged normal if it is sufficiently closer to the winner, and flagged anomalous if its distance from the winner is more than a preset threshold.

3   Related Work

In the work cited in this paper, SOM-based profiles of various network services like web, email, etc., are built to perform anomaly-based intrusion detection. Using network-service profiles to perform intrusion detection is not new however. The paper [7] discusses the approach used to build statistical profiles of network services for the EMERALD [20] intrusion detection system. The paper [16] discusses a Neural network based approach to develop connection signatures of common network services.

Self-Organizing Maps have also been used in the past in the intrusion detection domain for various purposes. The paper [10] describes a Multi-level Perceptron/SOM prototype used to perform misuse-based intrusion detection. The paper [23] describes a system that uses SOMs as a monitor-stack to profile network data at various layers of the TCP/IP protocol stack. This system was used to detect buffer-overflow attacks by building profiles of application data based on percentage of bytes that were alphabetical, numerical, control, or binary. The paper [15] describes a system that uses Neural networks using the Resilient Propagation Algorithm (RPROP) to detect intrusions that uses SOMs for clustering and visualizing the data.

The paper [18] describes a host-based intrusion detection system that uses multiple SOMs to build profiles of user sessions, and uses them to detect abnormal user activities. The paper [17] describes an anomaly-based intrusion detection system that characterizes each connection based on the following features: Duration of the connection, Protocol type (TCP/UDP), Service type

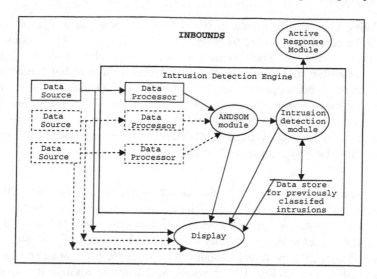

Fig. 2. INBOUNDS Architecture Diagram

(HTTP/SMTP/etc.), Status of the connection, Source bytes (Bytes sent from Source to Destination), and Destination bytes (Bytes sent from Destination to Source). SOMs based on these features were used to classify network traffic into normal or anomalous. In our approach cited in this paper, we characterize each network connection based on a different set of features, and build SOMs for each individual network service of interest.

4 SOM-Based Anomaly Detection

In this section, we describe the Anomalous Network-traffic Detection using Self-Organizing Maps (ANDSOM) module used by INBOUNDS for detecting intrusions. We briefly describe the design of the INBOUNDS system as a whole, and then describe the ANDSOM module in detail.

4.1 INBOUNDS Architecture

The INBOUNDS Architecture diagram is shown in Figure 2. Some of the modules of the INBOUNDS system are currently under development. The goal of this section is only to present a high-level view of the INBOUNDS system, so as to give proper context to describe the ANDSOM module.

The Intrusion Detection Engine is the heart of the INBOUNDS system. Multiple Data Source modules feed real-time network data into the engine. This engine makes a decision on whether a network connection looks normal or anomalous. The Display module shall display real-time network traffic seen in the network on which INBOUNDS is being run, with a GUI front-end. The Active Response module takes response actions against intrusions. The response actions include being able to add a rule in the network firewall (if available) to block the traffic, to rate-limit traffic, to close the TCP connection by sending a RST packet to the sender etc. The Intrusion Detection module is present as a place-holder for a module that can make the final decision on whether the connection being analyzed is intrusive or not. The goal of this module is to incorporate the results of other modules, beside the ANDSOM module, and come up with a final decision. The modules that could be added in future include signature-based intrusion detection systems like SNORT [3] and modules based on other paradigms like the Bayesian module under development.

Data Source Module. The Data Source module feeds live network data pack-ets to the Intrusion Detection Engine. The program *tcpurify* [9] runs as the Data Source module, captures network packets off the wire, removes the application data from the packet and reports only the first 64 bytes of each packet, covering the IP and TCP/UDP protocol headers. The *tcpurify* program can also obfus-cate the sender and receiver IP addresses and provide anonymity to the two hosts involved in the network connection during traffic analysis. This module is explained in detail in [22].

Data Processor Module. This module receives the raw packets from the Data Source modules as input and runs the *tcptrace* [19] program with the INBOUNDS module. The INBOUNDS module for *tcptrace* reports the following messages for every connection seen in the network.

Open messages are reported upon seeing a new connection being opened in the network. The Open (O) message is of the format:

```
O TimeStamp Protocol <src host:port> <dst host:port> Status
```

The TimeStamp field reports the time the connection was opened. The Pro-tocol field keeps track of if the protocol was TCP or UDP. Since UDP traffic doesn't have an implicit notion of connection unlike TCP, the Data Processor module groups UDP traffic between unique

$$< SourceIP, SourcePort, DestinationIP, DestinationPort >$$

4-tuples as connections, and uses a time-out mechanism to expire old connec-tions. The $< srchost : port >$, and $< dsthost : port >$ fields together identify the end-points involved in the connection. The Status field is reported as 0 if both SYN packets opening the connection were seen, and reported as 1 otherwise, for TCP connections. For UDP connections, the Status field is always reported as 0.

Update messages are reported periodically during the lifetime of the con-nection. The Update (U) message is of the following format:

```
U TimeStamp Protocol <src host:port> <dst host:port>

        INTER ASOQ ASOA QAIT AQIT
```

The period with which successive Update (U) messages are reported is tunable and defaults to 60 seconds. The INTER field reports the interactivity of the connection, defined as the number of questions per second seen during the past period. A sequence of data packets seen from the sender to the receiver constitute a single question until the receiver sends a packet carrying some data (pure TCP acknowledgments do not count), which would mark the end of the question. The answers are similarly defined for the receiver to sender direction. The ASOQ field reports the Average Size of Questions seen during the past period and the ASOA field reports the Average Size of Answers seen during the past period. The QAIT (Question-Answer Idle Time) field reports the idle time seen between seeing a question and an answer during the past period, averaged per second. The AQIT (Answer-Question Idle Time) similarly identifies the idle time between seeing an answer and a question, averaged per second, in the past period.

Close messages are reported when a previously open connection is closed in the network. The Close (C) message is of the following format:

```
C TimeStamp Protocol <src host:port> <dst host:port> Status
```

For TCP connections, the Status field is reported as 0 if both the FIN packets were seen during the connection close. If the connection was closed with a RST packet, the Status is reported as 1. UDP connections are reported as closed if they are found inactive for an expire-interval. The expire-interval is tunable, and defaults to 120 seconds. The Status field is always reported as 0 for UDP connections.

4.2   ANDSOM Module – Training

The ANDSOM module implements the SOM-based approach for intrusion detection. In the training phase, SOMs are built to model different network services like web, email, telnet etc. For example, if we are trying to model web traffic in our network, a training data set is first collected by capturing dumpfiles from the network having a large number of sample web connections. It is important to make sure that intrusions themselves do not get into the training data set, since such intrusions may be perceived as normal by the SOM being built. For this, the signature-based intrusion detection system SNORT is run on the dumpfile, and connections reported by SNORT as intrusive are removed. However, it is still possible that we could have intrusions missed by SNORT if it had no rules to detect them. To make our system robust against this possibility, we could use multiple training data sets to generate multiple SOMs for each network service and run training data sets against other maps to prune out anomalies from getting into our model, as discussed in [23].

The submodules that make up the ANDSOM module are explained below.

TRC2INP Submodule. This submodule receives the 'O', 'U', and 'C' messages generated by the Data Processor module as input and generates six-dimensional vectors characterizing network connections. The parameters constituting the six dimensions are INTER, ASOQ, ASOA, L_QAIT, L_AQIT, and DOC. The INTER, ASOQ, and ASOA dimensions are calculated by averaging the INTER, ASOQ, and ASOA values from the 'U' messages received during the lifetime of the connection. The dimensions L_QAIT, and L_AQIT represent log base 10 values of the average QAIT and AQIT parameters calculated from the 'U' messages received during the course of the connection. The DOC dimension reports the Duration of Connection, and is the difference between the TimeStamps reported in the 'O' and 'C' messages of the connection.

The rationale behind using log base 10 values of QAIT and AQIT is to be more robust to false-positives. Since the QAIT and AQIT values tend to be relatively low in magnitude compared to other dimensions, if the QAIT value of a connection was reported as 0.0008 for example, and if the mean value found in the training data set was 0.0002, the connection was perceived to be four times the mean and had a high probability of being found anomalous. However, this might turn out to be a false-alarm, and what we might actually need is the order of QAIT and AQIT, whether they are in milli-seconds or micro-seconds etc., than the actual values themselves. We observed false-positives similar to the above example during our experiments, and decided to use the log value of the dimensions to mitigate the problem.

Normalizer Submodule. Using the six-dimensional vectors reported by the TRC2INP module to build SOMs directly tends to be biased to certain dimensions, as different dimensional values tend to be in different units. Normalizing all dimensions to values from 0 to 1, for example, could help, but still the dimension with the most variance would tend to dominate the SOM formation. Hence we use the following variance normalization procedure in this submodule to normalize the six-dimensional vectors.

The goal of variance normalization is to normalize the six-dimensional vectors of the training data set so that, in the set of normalized vectors, each dimension has a variance of unity. This normalization process is done in two steps. In the first step, the mean (μ) and standard deviation (σ) values are calculated for each of the six dimensions in the training data set. In the second step, a six-dimensional vector $< d_1, d_2, d_3, d_4, d_5, d_6 >$ is normalized to $< n_1, n_2, n_3, n_4, n_5, n_6 >$, by

$$n_i = \frac{d_i - \mu_i}{\sigma_i}$$

where μ_i and σ_i are the mean and standard deviations of dimension i.

At the end of the normalization process, the mean and standard deviation values found are stored in a data file for use in real-time operation.

SOM Training. We used the public domain software packages SOM_PAK [5], and SOMTOOLBOX [4], during this phase. The SOM_PAK is a set of C programs that implement various stages of the SOM algorithm. The SOMTOOL-

BOX is a Toolbox for the MATLAB package, which we used for its graphical visualization functions.

SOM Initialization The SOMs were initialized with the *som_lininit* function from the SOMTOOLBOX. This function uses Principal Component Analysis [14] to arrive at the SOM dimensions by calculating the eigen values and eigen vectors of the auto-correlation matrix of the training data set. The orientation corresponding to the two largest eigen values, which are the directions in which the data set exhibits the most variance, is found. The ratio between the SOM dimensions are chosen based on the ratio of the two largest eigen values. The actual dimensions are chosen depending on this ratio and on the number of vectors in the training data set, and is explained in further detail in [22].

The SOM was chosen to be of hexagonal topology, and an Euclidean distance measure was used. After choosing the dimensions, the *som_lininit* function initializes the neurons in the SOM to values linearly chosen from the range of values in the training data set.

Initial Training Phase The *vsom* program from the SOM_PAK package was used to train the neurons in the SOM. The number of iterations of training in this phase were chosen to be low, in the order of a few thousands. In our experiments, for each network service, we typically had a few thousand samples, and this phase was done so that each sample was shown at most once to the SOM being built. The Gaussian neighborhood function was used with an initial neighborhood radius as the lower of the SOM dimensions. The neighborhood radius decreased linearly to 1 at the end of the training. The learning rate factor $\alpha(t)$ was chosen to be 0.9 and reduced linearly to 0 at the end of training.

Final Training Phase The *vsom* program was used again in the final training phase, and the number of iterations of training was chosen to be high, in the range of 100,000s. The number of iterations was set to be 500 times the product of the lattice dimensions (based on the heuristic recommended in [25]). The Gaussian neighborhood function with a low initial neighborhood radius of 5, and a low learning rate factor of 0.05 were set, and the map was fine-tuned in the Final Training Phase.

SOM Validation. We evaluate the SOM at the end of the training phase, by feeding back the training data set to the SOM, and calculating the distance to winner for each of the samples. We validate the SOM if at least 95.44% of sample vectors in the training data set had a winner within 2 units of distance. This heuristic assumes the training data set to follow Gaussian distribution. If the data in the training data set were to follow Gaussian distribution strictly, 95.44% of the samples must fall within 2 units of standard deviation from the mean, according to properties of Gaussian distribution. If the 95.44% heuristic is not met at the end of training, the samples that do not have a winner within 2 units are shown more often to the SOM, and the training is repeated.

Although this heuristic lets the SOM model capture the behavior exhibited by the bulk of traffic, it does not capture the out-lier behavior exhibited by fewer connections. These outliers may give rise to false-positives with our model. If we were to raise the heuristic and try to capture more outliers into our model, we could get rid of some false-positives, but would be subjecting ourselves to more false-negatives. Note that to include an out-lier in our model, we need a SOM neuron within 2 units of standard deviation from it in six-dimensional space, as all connections with winner more than 2 units distant will be classified as anomalous. When we have such a neuron, all connection samples within the six-dimensional hyper-sphere of radius 2 units from the neuron will be classified as normal traffic. If an attack were to fall in such a hyper-sphere surrounding such a neuron, it would give rise to a false-negative. Thus, as we increase our heuristic value, we would add a lot of such hyper-spheres for the outliers into our model and the SOM would tend to get more and more general in nature, losing its specificity of modeling only the network service of interest.

We believe that our 95.44% Gaussian heuristic is a reasonable value to capture the characteristics exhibited by the bulk of traffic. However, our experiments need to be repeated with various threshold percentages for the heuristic as a future work, to study the trade-off more thoroughly.

4.3 ANDSOM Module – Operation

During real-time operation phase, the ANDSOM module receives the 'O', 'U', and 'C' messages of connections from the Data Processor module. These messages are converted to six-dimensional vectors by the TRC2INP module. If a SOM was built for that network service, it is normalized based on the mean (μ_i) and standard deviation (σ_i) values found from the training data used to build the SOM. The normalized vector is then fed to the SOM, and the winner is found. The network connection is classified as anomalous, if the distance to the winner was more than 2 units.

5   Experimental Results

In this section, we describe our experiments with the SOM models for Domain Name System (DNS) and web (Hyper-Text Transfer Protocol) traffic, and analyze the performance of the models built.

5.1   DNS

DNS [21] traffic runs on top of both TCP and UDP. Although some DNS connections are observed on top of TCP, typically when two name servers transfer bulk domain information, the bulk of DNS traffic is found to be on top of UDP, and involve simple query-response of domain information. We collected dump-files from our network yielding 8857 sample DNS connections, and a SOM of

Table 1. DNS Training Data Statistics

Dimensions	Mean	Standard Deviation
INTER	0.653	0.701
ASOQ	29.082	19.831
ASOA	112.352	94.651
L_QAIT	-1.142	1.376
L_AQIT	-0.016	0.186
DOC	2.033	1.056

Table 2. DNS Exploit Vector

INTER	ASOQ	ASOA	L_QAIT	L_AQIT	DOC
1.989	493.000	626.000	-2.847	-2.375	1.006

Table 3. DNS Normalized Exploit Vector

INTER	ASOQ	ASOA	L_QAIT	L_AQIT	DOC
1.906	23.393	5.427	-1.239	-12.664	-0.973

dimensions 19x25 was built and linearly initialized. The mean and standard deviation values of this data set found by the Normalizer submodule shown in Table 1 illustrate the traits of DNS traffic found in our network.

The mean INTER value of 0.65 and the DOC value of 2 seconds, indicate that a DNS connection has 1.3 questions asked during the course of a connection. This is expected since the bulk of DNS connections involve a single query-response. The relative mean values of ASOQ and ASOA indicate that the answers tend to be much bigger than the questions, which is expected since DNS responses tend to be much bigger than DNS queries in general. The mean L_QAIT indicates that the QAIT value tends to be in hundredths of second per second. The L_AQIT value close to 0 corresponds to an AQIT value close to a second per second and is expected because single query-response traffic has no request (question) following a response (answer). The AQIT value is hence reported as the maximum value of 1 second per second for these connections, causing the mean L_AQIT value to be close to 0.

For testing the SOM model, we generated anomalous DNS traffic with an attack based on an exploit of the BIND [11] DNS server. BIND server version 8.2.x was run as a vulnerable server in our test-bed. The exploit [1], available in the public domain, is based on the buffer-overflow vulnerability [6] in processing Transaction Signatures found in 8.2.x versions.

Table 2 shows the six-dimensional values of the DNS exploit vector, and Table 3 shows the normalized values of the DNS exploit vector, based on the mean and standard deviation values found in the training data set. We can observe from these tables that the ASOQ value of 493 bytes is highly anomalous with a distance of 23.393 standard deviations, since the training data set had a mean ASOQ value of 29 bytes. The ASOA value of 626 bytes is also anomalous

Table 4. DNS Winner Neuron

INTER	ASOQ	ASOA	L_QAIT	L_AQIT	DOC	Distance
0.708	6.072	-0.799	0.150	-0.212	-0.128	22.314

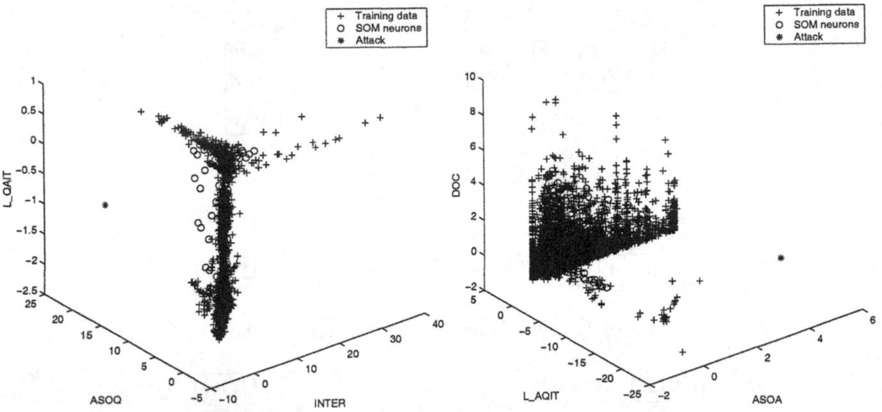

(a) View 1 (b) View 2

Fig. 3. DNS Exploit View (Units: Standard-Deviations from Mean)

from the training data set with 5.427 standard deviations away from the mean ASOA of 112.35 bytes. Further, the L_AQIT value of the -2.375 indicates that the actual AQIT was in the order of milli seconds per second. This happens to be highly anomalous with a normalized value of -12.664 standard deviations because the mean L_AQIT was in the order of -0.016, corresponding to an AQIT value of close to one second per second.

The winner neuron for the DNS exploit, and its distance to the winner in six dimensional space, are shown in Table 4. We can see that the winner neuron was at a distance of 22.314 standard deviations in the six-dimensional space, resulting in the DNS exploit being successfully classified with our intrusion threshold of 2 units.

To aid in the visualization of the six-dimensional space, we split the space into two three-dimensional views. The dimensions that take the X, Y, and Z axes of the two views were chosen arbitrarily with the goal of showing the attack point from the training data points clearly. The two three-dimensional views are shown in Figure 3.

5.2 HTTP

We built a SOM to model web traffic based on the HTTP [8] [13] protocol. A training dataset of 7194 HTTP connections collected from our network was used, and a SOM of dimensions 16x27 was built and linearly initialized. The mean and standard deviation values of the training data set found by the Normalizer submodule are shown in Table 5.

Table 5. HTTP Training Data Statistics

Dimensions	Mean	Standard Deviation
INTER	0.829	0.773
ASOQ	589.120	743.973
ASOA	6802.338	59463.781
L_QAIT	-1.383	0.874
L_AQIT	-3.714	3.324
DOC	9.463	27.244

The mean interactivity of a HTTP connection is close to 0.8 questions per second. The mean size of questions is an order of magnitude smaller than the size of the answers, implying that more data seems to come from web-servers to web-clients than in the other direction. However ASOQ and ASOA tend to be highly variant as indicated by their high standard deviations. The QAIT seems to be in hundredth-s of a second per second, which could correspond to the fact that web-servers tend to be across the Internet causing the delay between the questions and answers. The AQIT value is in the order of ten-thousandths of a second per second and seems to indicate the fact that it takes very less time for a web-client to generate the next question, once the answer to a previous question is received. The mean duration of a HTTP connection is 9 seconds, although this duration is found to be highly variant with a standard deviation of 27.

We used the HTTP Tunnel [2] program to generate anomalous HTTP traffic in the network. The HTTP Tunnel program creates application-layer HTTP tunnels between two hosts, and lets any type of traffic to be run on top of HTTP. The HTTP tunnel program can be used by attackers inside an organization to break firewall rules. For example, assuming an organization firewall allows traffic to a host A on HTTP port 80, a malicious user inside the organization could setup an HTTP tunnel server on host A, and could let a user outside the organization on host B establish a telnet session to A by encapsulating all data as HTTP. The HTTP tunnel program uses the HTTP POST and GET methods to establish a duplex connection between two hosts; the POST method is used by the tunnel client on B to send data to A, and the GET method is used by the client on B to fetch data from A.

We used this program for our experiment by running a tunnel server in our test-bed, and establishing a telnet session to it from a tunnel client across the Internet. Although this traffic shows up as HTTP, we expect our model to classify it as anomalous since its connection characteristics might be different from normal HTTP traffic. The telnet connection was run on the HTTP tunnel for approximately 10 minutes, during which 13 connections (3 POST connections and 10 GET connections) were opened. We present the GET and POST connections that turned out to be highly anomalous amongst the 13 connections. The six dimensional vectors of those GET and POST connections are shown in Table 6 and the normalized values of these vectors are shown in Table 7.

In the HTTP GET connection, a single query is made at the beginning of the connection by the client, and all replies from the server form a single answer.

Table 6. HTTP Tunnel Traffic

	INTER	ASOQ	ASOA	L_QAIT	L_AQIT	DOC
GET	0.004	17.200	22860.200	-5.699	-5.854	247.687
POST	0.023	491.667	0.000	-5.523	-10.000	307.706

Table 7. HTTP Normalized Tunnel Traffic

	INTER	ASOQ	ASOA	L_QAIT	L_AQIT	DOC
GET	-1.068	-0.769	0.270	-4.937	-0.644	8.744
POST	-1.044	-0.131	-0.114	-4.735	-1.891	10.947

Hence, the QAIT value is calculated only once, when the first data packet is seen on the tunnel from the server after the GET request is made. Such a QAIT value, calculated and normalized to a 60 second update interval, turns out to be very low, in the order of micro-seconds, which results in the L_QAIT value of -5.699, which is considered to be highly anomalous, being approximately -4.94 standard deviations from the mean. The duration of the connection (DOC) happens to be 247 seconds and is found to be highly anomalous with a distance of 8.74 standard deviations.

Similarly, since the POST connection lasts for 307 seconds approximately, the DOC dimension is considered highly anomalous. The ASOA value is found to be 0 bytes in Table 6 because all data in the POST connection flows from the tunnel client to the tunnel server, with only pure TCP ACKs arriving from the tunnel server. The L_AQIT value is also calculated to be -10.000 since no sample was available to calculate AQIT as there were no answers. The AQIT is found to be its initial value of 0 at the end. Since log base 10 of 0 is negative infinity, a low value of -10.000 is reported by the TRC2INP submodule. The L_QAIT is found to be anomalous with the value of -5.523, which corresponds to a QAIT value in microseconds. This again is due to the fact that no data flowed in the opposite direction, causing all data from tunnel client to server to be perceived as one question. The QAIT value was calculated when the FIN packet was seen on the connection. This happens to be low, as the first FIN packet seen is also sent from the tunnel client.

To summarize, both the GET and POST connections are found to be anomalous because the packet flow in both directions is found to be almost completely uni-directional, which is unusual for HTTP traffic, and because of the fact that the connections last a much longer time compared to the normal HTTP traffic used in training. The same winner neuron was found for both the GET and POST connection traffic, which is presented in Table 8.

Both the connections are classified as intrusions with the intrusion threshold of 2 units. The two three-dimensional views of six-dimensional space for HTTP traffic, are shown in Figure 4.

5.3   Performance Analysis

In this section, we present the Run-time and Modeling analyses of our system. Run-time analysis is aimed at estimating the feasibility of using the SOM-based

Table 8. HTTP Winner Neuron

	INTER	ASOQ	ASOA	L_QAIT	L_AQIT	DOC	Distance
GET	-0.953	-0.389	0.022	-1.460	1.131	5.895	4.855
POST	-0.953	-0.389	0.022	-1.460	1.131	5.895	6.743

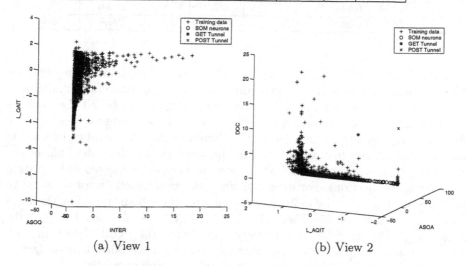

(a) View 1 (b) View 2

Fig. 4. HTTP Exploit View (Units: Standard-Deviations from Mean)

approach real-time, and the Modeling analysis is aimed at evaluating the efficiency with which the traffic characteristics of a network-service are modeled by its SOM.

Run-Time Analysis. We performed an off-line evaluation of the modules of the INBOUNDS system to estimate its run-time performance. Traffic from our department network was captured in dumpfiles of varying durations (15 min, 30 min, 45 min, 1 hour, 2 hours, and 3 hours), and the Data Processor module was run off-line on them to generate the 'O','U', and 'C' messages [Sec. 4.1]. These messages were fed to the TRC2INP module to generate six-dimensional vectors of network connections. The *locator* module normalized the vectors based on the HTTP training statistics (mean and standard deviation of the dimensions), fed it to the HTTP SOM, determined the winner neuron and the distance to it. The connection is classified anomalous if this distance was more than 2 units. Communication between the modules was through pipes, with each module reading its input from STDIN and writing out its output to STDOUT. Finally, as the goal was just to estimate the peak run-time performance, traffic from all network services found (not necessarily HTTP) was fed to the HTTP SOM.

Here, we present the results of the 1-hour, 2-hour, and 3-hour dumpfiles. The tests were performed on a GNU/Linux system running on a 800 MHz Pentium III processor with 256 MB RAM. The reader is referred to [22] for a more detailed analysis of the evaluation.

Table 9. Off-line Run-time Performance Analysis

Duration (Hours)	Bytes	Avg. Data Rate (Mbps)	Packets	Conns.	Proc. Time (sec)	Proc. Rate (Mbps)
1	1,096,577,208	2.44	2,536,807	10,704	57.11	153.61
2	1,954,570,814	2.17	5,322,218	87,817	214.6	72.86
3	2,810,266,341	2.08	7,686,773	124,935	295.6	76.06

Table 9 illustrates the total bytes seen for various durations of capture, the Average Data Rate seen in that duration, total number of packets seen, the total number of connections found, total Processing Time taken by all the modules together, and the corresponding Processing Rate of the modules. The net processing time depends on the size of the dumpfile and the number of packets and connections per unit time found in the network. Further, the bulk of the processing time is spent on the Data Processor module that needs to keep state of all active connections. For example, when the experiments were repeated to evaluate the time taken by individual modules for the 3-hour dumpfile, the Data Processor module took 254.9 seconds, the TRC2INP module took 21.9 seconds, while the *locator* module that actually implements the SOM algorithm took just 11.24 seconds. The SOM algorithm itself seems to be fairly light-weight in that once a trained SOM is available, it merely involves normalizing the vector based on the service statistics (mean and standard deviation of the dimensions) and computing the distance from the normalized vector to all the neurons in the SOM (taking linear time in the number of neurons in the SOM) and determining the winner.

Modeling Analysis. To determine the modeling efficiency of the SOMs constructed, the amount of false-positives generated for the vectors from the training data set for different values of threshold (distance to the winner on which a connection is considered anomalous) was measured.

The percentage of false-positives generated for the DNS and HTTP SOMs shown in Figure 5 show the false-positive percentages as the threshold value is increased from 0.1 in steps of 0.1 until the threshold required to classify all the vectors in the training data set are classified as normal. For the threshold of 2 units used in our modules, which was sufficient to classify the attacks studied as anomalous, 1.18% and 1.16% of the DNS and HTTP training data set vectors give rise to false positives. The false-positive percentage drops exponentially, and increasing the threshold beyond 2 units seems to yield limited drops in the percentages of false-positives.

We also tested the HTTP SOM for streaming music and chat programs as these programs tend to run on HTTP port 80, and hence could be perceived as HTTP traffic. Streaming music connections (running on TCP) tend to be classified as anomalous, giving rise to false-positives. Such connections exhibit high ASOA values since unidirectional streams are treated as single huge Answers from the server to the client. Chat sessions are classified as anomalous too based

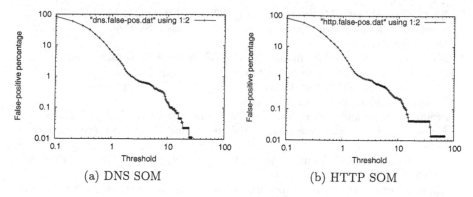

(a) DNS SOM   (b) HTTP SOM

Fig. 5. SOM Sensitivity

on the DOC dimension when they last for more than a couple of minutes, since the Mean and Standard-deviation values of DOC for the HTTP training data set were 9.5 seconds and 27.2 respectively. Although we can mitigate the false-positives rising out of such streaming music and chat sessions by adding multiple samples of them to the training data set and repeating the SOM training process, this could make the HTTP SOM to be more generic in nature, yielding false-negatives to attacks that resemble music streams/chat sessions.

6   Conclusions

The ability of the SOM based approach to correlate multiple aspects of a network connection (reported by the six parameters) to decide if it looks normal or abnormal, makes it a powerful technique for anomaly detection. The SOM model we built to characterize SMTP (email) traffic was also successful in detecting a Sendmail [24] buffer overflow attack, and is described in [22]. The SOM based approach seems to be particularly well suited to detect buffer-overflow attacks, as they tend to differ from the normal traffic behavior on the six dimensions.

However, the ANDSOM module may not detect attacks that resemble normal operational behavior. An intrusion massaged to resemble normal traffic might go un-noticed. Another limitation is that although the behavior exhibited by the bulk of traffic for a network service can be modeled, corner-case behavior occurring infrequently may be classified as intrusions, giving rise to false-positives.

For future work, it could be interesting to study the effects of modification to the SOM algorithm, including trying other neighborhood functions and different map topologies. It would also be interesting to construct and validate maps with various values of threshold with the Gaussian heuristic, and also by assuming other distributions of data besides Gaussian for the training data set.

References

1. Bind named 8.2.x Remote Exploit.
   http://downloads.securityfocus.com/vulnerabilities/exploits/tsig.c.

2. HTTP Tunnel. http://www.nocrew.org/software/httptunnel.html.
3. Snort - The Open Source Network Intrusion Detection System. http://www.snort.org.
4. SOM Toolbox for Matlab. http://www.cis.hut.fi/projects/somtoolbox.
5. SOM_PAK. http://www.cis.hut.fi/research/som_lvq_pak.shtml.
6. VU#196945 ISC BIND 8 Buffer Overflow in TSIG Handling Code. http://www.kb.cert.org/vuls/id/196945.
7. Phillip A.Porras and Alfonso Valdes. Live Traffic Analysis of TCP/IP Gateways. In *Proceedings of the ISOC Symposium on Network and Distributed Systems Security*, 1998.
8. T. Berners-Lee, R. Fielding, and H. Frystyk. Hypertext Transfer Protocol – HTTP/1.0, May 1996. RFC 1945.
9. Ethan Blanton. TCPurify. http://irg.cs.ohiou.edu/~eblanton/tcpurify.
10. James Cannady and Jim Mahaffey. The Application of Artificial Intelligence to Misuse Detection. In *Proceedings of the First Recent Advances in Intrusion Detection (RAID) Conference*, 1998.
11. Internet Software Consortium. Bind. http://www.isc.org/products/BIND.
12. Internet Software Consortium. Internet Domain Survey, Jan 2003. http://www.isc.org/ds/WWW-200301/index.html.
13. R. Fielding, J. Gettys, J. Mogul, H. Frystyk, L. Masinter, P. Leach, and T. Berners-Lee. Hypertext Transfer Protocol – HTTP/1.1, June 1999. RFC 2616.
14. J.Hollmen. Principal Component Analysis. http://www.cis.hut.fi/~jhollmen/dippa/node29.html.
15. Chaivat Jirapummin, Naruemon Wattanapongsakorn, and Prasert Kanthamanon. Hybrid Neural Networks for Intrusion Detection System, 2002.
16. K.Tan and B.Collie. Detection and Classification of TCP/IP Network Services. In *Proceedings of the 13th Annual Computer Security Applications Conference*, 1997.
17. Peter Lichodzijewski, A.Nur Zincir-Heywood, and Malcolm I.Heywood. Dynamic Intrusion Detection Using Self-Organizing Maps. In *The 14th Annual Canadian Information Technology Security Symposium (CITSS)*, 2002.
18. Peter Lichodzijewski, A.Nur Zincir-Heywood, and Malcolm I.Heywood. Host-based Intrusion Detection Using Self-Organizing Maps. In *The IEEE World Congress on Computational Intelligence, International Joint Conference on Neural Networks, IJCNN'02*, 2002.
19. Shawn Ostermann. Tcptrace - TCP Connection Analysis Tool. http://www.tcptrace.org.
20. P.A.Porras and P.G.Neumann. EMERALD: Event Monitoring Enabling Responses to Anomalous Live Disturbances. In *Proceedings of the National Information Security Conference*, pages 353–365, Oct 1997.
21. P.Mockapetris. Domain Names - Concepts and Facilities, November 1987. RFC 1034.
22. Manikantan Ramadas. Detecting Anomalous Network Traffic with Self-Organizing Maps. Master's thesis, Ohio University, Mar 2003. http://irg.cs.ohiou.edu/~mramadas/documents/MS-Thesis/thesis.pdf.
23. Brandon Craig Rhodes, James A.Mahaffey, and James D.Cannady. Multiple Self-Organizing Maps for Intrusion Detection. In *Proceedings of the 23rd National Information Systems Security Conference*, 2000.
24. The Sendmail Consortium. Sendmail. http://www.sendmail.org.
25. T.Kohonen. *Self Organizing Maps*. Springer, third edition, 2001.

An Approach for Detecting Self-propagating Email Using Anomaly Detection*

Ajay Gupta and R. Sekar

Department of Computer Science
Stony Brook University, Stony Brook, NY 11794
{ajay,sekar}@cs.sunysb.edu

Abstract. This paper develops a new approach for detecting self-propagating email viruses based on statistical anomaly detection. Our approach assumes that a key objective of an email virus attack is to eventually overwhelm mail servers and clients with a large volume of email traffic. Based on this assumption, the approach is designed to detect increases in traffic volume over what was observed during the training period. This paper describes our approach and the results of our simulation-based experiments in assessing the effectiveness of the approach in an intranet setting. Within the simulation setting, our results establish that the approach is effective in detecting attacks all of the time, with very few false alarms. In addition, attacks could be detected sufficiently early so that clean up efforts need to target only a fraction of the email clients in an intranet.

1 Introduction

Email viruses have become one of the major Internet security threats today. An email virus is a malicious program which hides in an email attachment, and becomes active when the attachment is opened. A principal goal of email virus attacks such as Melissa [1] is that of generating a large volume of email traffic over time, so that email servers and clients are eventually overwhelmed with this traffic, thus effectively disrupting the use of the email service. Future viruses may be more damaging, taking actions such as creating hidden back-doors on the infected machines that can be used to commandeer these machines in a subsequent coordinated attack.

Current approaches for dealing with email viruses rely on the use of anti-virus software at the desktops, network servers, mail exchange servers and at the gateways. Detection of email viruses is usually based on a signature-based approach, where the signature captures distinguishing features of a virus, such as a unique subject line or a unique sequence of bytes in its code. This approach is effective against known email viruses, but is ineffective against unknown (i.e., newly released) viruses. To overcome this drawback, techniques have been recently developed that focus on virus behavior rather than its representation. Such "behavior-blocking" approaches detect viruses by using signatures of behavior, such as fast generation of emails or self-replication.

Although behavior-blocking is more effective against unknown viruses, it can still be fooled by carefully designed viruses that propagate slowly, or replicate after a period. For instance, if system is set to block the behavior that an email attachment should not cause generation of more than k other email messages, a virus that generates only

---

* This research was supported in part by NSF under grant CCR-0098154 and the Defense Advanced Research Agency (DARPA) under contract number N66001-00-C-8022.

G. Vigna, E. Jonsson, and C. Kruegel (Eds.): RAID 2003, LNCS 2820, pp. 55–72, 2003.

$k-1$ copies will go undetected. Similarly, an email attachment that causes time-delayed propagation may also go undetected. More generally, a virus can employ a combination of low propagation factor, high incubation period, and randomization to evade behavior-blocking approaches.

An alternative approach for detection is one that focuses on the ultimate effect of self-propagating email viruses: increase in email traffic. Simple adaptations on the part of the virus, such as reducing the propagation factor below a certain threshold, introducing time delays or other randomizations do not alter this ultimate effect. For this reason, our approach is based on detecting email viruses based on increases in the volume of email traffic generated.

Given the variations in email traffic from one site to another, and from one time to another, it is difficult for manual development of characterizations of excessive email traffic. An alternative approach is to use machine learning — the system is trained to learn characteristics of normal email traffic, and then detect significant increases. In the context of intrusion detection, such *anomaly detection* approaches have been associated with relatively high false-alarm rates, as well as a moderate rate of false negatives (i.e., missed attacks). In this paper, we develop and study an approach that appears to be capable of detecting attacks with very low false alarm rate, while still being able to detect attacks reasonably early.

This paper first presents our approach for anomaly-based detection of the self-propagating email viruses. It begins with an overview of our approach in Section 2. We have studied the performance of this approach using two complementary experiments, both based on simulation. The first experiment focuses on creating stealthy virus behaviors, but uses a simplistic user model. The second experiment strives for more realistic user models, as well as more accurate reproduction of the behaviors of different software components of the email system, but the virus models are not as stealthy or variable as the first experiment.

Section 3 describes our first experiment. Our experimental results show that viruses similar to the ones that are prevalent currently, can be detected early. This is because such viruses are very "noisy." For stealthier viruses that use a small replication factor, detection is still achieved fairly early in our simulation, when a minority of email clients are infected. For the most stealthy viruses that use a combination of low replication factor and delayed propagation, a majority of the network is infected by the time of detection. In all cases, detection is achieved before the time the email server experiences a high overload. Since our technique promises to provide low false alarm rates, there is a potential to launch automated responses at detection time so as to quarantine emails with attachments on the mail server[1]. At this point, a more careful investigation of the virus can be performed, followed by a cleanup phase (on the email clients) if a virus is indeed present. Note that early detection of the virus reduces the cleanup costs significantly, as only a fraction of the computers in an organization need to be cleaned up.

The second experiment, described in Section 4, used a more elaborate user model. Moreover, an actual email system was used so as to make the simulation results more realistic. The goal of the experiment, conducted as part of a DARPA-sponsored research

---

[1] Such a quarantine will be effective in arresting further spread of the virus, assuming that viruses can spread only through attachments.

program, was to study the effectiveness of automated response to check the spread of such viruses. A number of signature and behavior based detectors were used in combination with our anomaly detector. The signature and behavior based detectors were tuned for early detection, but this meant that the more stealthy viruses would not be caught by them. The anomaly detector was therefore tuned for delayed but certain detection. The detection delay was artificially increased so that the anomaly detector will not raise an alarm until it is certain that any responses based on other detectors have failed. For this reason, our primary effectiveness criteria in this experiment was detection, rather than early detection. Of the hundreds of experiments conducted in this set up, there were 7 cases where the virus was not checked by other detectors, and in each of these cases, our anomaly detector was able to detect the attack. These experimental results show that our approach is effective, subject to the accuracy of the simulation models used in the experiment. They also indicate that our approach can complement other "behavior-blocking" approaches, which are typically tuned for early detection but may be fooled by stealthy viruses.

Some of the key benefits of our approach are:

– *Accurate detection.* In our simulation-based experiments, our approach demonstrated near-zero false alarm rates with zero false negatives (i.e, 100% detection). The latter is possible because of the nature of self-propagating email, wherein the email traffic keeps increasing until it is detected.

– *Robust against polymorphic and stealthy viruses.* Our technique is unaffected by polymorphic viruses. It promises to reliably detect stealthy viruses that pose challenges to previously developed detection techniques, although the detection may be delayed.

A practical benefit of our approach is that it has a low runtime overhead. Moreover, its learning phase is robust enough to operate without expert supervision.

While the above results are promising, they are tempered by the fact that they are based exclusively on simulated behaviors of email users. The first experiment used a particularly simple model for user behaviors: each user was modeled as a Poisson process. The second experiment used a non-uniform model taking into account such factors as address books. User behavior was simulated using a 3-state ("reading email," "composing email," and "idle") Markov process that makes random transitions between states that is governed by a set of transition probabilities. Thus the user model was much more realistic in this experiment. Nevertheless, it is well known in the context of anomaly detection that real system behavior tends to exhibit more variability than what can be observed in a simulation. Thus, the results obtained using simulation experiments cannot be directly extrapolated to real operating environments. Our ongoing work aims to address this weakness by using simulation only for the purpose of modeling viruses; normal email traffic will be taken from actual mail server logs.

2 Overview of Approach

Our approach is based on *specification-based anomaly detection* [36], a technique that combines state-machine specifications of network protocols with statistical machine-learning. In this case, the protocol models the interaction between email clients in an organization with the email server of the same organization. These interactions are called

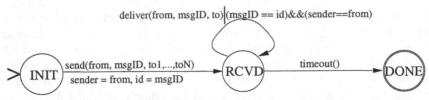

Fig. 1. A State Machine Modeling Email Server Operation

events. The state machine (implicitly) classifies events into different categories based on the transition taken by them in the state machine. Machine learning techniques are then used to learn statistics associated with each of these classes. Several choices exist for such statistics, including: average number of attachments to an email, size of a message, etc. Our focus, however, was on characteristics that are necessarily associated with increased email traffic, and hence we chose statistics relating to frequency of taking different transitions. The fact that this simple measure was effective supports the claim of [36] that the use of protocol state machines simplifies feature selection, i.e., even a naive choice of features produces good results.

The first step in our approach is to develop a state machine modeling the behavior of an email service, as observed at a mail server. For the rest of this paper, we concern ourselves mainly with email service within an intranet. We assume that all email clients transfer each of their outgoing messages to the intranet mail server, which in turn forwards the messages to each of the recipients[2]. Since we are only concerned with emails within the intranet, the email server simply queues each message received from any client on the mail queues associated with the respective recipients.

Figure 1 shows the simplified model of email server behavior described in the preceding paragraph. The state machine has three states that are identified as $INIT$, $RCVD$ and $DONE$. The reception of an email from a client $from$ at the server is modeled using the event $send$ that takes several parameters: the first parameter identifies the sender, the second is a unique identifier for the message, and the rest of the parameters denote the recipients of the message. The contents of the message are not modeled in this state machine. When the server receives this message, it forwards the message to each of the email recipients. This forwarding operation is modeled using the $deliver$ event, which takes the sender name, the message identifier and the recipient names as parameters. This event may occur zero or more times, depending on the number and email ids of the recipients. Note that there is no easy way to relate the number of recipients in the $send$ message with the number of recipients to which the message is forwarded by the server. The number of actual recipients of a message may be more (e.g., when a recipient name corresponds to a mailing list), or less (e.g., when a recipient name is in error, or due to duplicates or mail aliases within the recipient list). For this reason, the state machine indicates that there may be zero or more instances of the $deliver$ event corresponding to each $send$ event. The correspondence between the $send$ and $deliver$ events is identified in the state machine by storing the message identifier and sender in two state variables id and $sender$, and then comparing these state variables with the arguments of the $deliver$ event.

---

[2] This assumption holds for most popular email clients such as Microsoft Outlook and Netscape Messenger.

The $DONE$ state in the state machine signifies the completion of the processing of a particular email from a client. Due to the difficulty outlined above in recognizing when such processing is completed, we use a time-out to model completion. The assumption being made here is that once an email is received by the server, it will be processed and the message sent to all recipients within a short period of time. The time-out value is set well above the expected time for such processing of email.

Formally, we use *extended finite state automata (EFSA)* to capture the state machine model shown in Figure 1. An EFSA is similar to a finite-state automaton in that it is characterized by a set of states, some times called *control states* of the automata, and a set of transitions between these states. EFSA differ from FSA in that (a) EFSA make transitions on events that may have arguments, and (b) EFSA can use a finite set of *state variables* in which values can be stored. The EFSA in Figure 1 consists of three control states $INIT$ (the start state), $RCVD$, and $DONE$ (the final state); three events *send*, *deliver* and *timeout*; and two state variables *sender* and *id*.

To understand how such EFSA specifications can be used for monitoring email traffic, consider the state machine diagram again. When an email is accepted by the mail server for delivery, a new instance of the state machine is created, and this instance makes a transition from $INIT$ to $RCVD$ state. The sender and message identifier are stored in the state variables associated with this instance. As copies of this message are delivered to the recipients, the *deliver* transition is taken. Finally, after a timeout period, a transition to the $DONE$ state is taken. This being a final state, the state machine instance is no longer needed, and is cleaned up, i.e., all resources allocated for this state machine instance are released. Note that in general, there will be multiple instances of the state machine active at any time. The number of such active instances is determined by how many email messages are sent by clients over the duration of the timeout period.

Now, we superimpose statistical machine learning over this state-machine specification of email server behavior. An obvious statistical property of interest is the frequency with which various transitions in the state machine are taken. A self-propagating email virus will cause an increase in many of these frequencies. We may also be interested in statistical properties across a *subset* of instances, rather than all instances. The instances of interest can be specified on the basis of state variable values. For instance, we may be interested in the number of emails sent to any recipient by a particular user C on the network. We will do this by selecting instances that have sender equal to C in their RCVD state, and identifying the number of times the transition on the *deliver* event was taken in these instances.

2.1 Statistics of Interest and Their Representation

In the state machine in Figure 1, there are two significant transitions, taking place on the *send* and *deliver* events respectively. We therefore choose frequencies of these two transitions as statistical information of interest, and maintain the following statistics:

 – frequency with which the *send* transition is taken, across all clients
 – frequency with which the *deliver* transition is taken, across all clients
 – for each client C, the frequency with which emails from C take the *send* transition
 – for each client C, the frequency with which emails *from C* take the *deliver* transition

Each of these statistics were maintained at multiple (of the order of ten) time scales, ranging from about a second to about an hour.

We could maintain average frequency information, but since most phenomena related to email can be bursty, we choose to maintain *frequency distributions* rather than averages. In particular, we define a time window w over which we count the number of times a transition is taken. Let $n_{T_1}, ..., n_{T_k}$ denote the counts associated with a transition over k successive time periods $T_1, ..., T_k$ that are w units long. Then a histogram of the values $n_{T_1}, ..., n_{T_k}$ is used to represent the frequency distribution over a time window w, as observed during a training period of duration $w * k$ units.

Since we do not know in advance the range of the values n_{T-1}, it is more convenient to use a histogram with geometric bin ranges, i.e., the range of values corresponding to jth bin in the histogram is a times the range of the $(j - 1)$th bin, for some factor a. In our experiments, a was set to $\sqrt{2}$. Thus, the histogram bins were $[0, 1), [1, 2), [2, 4), [4, 7), [7, 11), [11, 17), [17, 25)$ and so on.

As with other anomaly detection techniques, our approach consists of a training period, followed by a detection period. During the training period, a histogram H_t representing the frequency distribution observed during the training period is computed and stored. For detection, the histogram H_d computed during detection is compared with the histogram H_t. An anomaly is flagged if H_d is "more" than H_t. The notion of "more" can be defined in multiple ways, but we need some thing that can be computed efficiently, and moreover, represents a clear and significant change from H_d. For this reason, we compare the highest non-zero bin $HNZB_d$ in H_d with the highest non-zero bin $HNZB_t$ computed during training. The severity of the anomaly is defined to be $HNZB_d - HNZB_t$, provided $HNZB_d > HNZB_t$. Otherwise, no anomaly is flagged. The condition $HNZB_d > HNZB_t$ reflects our bias for detecting increased email traffic, as opposed to detecting a reduction in email traffic. Note that with this simple threshold criteria, there is no need to maintain entire histograms, but only the highest nonzero bins. More complex threshold criteria may take into account the entire histogram H_t to derive a threshold, so it is useful to compute and maintain histograms during training. During detection, however, the potential benefits of having the extra information will likely be more than offset by the additional storage needed to maintain histograms.

By choosing different values for the time window w, we can capture statistical information at different time scales. A small value of w will enable fast detection of intense attacks, as such attacks can be detected with a delay of the order of w. However, a slow but sustained attack may not be detected using a small time window. This is because there can be much more burstiness in email traffic at shorter time scales than larger time scales. Such burstiness means that the peak frequencies observed at shorter time scales will be much higher than average values, thus making it difficult to detect small increases in traffic. Since burstiness at higher time scales tends to be smaller, the difference between peak and average is smaller in those time scales, thus making it easier to detect modest increases in traffic. For this reason, we use several different time scales in our experiment, starting from 0.8 seconds and increasing to about 83 minutes, with each time scale being three to five times the previous one.

The above discussion separates the training phase from the detection phase. In a live system, user behaviors evolve over time, and this must be accommodated. The usual technique used in anomaly detection systems is to continuously train the system, while ensuring that (a) very old behaviors are "aged" out of the training profile, and (b) very recent behaviors do not significantly alter this profile. This technique can be incorporated into our approach as well, but we did not pursue this avenue as the change would have no direct effect on the results reported in this paper.

3 Experiment I

The primary goal of the first set of experiments was to study the effectiveness of our approach for detecting self-propagating email viruses. In particular, we wanted to study the false alarm rate and detection latency as the stealthiness of the virus is changed. This experiment us based on simple models of user behavior. (More complex and realistic user models are considered in Experiment II.)

One obvious way to study the effectiveness of the approach is to install it on a real mail server, such as the mail server in a university or a large company. Apart from issues of privacy that need to be addressed in such experiments, there is another serious impediment to such an approach: it is not practical to introduce viruses into such systems for the purpose of experimentation: it would seriously impact email service in the organization. Given the critical role that email has begun to assume in practically every large organization, such an approach is impractical.

Even if we were able to introduce such viruses in a real email system, existing email viruses are rather noisy: as soon as they are read, they send copies of themselves to all (or most) users in the address book. This causes a sharp spurt in email generation rate in the system, and would be immediately detected by our approach. To pose any challenge to our approach or to assess its capabilities, we would have to create new email viruses, which would be a significant task by itself. Therefore our experiment is based on simulation. Below, we describe the simulation environment, and proceed to present the results of the experiments.

An important aspect of these experiments is that the training, as well as detection took place in an unsupervised setting. No attempt was made to tune or refine the anomaly detector based on observed results. Such tuning or refinement could further improve the results.

3.1 Experimental Setup

For this experiment, we simulated an intranet with several hundred users. Three sizes of the intranet were considered: 400 users, 800 users and 1600 users. Our simulation could have been based on actual mail servers and mail clients that were driven by simulated users. However, the realism in the simulation is almost totally determined by the model used for user behavior, and is largely unaffected whether real email clients or mail servers were used[3]. On the other hand, leaving out real mail servers and clients in a simulation has several important benefits. First, we do not need a large testbed consisting of hundreds

---

[3] The only condition when the presence of real mail clients and servers can become important is when the system gets overloaded, due to propagation of email virus. In our experiments, the virus was always detected well before there was any significant increase in email traffic, and hence the absence of actual email servers and clients is unlikely to have affected the results we obtained.

of computers, real or virtual. Second, a light-weight simulation that avoids real mail servers and clients can complete in seconds instead of taking hours.

Our simulation used discrete time, where each cycle of simulation was chosen to correspond to roughly 0.2 seconds. This is a rather arbitrary number — our main concern in this context was to choose a small enough granularity that the results would be essentially the same as with a simulation based on continuous time.

Email users are modeled as Poisson processes, reading or sending emails at random during each simulation cycle. Specifically, in a single simulation cycle, the probability of a user sending email was set at 0.0006 and the probability of checking email was set at 0.0003. This means that users send out emails with a mean interval of about 5 minutes, and that they check emails with a mean interval of about 10 minutes. The recipients for each mail was determined at random, and the number of recipients was chosen using a positive normal distribution with a mean of 1 and standard deviation of 2. Whereas sending of mails was assumed to take place one at a time, email reading was modeled as a batch process — each attempt to read email reads most of the emails queued for the user. Moreover, for each message, the user randomly chooses to reply to the sender, reply to all recipients, or not reply at all. We have used identical models for all users in this experiment, while the experiment described in Section 4 uses a non-uniform model where different user behaviors are different.

In this experiment, we wanted to model not only the viruses prevalent today, all of which propagate very rapidly, but also stealthy viruses. For stealth, viruses may employ a combination of the following techniques:

- *low propagation factor,* i.e., when the virus is read, it does not cause generation of emails to a large number of users, such as the set of names in the address book of the reader. A high propagation factor makes the virus much more noticeable.
- *long incubation period,* the delay between when the virus is read and the time it causes propagation of email is large. The long delay makes it difficult to associate the propagation with the virus.
- *polymorphism,* the virus modifies itself, so that the emails generated do not look like the virus that was read. For additional stealth, the virus can propagate non-virus carrying emails as well as those carrying the virus.
- *matching user behavior,* i.e., the virus avoids sending out emails with a large recipient list, instead partitioning such messages into multiple ones with recipient lists of the size observed on normal messages.
- *randomization,* i.e., all of the above techniques are randomized — for instance, the incubation period is a random number over a range. Similarly, the propagation factor is a random number.

Of these techniques, polymorphism does not affect our approach, as it is not based on email content. Among the rest, propagation factor and incubation period were found to have the maximum impact on detection effectiveness, while randomization had modest effect. Matching of user behavior seemed to have no effect. Thus, our results discussion considers only two of the above factors: propagation factor and incubation period.

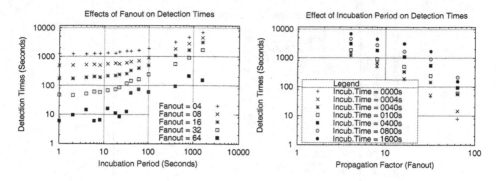

Fig. 2. Detection time as a function of incubation period and propagation factor.

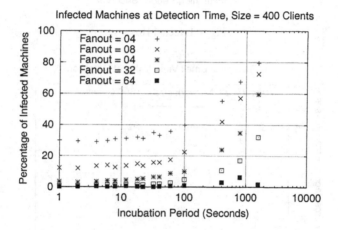

Fig. 3. Percentage of Infected Hosts

3.2 Metrics Used for detection

The first and most obvious metric is the detection time: the time between the introduction of the virus and the time of detection. Figure 2 shows how the detection time changes as the propagation factor (also known as fanout) and incubation period are changed. Note that longer incubation periods and lower propagation factors delay detection. The detection delay is somewhat mitigated by the fact that the virus itself propagates more slowly in these cases. We therefore look at other metrics that factor out the speed at which a virus spreads. Some of these metrics are:

- percentage of clients that are infected at the time of detection
- percentage of email traffic due to viruses at the time of detection

The first of these metrics is related to the costs for cleaning up after the virus infection. The other metric relates to the load on the email server, and the degree to which its function is degraded by the virus.

Figure 3 shows the percentage of infected hosts at the time of detection of the attack. The results are for an intranet consisting of 400 clients. This figure shows that for noisy

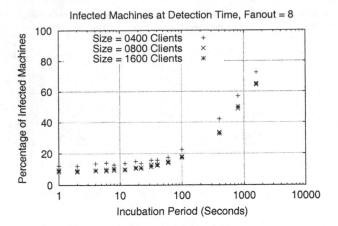

Fig. 4. Infected Hosts

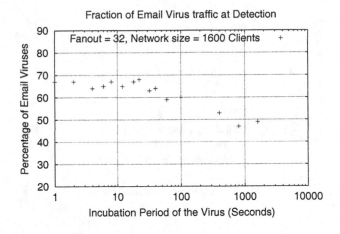

Fig. 5. Percentage of Virus Carrying Emails

viruses, detection occurs early, but very stealthy viruses, especially those that use a combination of large incubation periods and low propagation factors, can potentially infect most of the network before being detected. Figure 4 shows that for a given value of propagation factor (fixed at 8 for this graph), and incubation period, the fraction of infected hosts is lower when the number of clients in the intranet is higher.

Figure 5 shows the fraction of email traffic that is due to the viruses as of the time of detection. Specifically, we calculated the fraction of email traffic due to viruses in the few seconds (2 seconds) preceding the detection. Note that the virus traffic is in the 40% to 70% range, which means that the email server is only slightly overloaded. Due to burstiness of emails, servers are typically designed to handle a few to several times the average rate at which emails are generated in the system. For this reason, a 40% to 70% increase in email traffic is not very significant.

3.3   False Alarms

False alarm rates were computed using two different criteria:

- *Criteria 1*: Count even a single alarm as a false alarm: Using this criteria, there were a total of 3 false alarms across 8 runs, or a rate of about 0.38 false alarms per hour.
- *Criteria 2*: Apply a threshold criteria, and count a false alarm when the threshold is exceeded. This threshold is established through experimentation. We found that by registering an alarm when more than 3 alarms are reported over a period of two seconds, zero false alarm rate could be achieved in our simulation.

We note that in the detection results reported earlier, Criteria 2 was used. Thus, those detection results were obtained with zero false alarm rate.

Runtime Performance and Memory Usage.

The whole implementation was done in Java. With 400 clients, about 800 frequency distributions were maintained, each over 8 time scales. Due to these structures the total memory use of the Java program was 30MB. When run on a Intel Pentium III system operating at 1GHz, it was able to simulate about 500 cycles per second, i.e., simulate 100 seconds in one second of operation. In addition to the simulation, the anomaly detector was processing about 100 messages per second. This performance was adequate to provide fast simulation. If used in a live environment, these performance results show that the anomaly detector will consume 1% of CPU on a similar system.

4   Experiment II

This experiment was conducted as part of the DARPA SWWIM program. The SWWIM Autonomic Response Architecture (SARA) experiment was conducted by a collaborative team of organizations, each responsible for a key function. This experiment differed from the previous experiment in several aspects. First, the user models were asymmetric, i.e., the behavior models for different users were different. Second, the experiment was conducted with real email servers (sendmail) and clients. Third, the simulation as well as the viruses were designed by a third party that had no vested interest in how the detectors from different organizations performed.

The overall goal of the SARA experiment was to evaluate the value of orchestrated response to attacks. The system consisted of several virus detection components, response components in the form of mail server and client enhancements to purge suspected messages, and an orchestrator. The orchestrator took its input from the detection components, evaluated the system state based on these inputs, selected a response action, and communicated these actions to the response components. Several detection components were built, including (a) simple behavior based detectors that looked for more than a certain number emails within a certain time period or within a certain time period after an attachment was opened, (b) more complex behavior based detectors that were tuned to detect the tree-like flow of emails produced by email viruses, and (c) our anomaly detector.

Early on in the experimental design, it was decided that the above detectors would be used in different stages of virus spread: the behavior based techniques will be used for early detection, at which point the system would attempt a carefully orchestrated sequence of responses. But these detectors can be fooled by stealthy viruses, at which point, the results from the anomaly detector would be used to identify the spread of the virus. Note that the anomaly detector cannot provide precise identification of offending email messages — the only thing that can be said is that a predominant number of email messages causing an alarm are bound to be viruses. Due to the absence of precise identification of virus-carrying emails, and given the time constraints associated with the conduct of this experiment, it was decided that the orchestrator would simply shutdown the system if the only information it had was from the anomaly detector. Clearly, this is a response of last resort, and not to be attempted unless every thing else failed. In particular, the orchestrator should be allowed to try intelligent responses based on inputs from other detectors; and only when all of this failed, it should consider shutting down the system. In order to make sure that these responses were given adequate time to work, it was decided that the anomaly detector would artificially delay detection until such time it became clear that the virus was established in spite of an orchestrated response.

4.1 Experimental Setup

The experiment was carried out using a "full scale" simulation of an email system for a single subnet of 400 clients. This included an email server (modified version of sendmail) and 400 email clients. The detection, response, and orchestration components communicated and worked in conjunction with the email server and clients.

Similar to Experiment I, the actions of users were emulated by 400 "bots." However, these bots were significantly more complex than user models used in Experiment I. In particular, user behavior was simulated by 400 bots that were implemented as processes that run concurrently. User behavior was modeled using a three-state Markov model, with the states corresponding to the user reading email, composing email and being idle. The bots will make transitions at random among these states, with a specified probability for each of the six possible transitions. In this manner this model avoids the pitfalls associated with a Poisson model used in Experiment I.

A second important improvement in the user model is that it is asymmetric, and it captures the concept of *address books*. When a user composes email, the set of recipients is assumed to come from his or her address book. The address book size is unlimited, i.e., it can be as large as the user population. These factors mean that it is much more common for emails with a large number of recipients to be generated in this experiment.

Several different types of viruses were used in the experiment. These virus types are shown in Figure 6. Higher numbered viruses were intended to be progressively more stealthy.

4.2 Detection Effectiveness

Hundreds of simulation runs were carried out with the above types of viruses. Due to the fact that the anomaly detector was tuned explicitly for delayed detection of viruses, no alarms were generated in those runs where the orchestrator was able to contain the virus. There were seven runs in which the orchestrator was unable to contain the virus. It is significant that in every one of these cases, the anomaly detector was able to detect the virus, as shown in Figure 7. In most cases, the detection took place 2 or 3 minutes after the detection of virus.

In some cases, the detection was rather slow. For virus 4b.v2, the delay was due to the fact that it had a very long incubation period, so it was not propagating fast until

Virus type	Description
1	Static
2a	Randomized Addresses - (taken from sent items)
2b	Randomized Addresses - (taken from received items)
3a	Randomized - (random number of recipients)
3b	Delayed Randomized (random no. of recipients and time delay)
4a	Polymorphic - (virus attachments all end in .vbs)
4a.v1	Polymorphic - (virus attachments have variable extensions)
4b	Persistent Polymorphic - (virus attachments all end in .vbs, lives forever)
4b.v1	Persistent Polymorphic - (fast propagating version)
4b.v2	Persistent Polymorphic - (slow propagating version)
4b.v3	Persistent Polymorphic - (medium propagating version)
4b.v4	Persistent Polymorphic - (viruses have variable extensions, lives forever)

Fig. 6. Properties of Viruses Used

Virus type	Time of (post-virus release) detection	Percentage of traffic consumed by virus
2b	3.7 min	< 5 percent
4a	36.4 min	< 5 percent
4b	3.0 min	< 5 percent
4b	2.2 min	< 5 percent
4b	3.3 min	< 5 percent
4b	3.1 min	< 5 percent
4b.v2	22.7 min	< 5 percent

Fig. 7. Virus Detection

around 20 minutes after its introduction. Thus, detection took only two minutes after the virus became active. In the case of virus 4a, the orchestrator was initially able to contain the virus, and hence no alarms were reported by the anomaly detector. However, after about 30 minutes of containment, the orchestrator lost control of the virus, which subsequently took over the system. The detection occurred a few minutes after the point when the virus got away.

4.3 False Alarm Analysis

As for Experiment I, false alarm rates were measured in two ways:

- *Criteria 1*: Count even a single alarm as a false alarm: Using this criteria, there were a total of 18 false alarms across 6 runs, or a rate of about 0.3 false alarms per hour. (Compare this to the 0.38 false alarms per hour obtained using this same criteria in Experiment I.)
- *Criteria 2*: Set a threshold via experimentation. In this case, the threshold was set so that not only do we mask false alerts, but also true alarms that are not sufficiently severe to warrant a system shutdown. (Recall that the only response used in the experiment was to shutdown the mail server when the anomaly detector produced

an alarm.) For this reason, the threshold was much higher than in Experiment I. Specifically, we identified a threshold of 50 or more alarms in a period of 256 seconds. Using this criteria, no false alarms were observed. (In fact, the maximum number of alarms produced within a period of 256 seconds in any of these six runs was 14, which is well below the 50 threshold.)

We note that in the detection results reported in Figure 7, Criteria 2 was used. Thus, those detection results were obtained with zero false alarm rate.

4.4 Runtime Performance and Memory Usage

The anomaly detector performance and memory usage in this experiment was similar to that reported for 400 clients in experiment I.

5 Related Work

Self-propagating malicious programs have been analyzed ever since they came into existence starting with the Morris worm [2]. Along with the growth of the Internet, the threat of worms spreading into computer networks has also increased. To understand and predict the propagation of such worms has become an increasingly important research topic. Propagation analysis and detection has also been carried out for more recent Code Red [12] and Melissa [1] viruses, where the email is used as the vehicle of propagation for these malicious executables.

Incidents of virus propagation through the cyber realm have been viewed and modeled using epidemiological modeling, mapping the Internet to mathematical models of ecological systems [15]. Models have been developed to accurately predict the propagation of worms and viruses through the networks. One such example is a variation of Kermack-Mckendrick model, used to predict the propagation of the Code Red virus through the Internet [39]. At IBM, Kephart and White have developed systems for detection using these models [7],[8] [9]. In addition to borrowing ideas from mathematical epidemiology, the model has been extended by incorporating network topological effects, using power-law relationships [20] which try to give some structure to the apparent randomness of the Internet. [10] studies the propagation of viruses when a subset of the hosts are immune to the virus. [18] studies the problem of network availability in the face of viral attacks. The focus of all these efforts were to study the propagation of viruses, whereas the focus of this paper is the development of an effective detection technique.

Anomaly detection techniques have long been used for intrusion detection [13, 27, 25, 32–34, 16, 36]. The approach developed in this paper is closely related to [36]. In both approaches, a protocol state machine specification forms the basis for detection. This state machine is used to transform events (such as network packets, or sending or delivery of emails) into frequency distributions that characterize normal behavior. The training and detection phases are robust, and can operate without any supervision. These factors contrast with most other anomaly detection approaches, especially at the network level, where considerable knowledge and ingenuity was needed to identify the set of "features" to be included in normal behavior characterization. Moreover, many of these techniques required expert supervision to make sure that the normal behavior characterization learned by the technique was indeed appropriate.

The Malicious Email Tracking (MET) system [17] was developed to track the flow of malicious emails such as self-replicating viruses through a network. It was designed as a system to track flow of malicious email traffic on wide area network without having to sample most of the emails exchanged in the network. However, its techniques for detecting malicious emails, such as the use of MD5 sums for identification of the propagation of the same virus, can be defeated by polymorphic viruses such as those considered in this paper.

While MET is focused specifically on emails, the earlier Graph-based intrusion detection system (GrIDS) [31] work was focused on the more general problem of large-scale automated attacks that propagate over the network. GrIDS is based on assembling the activities on different network nodes into *activity graphs* that show the spread of attacks through a network. It can also support policy-based detection of attacks by detecting policy violations in the activity graph.

[6] uses a data mining approach to detect malicious executables embedded within emails. Short sequences of machine instructions are the features used in this approach. A Naive Bayes classifier, trained on a set of malicious and a set of benign executables, was used to detect whether an attachment contained malicious code. This approach assumes that there are similarities among the binary code of malicious executables. While this is shown to be true for viruses known today, it is easy enough to write stealthy viruses that can escape detection by this technique.

The Email Mining Toolkit (EMT) [35] work complements MET in that it uses data mining to synthesize the behavior profiles of users that is used by MET to detect malicious email. EMT models "normal behavior" of each email user in terms of several characteristics such as the identities of the other users they communicate with, and the frequencies with which they communicate with these users. It can detect not only viruses, but also changes in communication patterns that may result due to misuse or other malicious user behavior. However, for the purpose of virus detection, this technique is likely to have higher latency than the technique proposed in this paper. This is because the sending of a single message, or even a few virus messages, cannot be considered a significant departure from normal communication pattern without increasing the false alarm rate.

6   Conclusions and Future Work

In this paper, we presented a new technique for detecting self-propagating email viruses using statistical anomaly detection. Our results suggest that the kinds of viruses prevalent today can be detected before a significant fraction of the network is infected. Our approach degrades gracefully when facing more stealthy viruses that use a combination of low propagation factor, high incubation period and randomization. We note that an email virus writer has to be careful in designing a stealthy virus: if it uses too low a propagation factor, then it may "die" in the presence of hosts that are immune to the virus (e.g., Microsoft Outlook viruses sent to Netscape or Lotus Notes users). A high incubation period also delays the spread of the virus, which provides more opportunities for a vigilant user or system administrator to notice the virus. Thus it is likely that very stealthy viruses are not very stable.

When we began this work, we assumed that an anomaly detection technique such as ours will have a significant latency in detection, by which time most of the network may be infected. While this assumption turned out to be true for the most stealthy of the viruses used in our experiments, our results suggest that for a majority of the viruses, it is potentially feasible to detect attacks when only a minority of the network is infected. Note that with early detection, the costs associated with cleaning up such viruses can be reduced.

While the results presented in this paper are promising, their main weakness is that they are all based on simulation. Real systems often display behaviors that are more complex and variable than those exhibited in simulations. This factor can artificially inflate the effectiveness of anomaly detection systems during simulations. In order to really assess the effectiveness of the approach, it is necessary to evaluate it using realistic email traffic. Our ongoing work develops techniques where email traffic is no longer simulated, but is taken from mail server logs. The virus models will continue to be simulated. The traffic presented to the anomaly detector is obtained by superimposing the background traffic from the logs with simulated virus email traffic.

A second difficulty in extrapolating the simulation results is that on real systems, email traffic crosses organization boundaries frequently. In particular, a virus may propagate from one user to any other user on the Internet, and not just on the intranet of the user's organization. At the same time, it is not realistic to assume that our anomaly detector can be deployed Internet-wide. Thus, a question arises as to how well an Internet-wide virus propagation can be detected by an anomaly detector observing the behavior of email on an intranet. This is another question that needs to be addressed in future research.

References

1. CERT/CC Co-ordination Center Advisories, Carnegie Mellon, 1988-1998, http://www.cert.org/advisories/index.html.
2. Eugene H. Spafford, The Internet worm program: an analysis, Tech. Report CSD-TR-823, Department of Computer Science, Purdue University, 1988.
3. Terran Lane, Carla E. Brodley, Temporal Sequence Learning and Data Reduction for Anomaly Detection, ACM Transactions on Information and System Security, 1998.
4. T. Lunt, A. Tamaru, F. Gilham, R. Jagannathan, P. Neumann, H. Javitz, A. Valdes, T. Garvey, A real-time intrusion detection expert system (IDES) - final technical report. Technical report, Computer Science Laboratory, SRI International, Menlo Park, California, February 1992.
5. T. Heberlein, G. Dias, K. Levitt, B. Mukherjee, J. Wood, D. Wobler, A Network Security Monitor , Proceedings IEEE Symposium on Research in Computer Security and Privacy, 1990.
6. Matthew G. Schultz, Eleazar Eskin, and Salvatore J. Stolfo. "Malicious Email Filter - A UNIX Mail Filter that Detects Malicious Windows Executables." Proceedings of USENIX Annual Technical Conference, 2001.
7. J.O. Kephart, S.R. White, Directed-graph Epidemiological Models of Computer Viruses, IBM T.J. Watson Research Center, IEEE Computer Society Symposium on Research in Security and Privacy, pp. 343-359, 1991.
8. J.O. Kephart, David M. Chess, S.R. White, Computers and Epidemiology, IBM T.J. Watson Research Center, IEEE Spectrum, May 1993.

9. J.O. Kephart, G.B. Sorkia, M. Swimmer, S.R. White, Blueprint for a Computer Immune System. Technical report, IBM T.J. Watson Research Center, Yorktown Heights, New York, 1997.

10. Chenxi Wang, John C. Knight, Matthew C. Elder, On Computer Viral Infection and the Effect of Immunization, Department of Computer Science, University of Virginia, ACSAC 2000.

11. Klaus Julisch, Mining Alarm Clusters to Improve Alarm Handling Efficiency, IBM Research, Zurich Research Laboratory, ACSAC 2001.

12. Stuart Staniford, Analysis of spread of July infestation of the Code Red worm, UC Davis, http://www.silicondefense.com/cr/july.html.

13. D. Anderson, T. Lunt, H. Javitz, A. Tamaru, and A. Valdes, Next-generation Intrusion Detection Expert System (NIDES): A Summary, SRI-CSL-95-07, SRI International, 1995.

14. S. Staniford, V. Paxson, N. Weaver, How to Own the Internet in Your Spare Time, Usenix Security Symposium, 2002.

15. Jane Jorgensen, P. Rossignol, M. Takikawa, D. Upper, Cyber Ecology: Looking to Ecology for Insights into Information Assurance, DISCEX 2001. Proceedings , Volume 2 , 2001.

16. Carol Taylor, Jim Alves-Foss, NATE, Network Analysis of Anomalous Traffic Events, A Low-cost Approach, New Security Paradigms Workshop, 2001.

17. Manasi Bhattacharyya, Shlomo Hershkop, Eleazar Eskin, and Salvatore J. Stolfo, MET: An Experimental System for Malicious Email Tracking, Workshop on New Security Paradigms, 2002 (NSPW-2002).

18. Meng-Jang Lin, Aleta M. Ricciardi, Keith Marzullo, A New Model for Availability in the Face of Self-Propagating Attacks, Workshop on New Security Paradigms, 1998.

19. Wenke Lee, Salvatore J. Stolfo, Kui W. Mok, A Data Mining Framework for Building Intrusion Detection Models, IEEE Symposium on Security and Privacy, 1999.

20. M. Faloutsos, P. Faloutsos, C. Faloutsos, On Power-Law Relationships of the Internet, ACM SIGCOMM, 1999.

21. M.G. Schultz, E.Eskin, E. Zadok, Data Mining Methods for Detection of New Malicious Executables, IEEE Symposium on Security and Privacy, May 2001.

22. Ian Whalley, Bill Arnold, David Chess, John Morar, Alla Segal, Morton Swimmer, An Environment for Controlled Worm Replication and Analysis, IBM TJ Watson Research Center, Sept 2000.

23. L. Heberlein et al, A Network Security Monitor, Symposium on Research Security and Privacy, 1990.

24. J. Hochberg et al, NADIR: An Automated System for Detecting Network Intrusion and Misuse, Computers and Security 12(3), May 1993.

25. W. Lee and S. Stolfo, Data Mining Approaches for Intrusion Detection, USENIX Security Symposium, 1998.

26. V. Paxson, Bro: A System for Detecting Network Intruders in Real-Time, USENIX Security Symposium, 1998.

27. P. Porras and P. Neumann, EMERALD: Event Monitoring Enabled Responses to Anomalous Live Disturbances, National Information Systems Security Conference, 1997.

28. Inc. Network Flight Recorder. Network flight recorder, http://www.nfr.com, 1997.

29. G. Vigna and R. Kemmerer, NetSTAT: A Network-based Intrusion Detection Approach, Computer Security Applications Conference, 1998.

30. G. Vigna, S.T. Eckmann, and R.A. Kemmerer, The STAT Tool Suite, in Proceedings of DISCEX 2000, IEEE Press, 2000.

31. Staniford-Chen, S. et al, GrIDS: A Graph-Based Intrusion Detection System for Large Networks. Proceedings of the 19th National Information Systems Security Conference, Baltimore, 1996.

32. S. Forrest, S. Hofmeyr and A. Somayaji, Computer Immunology, Comm. of ACM 40(10), 1997.

33. A. Ghosh, A. Schwartzbard and M. Schatz, Learning Program Behavior Profiles for Intrusion Detection, 1st USENIX Workshop on Intrusion Detection and Network Monitoring, 1999.

34. R. Sekar, M. Bendre, P. Bollineni and D. Dhurjati, A Fast Automaton-Based Approach for Learning Program Behaviors, IEEE Symposium on Security and Privacy, 2001.

35. Salvatore J. Stolfo, Shlomo Hershkop, Ke Wang, Olivier Nimeskern, Chia-Wei Hu, Behavior Profiling of Email, submitted to 1st NSF/NIJ Symposium on Intelligence and Security Informatics(ISI 2003).

36. R. Sekar, A. Gupta, J. Frullo, T. Shanbhag, A. Tiwari, H. Yang, S. Zhou, Specification-based anomaly detection: a new approach for detecting network intrusions, ACM Computer and Communication Security Conference, 2002.

37. R. Sekar, Y. Guang, T. Shanbhag and S. Verma, A High-Performance Network Intrusion Detection System, ACM Computer and Communication Security Conference, 1999.

38. R. Sekar and P. Uppuluri, Synthesizing Fast Intrusion Prevention/Detection Systems from High-Level Specifications, USENIX Security Symposium, 1999.

39. C.C. Zou, W. Gong, Don Towsley, Code Red Worm Propagation Modeling and Analysis, ACM Computer and Communication Security Conference, 2002.

Statistical Causality Analysis of INFOSEC Alert Data

Xinzhou Qin and Wenke Lee

College of Computing
Georgia Institute of Technology
Atlanta, GA 30332
{xinzhou,wenke}@cc.gatech.edu

Abstract. With the increasingly widespread deployment of security mechanisms, such as firewalls, intrusion detection systems (IDSs), antivirus software and authentication services, the problem of alert analysis has become very important. The large amount of alerts can overwhelm security administrators and prevent them from adequately understanding and analyzing the security state of the network, and initiating appropriate response in a timely fashion. Recently, several approaches for alert correlation and attack scenario analysis have been proposed. However, these approaches all have limited capabilities in detecting new attack scenarios. In this paper, we study the problem of security alert correlation with an emphasis on attack scenario analysis. In our framework, we use clustering techniques to process low-level alert data into high-level aggregated alerts, and conduct *causal analysis* based on statistical tests to discover new relationships among attacks. Our statistical causality approach complements other approaches that use hard-coded prior knowledge for pattern matching. We perform a series of experiments to validate our method using DARPA's Grand Challenge Problem (GCP) datasets and the DEF CON 9 datasets. The results show that our approach can discover new patterns of attack relationships when the alerts of attacks are statistically correlated.

Keywords: Intrusion detection, alert correlation, attack scenario analysis, time series analysis

1 Introduction

Information security (INFOSEC) is a complex process with many challenging problems. Deploying INFOSEC mechanisms, e.g., authentication systems, firewalls, intrusion detection systems (IDSs), antivirus software, and network management and monitoring systems, is just one of the necessary steps in the security process. INFOSEC devices often output a large amount of low-level or incomplete alert information because there is a large number of network and system activities being monitored and multiple INFOSEC systems can each report some aspects of the same (coordinated) security event. The sheer quantity of alerts from these security components and systems also overwhelms security administrators. The large number of low-level or incomplete alert information can

G. Vigna, E. Jonsson, and C. Kruegel (Eds.): RAID 2003, LNCS 2820, pp. 73–93, 2003.

prevent intrusion response systems and security administrators from adequately understanding and analyzing the security state of the network, and initiating appropriate response in a timely fashion. From a security administrator's point of view, it is important to reduce the redundancy of alarms, intelligently integrate and correlate security alerts, construct attack scenarios (defined as a sequence of related attack steps) and present high-level aggregated information from multiple local-scale events. Correlating alerts of the related attack steps to identify an attack scenario can also help forensic analysis, response and recovery, and even prediction of forthcoming attacks.

Recently there have been several proposals on alert correlation (e.g., [4, 7, 10, 22, 25, 27]). Most of these proposed approaches have limited capabilities because they rely on various forms of predefined knowledge of attack conditions and consequences. They cannot recognize a correlation when an attack is new (previously unknown) or the relationship between attacks is new. In other words, these approaches in principle are similar to *misuse detection* techniques, which use the "signatures" of known attacks to perform pattern matching and cannot detect new attacks. It is obvious that the number of possible correlations is very large, potentially a combinatorial of the number of (known and new) attacks. It is infeasible to know *a priori* and encode all possible matching conditions between attacks. To further complicate the matter, the more dangerous and intelligent adversaries will always invent new attacks and novel attack sequences. Therefore, we must develop significantly better alert correlation algorithms that can discover sophisticated and new attack sequences.

In this paper, we study the problem of INFOSEC alert analysis with an emphasis on attack scenario analysis. The analysis mechanism is based on time series and statistical analysis. We reduce the high volume of raw alerts by combining low-level alerts based on alert attributes. Clustering techniques are used to group low-level alert data into high-level alerts. We prioritize alerts based on the relevance of attacks to the protected networks and hosts and the impacts of attacks on the mission goals. We then conduct causality analysis to correlate alerts and construct attack scenarios. We perform a series of experiments to validate our method using DARPA's Grand Challenge Problem (GCP) datasets and the DEF CON 9 datasets. Our results show that our approach can discover new patterns of alert relationships without depending on prior knowledge of attack scenarios. Our statistical approach complements other approaches in that our correlation approach does not depend on the hard-coded prior knowledge for pattern matching and can discover new attack relationships when the alerts of attacks are statistically correlated.

The emphasis of this paper is on statistical causality analysis. The remainder of this paper is organized as follows. In Section 2, we introduce Granger Causality Test, a time series analysis method. Our alert correlation steps and algorithms are presented in Section 3. In Section 4, we report the experiments and results on the GCP datasets and the DEF CON 9 datasets. Section 5 discusses related work. We summarize our work and future work in Section 6.

2   Granger Causality Analysis

Time series analysis aims to identify the nature of a phenomenon represented by a sequence of observations. The objective requires the study of patterns of the observed time series data. Time series analysis has been widely used in many applications, e.g., earthquake forecasting and economy analysis. In this section, we introduce time series based causal analysis, and in particular, the Granger Causality Test [11].

2.1   Time Series Analysis

A time series is an ordered finite set of numerical values of a variable of interest along the time axis. It is assumed that the time interval between consecutively recorded values is constant. We denote a univariate time series as $x(k)$, where $k = 0, 1, \ldots, N - 1$, and N denotes the number of elements in $x(k)$.

Time series causal analysis deals with analyzing the correlation between time series variables and discovering the causal relationships. Causal analysis in time series has been widely studied and used in many applications, e.g., economy forecasting and stock market analysis. Network security is another application in which time series analysis can be very useful. In our prior work [1, 3], we have used time series-based causality analysis for pro-active detection of Distributed-Denial-of-Service (DDoS) attacks using MIB II [26] variables. We based our approach on the Granger Causality Test (GCT) [11]. Our results showed that the GCT is able to detect the "precursor" events, e.g., the communication between Master and Slave hosts, without prior knowledge of such communication signatures, on the attacker's network before the victim is completely overwhelmed (e.g., shutdown) at the final stage of DDoS.

In this work, we apply the GCT to INFOSEC alert streams for alert correlation and scenario analysis. The intuition is that attack steps that do not have well-known patterns or obvious relationships may nonetheless have some statistical correlations in the alert data. For example, there are one or more alerts for one attack only when there are also one or more alerts for another attack. We can apply statistical causality analysis to find such alerts to identify an attack scenario. We next give some background on the GCT.

2.2   Granger Causality Test

The intuition of Granger Causality is that if an event X is the cause of another event Y, then the event X should precede the event Y. Formally, the Granger Causality Test (GCT) uses statistical functions to test if *lagged* information on a time-series variable x provides any statistically significant information about another time-series variable y. If the answer is yes, we say variable x Granger-causes y. We model variable y by two auto-regression models, namely, the Autoregressive Model (AR Model) and the Autoregressive Moving Average Model (ARMA Model). The GCT compares the residuals of the AR Model with the residuals of the ARMA Model. Specifically, for two time series variables y and x with size N, the Autoregressive Model of y is defined as:

$$y(k) = \sum_{i=1}^{p} \theta_i y(k - i) + e_0(k) \tag{1}$$

The Autoregressive Moving Average Model of y is defined as:

$$y(k) = \sum_{i=1}^{p} \alpha_i y(k - i) + \sum_{i=1}^{p} \beta_i x(k - i) + e_1(k) \tag{2}$$

Here, p is a particular lag length, and parameters α_i, β_i and θ_i ($1 \leq i \leq p$) are computed in the process of solving the Ordinary Least Square (OLS) problem (which is to find the parameters of a regression model in order to have the minimum estimation error). The residuals of the AR Model is $R_0 = \sum_{k=1}^{T} e_0^2(k)$, and the residuals of the ARMA Model is $R_1 = \sum_{k=1}^{T} e_1^2(k)$. Here, $T = N - p$.

The AR Model, i.e., Equation 1, represents that the current value of variable y is predicted by its past p values. The residuals R_0 indicate the total sum of squares of error. The ARMA Model, i.e., Equation 2, shows that the current value of variable y is predicted by the past p values of both variable y and variable x. The residuals R_1 represents the sum of squares of prediction error.

The Null Hypothesis H_0 of GCT is $H_0 : \beta_i = 0, i = 1, 2, \cdots, p$. That is, x does not affect y up to a delay of p time units. We denote g as the Granger Causality Index (GCI):

$$g = \frac{(R_0 - R_1)/p}{R_1/(T - 2p - 1)} \sim F(p, T - 2p - 1) \tag{3}$$

Here, $F(a, b)$ is Fisher's F distribution with parameters a and b [14]. F-test is conducted to verify the validity of the Null Hypothesis. If the value of g is larger than a critical value in the F-test, then we reject the Null Hypothesis and conclude that x Granger-causes y. Critical values of F-test depends on the degree of freedoms and significance value. The critical values can be looked up in a mathematic table [15].

The intuition of GCI (g) is that it indicates how better variable y can be predicted using histories of both variable x and y than using the history of y alone. In the ideal condition, the ARMA model precisely predicts variable y with residuals $R_1 = 0$, and the GCI value g is infinite. Therefore, the value of GCI (g) represents the strength of the causal relationship. We say that variable $\{x_1(k)\}$ is more likely to be causally related with $\{y(k)\}$ than $\{x_2(k)\}$ if $g_1 > g_2$ and both have passed the F-test, where g_i, $i = 1, 2$, denotes the GCI for the input-output pair (x_i, y).

Applying the GCT to alert correlation, the task is to determine which hyper alerts among $B_1, B_2, \ldots, B_l$ are the most likely to have the causal relationship with hyper alert A (a hyper alert represents a sequence of alerts in the same cluster, see Section 3). For a hyper alert time series, say A, each $A(k)$ is the number of alerts occurring within a certain time period. In other words, we are testing the statistical correlation of alert instances to determine the causal relationship between alerts. For each pair of hyper alerts $(B_i, A), i = 1, 2, \ldots, l,$ we compute the GCI value g_i. We record the alerts whose GCI values have passed the F-test as the candidates, and rank order the candidate alerts according to their GCI values. We can then select the top m candidate alerts and regard them as being causally related to alert A. These (candidate) relationships can be subject to more inspection by other analysis techniques such as probabilistic reasoning or plan recognition.

The main advantage of using statistical causality test such as GCT for alert correlation is that this approach does not require *a priori* knowledge about attack behaviors and how the attacks could be related. This approach can identify the correlation between two attack steps as long as the two have a high probability (not necessarily high frequency) of occurring together. We believe that there is a large number of attacks, e.g., worms, that have attack steps with such characteristics. Thus, we believe that causal analysis is a very useful technique. As discussed in [1, 3, 2], when there is sufficient training data available, we can use GCT off-line to compute and validate very accurate causal relationships from alert data. We can then update the knowledge base with these "known" correlations for efficient pattern matching in run-time. When GCT is used in real-time and finds a new causal relationship, as discussed above, the top m candidates can be selected for further analysis by other techniques.

3   Alarm Correlation

In this section, we describe our framework for alert correlation and attack scenario construction. Specifically, the steps include alert aggregation and clustering, alert prioritization, alert time series formulation, alert correlation, and scenario construction.

3.1   Alert Aggregation and Clustering

One of the issues with deploying multiple security devices is the sheer amount of alerts output by the devices. The large volume of alerts makes it very difficult for the security administrator to analyze attack events and handle alerts in a timely fashion. Therefore, the first step in alert analysis is alert aggregation and volume reduction.

In our approach, we use alert fusion and clustering techniques to reduce the redundancy of alerts while keeping the important information. Specifically, each alert has a number of attributes such as *timestamp, source IP, destination IP, port(s), user name, process name, attack class,* and *sensor ID,* which are defined in the standard document "Intrusion Detection Message Exchange Format (IDMEF)" [12] drafted by the IETF Intrusion Detection Working Group.

In alert fusion, there are two steps. First, we combine alerts that have the same attributes except timestamps. The timestamps can be slightly different,

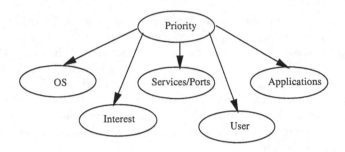

Fig. 1. Alert Priority Computation Model

e.g., 2 seconds apart. Second, based on the results of step 1, we aggregate alerts with the same attributes but are reported from different heterogeneous sensors. The alerts varied on time stamp are fused together if they are close enough to fall in a pre-defined time window.

Alert clustering is used to further group alerts after alert fusion. Based on various clustering algorithms, we can group alerts in different ways according to the *similarity* among alerts, (e.g., [27] and [17]). Currently, based on the results of alert fusion, we further group alerts that have same attributes except time stamps into one cluster. After this step, we have further reduced the redundancy of alerts.

A *Hyper Alert* is defined as a time ordered sequence of alerts that belong to the same cluster.

For example, after alert clustering, we have a series of alerts, $A_1, A_2...A_n$ in one cluster that have the same attributes along the time axis, and we use hyper alert A to represent this sequence of alerts.

3.2   Alert Prioritization

The next phase of alert processing is to prioritize each hyper alert based on its relevance to the mission goals. The objective is that, with the alert priority rank, security analyst can select important alerts as the target alerts for further correlation and analysis. Specifically, the priority score of an alert is computed based on the relevance of the alert to the configuration of the protected networks and hosts as well as the severity of the corresponding attack assessed by the security analyst. Porras et al. proposed a more comprehensive mechanism of incident/alert rank computation model in a "mission-impact-based" correlation engine, named M-Correlator [25]. Because we focus on alert correlation and scenario analysis instead of alert priority ranking, and alert prioritization is just an intermediate step to facilitate further alert analysis, we adapted the priority computation model of M-Correlator with a simplified design.

Figure 1 shows our priority computation model that is constructed based on Bayesian networks [24]. We use Bayesian inference to obtain a belief over states (hypotheses) of interests. A Bayesian network is usually represented as a directed acyclic graph (DAG) where each node represents a variable, and the directed edges represent the causal or dependent relationships among the variables. A conditional probability table (CPT) [24] is associated with each child node. It encodes the prior knowledge between the child node and its parent node. Specifically, an element of the CPT at a child node is defined by $CPT_{ij} = P(child\_state = j | parent\_state = i)$ [24]. The belief in hypotheses of the root is related to the belief propagation from its child nodes, and ultimately the evidence at the leaf nodes.

Specifically, in our priority computation model, the root represents the priority with two hypothesis states, i.e., "high" and "low". Each leaf node has three states. For node "Interest", its three states are "low", "medium" and "high". For other nodes, the three states are "matched", "unmatched" and "unknown". The computation result is a value in [0,1] where 1 is the highest priority score.

We denote e^k as the kth leaf node and H_i as the ith hypothesis of the root node. Given the evidence from the leaf nodes, assuming conditional independence with respect to each H_i, the belief in hypothesis at the root is: $P(H_i \mid e^1, e^2, \ldots, e^N) = \gamma P(H_i) \prod_{k=1}^{N} P(e^k | H_i)$, where $\gamma = [P(e^1, e^2, \ldots, e^N)]^{-1}$ and γ can be computed using the constraint $\sum_i P(H_i | e^1, e^2, \ldots, e^N) = 1$. For example, for the hyper alert of *FTP Globbing Buffer Overflow* attack, we get evidence [high, matched, matched, unknown, unknown] from the corresponding leaf nodes, i.e., Interest, OS, Services/Ports, Applications and User, respectively. As Figure 1 shows, the root node represents the priority of hyper alert. Assume that we have the prior probabilities for the hypotheses of the root, i.e., $P(Priority = high) = 0.8$ and $P(Priority = low) = 0.2$, and the following conditional probabilities as defined in the CPT at each leaf node, $P(Interest = high | Priority = high) = 0.70$, $P(Interest = high | Priority = low) = 0.10$, $P(OS = matched | Priority = high) = 0.75$, $P(OS = matched | Priority = low) = 0.20$, $P(Services = matched | Priority = high) = 0.70$, $P(Services = matched | Priority = low) = 0.30$, $P(Applications = unknown | Priority = high) = 0.15$, $P(Applications = unknown | Priority = low) = 0.15$, $P(User = unknown | Priority = high) = 0.10$, $P(User = unkown | Priority = low) = 0.10$, we then can get $\gamma = 226.3468$, therefore, $P(Priority = high | Interest = matched, OS = matched, Service = matched, Applications = matched, User = unknown) = 0.9959$. We regard this probability as the priority score of the alert. The current CPTs are predefined based on our experience and domain knowledge. It is our future work to develop an adaptive priority computation model so that the CPTs can be adaptive and updated according to specific mission goals.

To calculate the priority of each hyper alert, we compare the dependencies of the corresponding attack represented by the hyper alert against the configurations of target networks and hosts. We have a knowledge base in which each hyper alert has been associated with a few fields that indicate its attacking OS, services/ports and applications. For the alert output from a host-based IDS, we will further check if the target user exists in the host configuration. The purpose of relevance check is that we can downgrade the importance of some alerts that are unrelated to the protected domains. For example, an attacker may launch an individual buffer overflow attack against a service blindly, without knowing if the service exists. It is quite possible that a signature-based IDS outputs the alert once the packet contents match the detection rules even though such service does not exist on the protected host. The relevance check on the alerts aims to downgrade the impact of such kind of alerts on further correlation analysis. The interest of the attack is assigned by the security analyst based on the nature of the attack and missions of the target hosts and services in the protected domain.

3.3   Alert Time Series Formulation

After the above processes, we formulate each hyper alert into a univariate time series. Specifically, we set up a series of time slots with equal time interval, denoted as T, along the time axis. Given a time range H, we can have $N = H/T$ time slots. Recall that each hyper alert A represents a sequence of alerts in the same cluster in which all alerts have the same attributes except timestamp, i.e., $A = [A_1, A_2, \ldots, A_n]$, where A_i represents an alert in the cluster. We denote $a(k)$, where $k = 0, 1, \ldots, N-1$, as the corresponding time series variable of hyper alert A. An element of the time series $a(k)$, denoted as a_i, is the number of alerts that fall in the ith time slot. Therefore, each element of a hyper alert time series variable represents the number of alert instances within the corresponding time slot. We currently do not use categorical variables such as port accessed and pattern of TCP flags as time series variables in our approach.

3.4   GCT Alert Correlation

The next phase of alert processing is to apply GCT for pair-wise alert correlation. Based on alert priority value and mission goals, the security analyst can specify a hyper alert as a target (e.g., alert *Mstream_DDOS* against a database server) with which other alerts are correlated. The GCT algorithm is applied to the corresponding alert time series. Specifically, for a target hyper alert Y whose corresponding univariate time series is $y(k)$, and another hyper alert X whose univariate time series is $x(k)$, we compute $GCT(x(k), y(k))$ to correlate these two alerts. For the target alert Y, we compute such pair-wise correlation with all the other alerts. As described in Section 2.2, the GCT index (GCI) g returned by the GCT function represents the evidence strength if X is causally related to Y. We record the alerts whose GCI values have passed the F-distribution test as candidates of causal alerts, and rank order the candidate alerts according to their GCI values. We then select the top m candidate alerts and regard them as being causally related to alert Y. These candidate relationships can be further inspected by other techniques or security analyst based on expertise and domain knowledge. The corresponding attack scenario is constructed based on the correlation results.

In alert correlation, identifying and removing background alerts is an important step. We use *Ljung-Box* [20] test to identify the background alerts. The assumption is that background alerts have characteristic of randomness. The *Ljung-Box* algorithm tests for such randomness via autocorrelation plots. The

Null Hypothesis is that the data is random. The test value is compared with critical values to determine if we reject or accept the Null Hypothesis.

However, in order to correctly remove the background alerts, expertise is still needed to verify that a hyper alert can be regarded as a background alert. In addition to expertise, we can also use other techniques, e.g., probabilistic reasoning, for further inspection and verification. This is part of our future work.

4   Experiments

To evaluate the effectiveness and validity of our alert correlation mechanisms, we applied our algorithms to the datasets of the Grand Challenge Problem (GCP) version 3.1 provided by DARPA's Cyber Panel program [6, 13], and datasets of the DEF CON 9 Capture The Flag (CTF) [9]. In this section, we describe our experiments with an emphasis on the GCP.

4.1   The Grand Challenge Problem (GCP)

The main motivation to use the GCP datasets is that the GCP has developed multiple innovative attack scenarios to specifically evaluate alert correlation techniques. In addition to the complicated attack scenarios, the GCP datasets also include many background alerts. This makes alert correlation and scenario construction more challenging. Other datasets, e.g., DEF CON 8 Capture The Flag (CTF) [8], have relatively simple scenarios [21]. In the GCP, multiple heterogeneous security systems, e.g., network-based IDSs, host-based IDSs, firewalls, and network management systems, are deployed in several network enclaves.

GCP alerts are in IDMEF (XML) format. We implemented our alert processing system in Java. It can consume XML format alerts directly.

As described in Section 3, we first fuse and cluster raw alerts into more aggregated and *hyper alerts*. In scenario I, there are a little more than 25,000 low-level raw alerts output by heterogeneous security devices in all enclaves. After alert fusion and clustering, we have around 2,300 hyper alerts. In scenario II, there are around 22,500 raw alerts that result in 1,800 hyper alerts.

The GCP definition includes complete information about the configuration of the protected networks and hosts including services, operating systems, user accounts, etc. Therefore, we can establish a configuration database accordingly. Information of mission goals enables us to identify the servers of interest and assign interest score for corresponding alerts targeting at the important hosts. The alert priority is calculated based on our model described in Section 3.2.

In formulating hyper alert time series, as described in Section 3, we set the time slot to 60 seconds. In the GCP, the whole time range is 5 days. Therefore, each hyper alert time series $x(k)$ has a size of 7,200, i.e., k=0, 1, 2, ..., 7,199.

In GCT alert correlation, the first step is to identify and remove the background alerts. As described in Section 3.4, we apply the *Ljung-Box* statistical test to all hyper alerts. We select the significance level $\alpha = 0.05$. However, in order to correctly remove the background alerts, expertise is still needed to verify that a hyper alert can be regarded as background alert. In the GCP, by using this mechanism, we can identify background alerts such as "HTTP_Cookie" and "HTTP_Posts". The next step is to select the alerts with high priority values as the target alerts. In this step, we set the threshold $\beta = 0.6$. Alerts with priority scores above β are regarded as important alerts and are selected as target alerts. We then apply the GCT to correlate each target alert with other alerts from which the background alerts identified by the *Ljung-Box* test are already excluded.

For performance evaluation, we define two measures: *true causality rate* $= \frac{\# \ of \ correct \ causal \ alerts}{total \ \# \ of \ causal \ relationships}$ and *false causal rate* $= \frac{\# \ of \ incorrect \ causal \ alerts}{total \ \# \ of \ causal \ alerts}$. Here, *causal alerts* refer to the causal alert candidates output by the GCT (i.e., passing the *F-test*) w.r.t. the target alerts. In experiments of the GCP, we refer to the documents with the ground truth to determine the causal relationships among the alerts.

In the GCP Scenario I, there are multiple network enclaves in which attacks are conducted separately. The attack scenario in each network enclave is almost the same. We selected a network enclave as an example to show the GCT correlation results.

In this network enclave, there are a total of 370 hyper alerts. Applying the *Ljung-Box* test on the hyper alerts, we identify 255 hyper alerts as background alerts. According to the alert priority values calculated based on the mission-goals and relevance to the protected networks and hosts, there are 15 hyper alerts whose priority values are above the threshold $\beta = 0.6$. Therefore, we have 15 hyper alerts as the target alerts, which are correlated with other alerts excluding the identified background alerts. As an example, we select three alerts that are related to the Database Server as the target alerts, i.e., *Loki*, *DB_NewClient* and *DB_IllegalFileAccess*. Alert *Loki* indicates that there is a stealthy data transfer via a covert channel. Alert *NewClient* means that a host on the network initiates a connection to a remote service that is suspicious and uncharacteristic. Therefore, alert *DB_NewClient* denotes the connection activity from the Database Server to an external suspicious site. Alert *DB_IllegalFileAccess* occurs when there is a file access (read or write) on the Database Server that violates the access policy. *DB* and *Plan* represent *Database Server* and *Plan Server* respectively. Table 1 shows the causal alert candidates correlated with target alert *Loki*. Table 2 shows the alert candidates that are causally related to target alert *DB_NewClient*. Table 3 shows the causal alerts related to target alert *DB_IllegalFileAccess*. Alert *DB_FTP_Globbing_Attack* indicates an *FTP Globbing buffer overflow* attack on the Database Server. Alert *DB_NewClient_Target* denotes an unusual connection activity from a host to the Database Server. Among the candidate alerts which have passed the F-test, we select the top 6 alerts according to their GCI values.

Figure 2 shows the correlation graph based on the correlation results of alerts *Loki*, *DB_NewClient* and *DB_IllegalFileAccess*. Here, some expert knowledge is needed to further inspect the causal alert candidates resulted from GCT correlation in order to construct the correlation graph. In this case, we do not include

Table 1. Alert Correlation by the GCT on the GCP Scenario I. Target Alert: Loki

$Alert_i$	Target Alert	GCT Index
HTTP_Java	Loki	22.25
DB_IllegalFileAccess	Loki	11.81
DB_NewClient	Loki	11.12
DB_NewClient_Target	Loki	10.84
DB_FTP_Globbing_Attack	Loki	10.84
HTTP_ActiveX	Loki	10.68

Table 2. Alert Correlation by the GCT on the GCP Scenario I: Target Alert: DB_NewClient

$Alert_i$	Target Alert	GCT Index
Loki	DB_NewClient	115.56
Plan_NewClient	DB_NewClient	14.50
Plan_Loki	DB_NewClient	13.06
HTTP_Java	DB_NewClient	12.84
DB_NewClient_Target	DB_NewClient	12.84
DB_FTP_Globbing_Attack	DB_NewClient	12.84
HTTP_ActiveX	DB_NewClient	12.84
DB_IllegalFileAccess	DB_NewClient	10.76

Table 3. Alert Correlation by the GCT on the GCP Scenario I: Target Alert: DB_IllegalFileAccess

$Alert_i$	Target Alert	GCT Index
HTTP_Java	DB_IllegalFileAccess	22.23
DB_NewClient	DB_IllegalFileAccess	14.87
Loki	DB_IllegalFileAccess	11.24
Plan_Loki	DB_IllegalFileAccess	11.13
HTTP_ActiveX	DB_IllegalFileAccess	10.71
Plan_NewClient	DB_IllegalFileAccess	9.08

alerts such as *HTTP_Java* and *HTTP_ActiveX* in the scenario construction because they are not likely to be correct causal alerts. In the correlation graph, the directed edges represent the causal relationships and the arrows show the causality directions. For example, Table 1 shows that alert *DB_FTP_Globbing_Attack* is a causal alert candidate with regard to alert *Loki*. Such causal relationship is shown by a directed edge originated from *DB_FTP_Globbing_Attack* pointing to *Loki* in Figure 2. A bi-directional edge indicates a mutual causal relationship between two alerts.

Figure 2 shows that there are multiple types of relationships among the alerts. First, there is a *straightforward* causal relationship that is obvious because of the nature of corresponding attacks. In Figure 2, we can see that alert *DB_FTP_Globbing_Attack* is causally related to alerts *Loki* and *DB_NewClient*, so is alert *DB_NewClient_Target*. Such causality indicates that the corres-

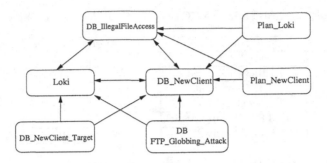

Fig. 2. The GCP Scenario I: Correlation Graph on Database Server

ponding activities represented by alert *DB_FTP_Globbling_Attack* and alert *DB _NewClient_Target* cause the activities indicated by alert *DB_NewClient* and *Loki*. The fact spreadsheet in the GCP document also supports the validity of such causality. The ground truth shows that the attacker first gets root access to the Database Server using the *FTP Globbling buffer overflow* attack, then transports the malicious agent to the Database Server. The activity of agent transfer is detected by an IDS that outputs alert *DB_NewClient_Target*. The buffer overflow attack and initial malicious agent transfer are followed by a series of forthcoming autonomous attacks from/against the Database Server. Such causal relationship is obvious and can also be discovered by other correlation techniques because once the attacker obtained the root access to the victim using the buffer overflow attack, he/she can easily launch other attacks from/against the target. Therefore, a simple rule is to correlate the buffer overflow attack with other following attacks at the same target.

Some *indirect* relationships among alerts can also be discovered by the GCT correlation. As shown in Figure 2, we can see that alerts *Plan_Loki* and *Plan NewClient* all have causal relationship with alerts *DB_IllegalFileAccess* (triggered by activities of illegal access to files at the Database Server) and *DB NewClient* (triggered by activities of connecting to a suspicious site). It is hard to correlate them together via traditional correlation techniques because they do not have a known relationship with the target alert *DB_NewClient*. From the ground truth in the GCP document, we can see that the attacker first compromises the Plan Server and then uses that host to break into the Database Server. Alert *Plan_NewClient* indicates that the attacker downloads malicious agent from the external site to the *Plan_Server*. Alert *Plan_Loki* indicates the attacker uploads sensitive information from the *Plan_Server* to the external site. The malicious code is later transferred to the Database Server after a buffer overflow attack against the Database Server originated from the Plan Server.

Figure 2 also shows a pattern of loop relationships among alerts. We can see that alerts *DB_IllegalFileAccess*, *Loki* and *DB_NewClient* have mutual causal relationships with each other. Such pattern indicates that the occurrences of these three alerts are tightly coupled, i.e., whenever we see one alert, we expect to see another one forthcoming. The fact spreadsheet validates our results. The

Table 4. Alert Correlation by the GCT on the GCP Scenario II: Target Alert: Plan_Service_Status

Alert$_i$	Target Alert	GCT Index
Plan_IIS_Generic_BufferOverFlow	Plan_Service_Status	20.21
Plan_Registry_Modified	Plan_Service_Status	20.18
IIS_Unicode_Attack	Plan_Service_Status	18.98
HTTP_Java	Plan_Service_Status	17.35
HTTP_Shells	Plan_Service_Status	16.28
HTTP_ActiveX	Plan_Service_Status	1.90

Table 5. Alert Correlation by the GCT on the GCP Scenario II: Target Alert: Plan_Host_Status

Alert$_i$	Target Alert	GCT Index
HTTP_Java	Plan_Host_Status	7.73
Plan_IIS_Generic_BufferOverflow	Plan_Host_Status	7.70
Plan_Registry_Modified	Plan_Host_Status	7.63
CGI_Null_Byte_Attack	Plan_Host_Status	7.56
Port_Scan	Plan_Host_Status	3.26
HTTP_RobotsTxt	Plan_Host_Status	1.67

malicious agent autonomously gets access to the sensitive files and collects data (alert *DB_IllegalFileAccess*), uploads the stolen data to an external site (alert *Loki*), then downloads new agent software (alert *DB_NewClient*) and installs it (alert *DB_IllegalFileAccess*) on the Database Server, and then begins another round of the same attack sequence. GCT correlation results show a loop pattern of causal relationship among the corresponding alerts because these activities occur together.

When we correlate each target alert with other alerts using the GCT, we have some false causal alert candidates. For example, *HTTP_Java, HTTP_ActiveX* in Table 1. Overall, in this experiment, the true causality rate is 95.06% (77/81) and false causality rate is 12.6% (10/87) in this network enclave.

We also use the same network enclave as an example to show our results in the GCP Scenario II. In this network enclave, there are a total of 387 hyper alerts. Applying the *Ljung-Box* test to the hyper alerts, we identify 273 hyper alerts as the background alerts. In calculating the priority of hyper alerts, there are 9 hyper alerts whose priority values are above the threshold $\beta = 0.6$. Therefore, we have 9 hyper alerts as the target alerts, which are correlated with other alerts excluding the identified background alerts. As before, based on the mission goals and alert priority, for example, we select two alerts, *Plan_Service_Status* and *Plan_Host_Status*, as the targets, then apply the GCT to correlate other alerts with them. Table 4 and Table 5 show the corresponding GCT results. We list the top 6 candidate alerts that have passed the F-test in the tables. The alerts *Plan_Host_Status* and *Plan_Service_Status* are issued by a network management

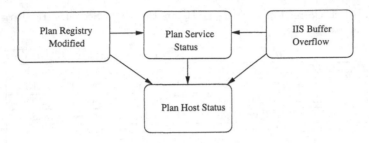

Fig. 3. The GCP Scenario II: Correlation Graph of Plan Server

system deployed on the network. The true causality rate is 93.15% (68/73) and false causality rate is 13.92% (11/79).

After finding the candidate alerts, we construct a corresponding correlation graph as shown in Figure 3. This figure shows that alerts *IIS_Buffer_Overflow* and *Plan_Registry_Modified* are causally related to alerts *Plan_Service_Status* and *Plan_Host_Status*. The GCP document verifies such relationship. The attacker launches *IIS Buffer Overflow* attack against the Plan Server in order to transfer and install the malicious executable code on it. The Plan Server's registry file is modified (alert *Plan_Registry_Modified*) and the service is down (alert *Plan_Service_Status*) during the daemon installation. Alert *Plan_Host_Status* indicates the "down" or "up" states of the Plan Server. The states are affected by the activities of the malicious agent installed on the Plan Server. Therefore, the ground truth described in the GCP document also supports the causal relationships among the corresponding alerts. These relationships are represented by directed edges pointing to alert *Plan_Host_Status* from alerts *IIS_Buffer_Overflow*, *Plan_Registry_Modified* and *Plan_Service_Status* in Figure 3.

However, the correlation result in the GCP Scenario II is not comprehensive enough to cover the complete attack scenarios. By comparing the alert streams with the GCP document, we notice that many malicious activities in the GCP Scenario II are not detected by the IDSs. Therefore, there are some missing intrusion alerts. In our approach, we depend on alert data for correlation and scenario analysis. When there is a lack of alerts corresponding to the intermediate attack steps, we cannot construct the complete attack scenario. In practice, IDSs or other security mechanisms can miss some attack activities. We will study how to deal with the "missing" attack steps in alert analysis and scenario construction.

4.2   DEF CON 9 Capture the Flag

As another case study, we applied our algorithms on the DEF CON 9 Capture The Flag (CTF) datasets. We use Snort to analyze the network traffic and output alerts for analysis. The DEF CON 9 CTF datasets are collected on 7 subnets. However, some datasets in subnet *Eth0* are corrupted. Therefore, we do not include them in our analysis. Because there is no information available about

Table 6. DefCon 9: Target Alert: DDOS_Shaft_Zombie_Host_A

$Alert_i$	Target Alert	GCT Index
FTP_Command_Overflow_Host_B_Src	DDOS_Shaft_Zombie	13.43
FTP_User_Overflow_Host_B_Src	DDOS_Shaft_Zombie	12.98
FTP_Command_Overflow_Host_C_Src	DDOS_Shaft_Zombie	11.43
WEB-CGI_ScriptAlias_Access	DDOS_Shaft_Zombie	11.12
TFT_GetPasswd_Host_B_Src	DDOS_Shaft_Zombie	10.88
FTP_Aix_Overflow_Host_B_Src	DDOS_Shaft_Zombie	10.83
EXPERIMENTAL_MISC_AFS_Access	DDOS_Shaft_Zombie	10.70
FTP_CWD_Overflow_Host_D_Src	DDOS_Shaft_Zombie	10.68
WEB-CGI_Wrap_Access	DDOS_Shaft_Zombie	10.54
FTP_Command_Overflow_Host_D_Src	DDOS_Shaft_Zombie	10.35
FTP_CWD_Overflow_Host_C_Src	DDOS_Shaft_Zombie	9.87
FTP_OpenBSDx86_Overflow_Host_D_Src	DDOS_Shaft_Zombie	7.86
WEB-CGI_WebDist_Access	DDOS_Shaft_Zombie	7.54

the network topology and host configuration, we cannot fully apply our model of alert priority computation on the datasets. Therefore, we select the target alerts for correlation based on domain knowledge.

As an example, we report results of alert analysis for *subnet 4*. Snort outputs more than 378,000 raw alerts. Scanning related alerts account for 91% of the total alerts. Alert *ICMP Redirect Host* accounts for about 3% of the total and alert *MISC Tiny Fragments* accounts for 5.9% of the total. Other alerts include Buffer Overflow, DDOS, DOS, DNS, TFTP, SNMP and Web-related attacks.

Applying our alert fusion and clustering algorithms, we can reduce the redundancy of low-level alerts dramatically, in particular, scanning alerts. The number of concrete high-level hyper alerts is about 1,300. We apply the *Ljung-Box* test with the significance level $\alpha = 0.05$ to all hyper alerts, and identify 754 hyper alerts as background alerts. For convenience, we denote the following: *Host_A* : 10.255.100.250, *Host_B* : 10.255.30.201, *Host_C* : 10.255.30.202, *Host_D* : 10.255. 40.237.

We first select the alert *DDOS Shaft Zombie* targeting at *Host_A*, and apply the GCT to correlate it with other alerts. Based on the correlation results, we select a causal alert as the next correlation target alert. For example, after each GCT correlation, we select the causal alert that is oriented from *host_C* as the target alert for the next GCT correlation. Table 6 through Table 8 show the corresponding GCT correlation results with regard to the selected target alerts, i.e., *DDoS_Zombie_Host_A, FTP_Command_Overflow_Host_C_Src, FTP_CWD_Overflow_Host_C_Src*. We construct the attack scenario graph based on GCT correlation results and alert analysis.

Figure 4 shows the attack scenario targeting *Host_A* according to the network activities in subnet 4. We can see that the attackers first launch a series of port scanning, e.g., *NMAP* and *RPC_Portmap*. Then multiple *FTP Buffer Overflow* attacks are launched against the target in order to get root access. The attackers also launch some Web-related attacks against the target. There are also some

Table 7. DefCon 9: Target Alert: FTP_Command_Overflow_Host_C_Src

$Alert_i$	Target Alert	GCT Index
Scan_NMAP_TCP	FTP_Command_Overflow_Host_C_Src	11.27
ICMP_Ping_NMAP	FTP_Command_Overflow_Host_C_Src	10.93
WEB-MISC_Perl_Command	FTP_Command_Overflow_Host_C_Src	10.75
Xmas_Scan	FTP_Command_Overflow_Host_C_Src	10.23
RPC_Portmap_Request	FTP_Command_Overflow_Host_C_Src	10.17
FIN_Scan	FTP_Command_Overflow_Host_C_Src	10.13
NULL_Scan	FTP_Command_Overflow_Host_C_Src	10.11

Table 8. DefCon 9: Target Alert: FTP_CWD_Overflow_Host_C_Src

$Alert_i$	Target Alert	GCT Index
Scan_NMAP_NULL	FTP_CWD_Overflow_Host_C_Src	12.72
ICMP_Ping_NMAP	FTP_CWD_Overflow_Host_C_Src	12.12
WEB-MISC_Perl_Command	FTP_CWD_Overflow_Host_C_Src	11.87
Xmas_Scan	FTP_Command_Overflow_Host_C_Src	11.63
SYN FIN_Scan	FTP_CWD_Overflow_Host_C_Src	11.27
NULL_Scan	FTP_CWD_Overflow_Host_C_Src	10.92

other attack scenarios that our algorithms are able to find; many of them are *port scanning* followed by *Buffer Overflow* attacks.

4.3 Discussion

In our experiments, the results from the GCP show that our approach can corre-late alerts of the attacks that have statistical causal relationships. The statistical causal correlations among alerts are not limited to the patterns of co-occurrences, e.g., alert *New_Client* and *Loki* in the GCP Scenario I. It also includes the case where the causal attack occurs only once, e.g., the sequential attacks in the scenario of the DEF CON 9. However, as the GCT results show, we have false causal alert candidates resulted from the GCT correlation that can result in false scenarios. One reason is that a large amount of background alerts can increase the false correlations. For example, we have a relatively high false causality rate in the GCP because the GCP has a lot of background alerts. Another reason is that, in our experiments, we do not have and use any training data sets. There-fore, it is different from traditional anomaly detection in which training data is used to construct the baseline that can reduce the false positive rate. In the DEF CON 9 dataset, our approach also finds some reasonable scenarios. Because of the nature of the DEF CON 9 dataset, we cannot comprehensively evaluate the success rate of our alert correlation method.

The key strength of our approach is that it can discover new alert correlations. Another advantage of our approach is that we do not require *a priori* knowledge about attack behaviors and how attacks are related when finding candidate alert correlations. In addition, our approach can also reduce the workload of security

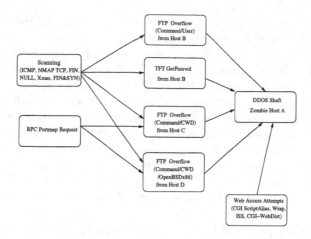

Fig. 4. DefCon 9: A scenario example of victim Host A

analysts in that they can focus on the causal alert candidates output by the GCT for further analysis. They do not have to assess all alerts and investigate all possible correlations. This is especially helpful when an attack is in progress and the security analysts need to figure out the attack scenarios in a timely fashion.

The time series used in our approach is based on the alert count instead of other categorical variables such as port access and pattern of TCP flag. The intuition is that if two attacks are related or have causal relationships, their occurrences should be tightly correlated because the causal attack triggers the resulting attack. Some experimental work and theoretical analysis have been presented in [1, 3, 2]. However, it is important to consider categorical variables when constructing attack scenarios. We will address this issue in our future work.

One challenge to our approach is background alert identification. Using the *Ljung-Box* test cannot cover all the background alerts. The limit of our approach is that we still need expert knowledge to further inspect the causal alert candidates resulted from GCT alert correlation when constructing attack scenarios. Human intervention has limits in automating attack scenario constructions. In future work, we will develop new correlation algorithms, in particular, probabilistic reasoning, and will integrate other existing correlation algorithms, e.g., *prerequisite-consequence* approach, for alert correlation in order to reduce the false correlation rate and improve the accuracy of scenario analysis.

5   Related Work

Recently, there have been several proposals on alert correlation and attack scenario analysis.

Porras et al. design a "mission-impact-based" correlation system, named M-Correlator [25]. The main idea is to evaluate alerts based on security interests and attack relevance to the protected networks and hosts. Related alerts are aggregated and clustered into a consolidated incident stream. The final result of the M-Correlator is a list of rank ordered security incidents based on the relevance and priority scores, which can be further analyzed by the security analyst. This approach focuses on the incident ranking instead of attack scenario analysis. The security analyst needs to perform further correlation analysis.

Valdes and Skinner [27] develop a probabilistic-based alert correlation mechanism. The approach uses similarities of alert attributes for correlation. Measures are defined to evaluate the degree of similarity between two alerts. Alert aggregation and scenario analysis are conducted by toughening or relaxing the similarity requirement in some attribute fields. However, it is difficult for this approach to correlate alerts that do not have obvious (or predefined) similarities in their attributes.

In the approach proposed by Debar and Wespi [7], alert clustering is applied for scenario construction. Two reasoning techniques are used to specify alert relationships. Backward-reasoning looks for *duplicates* of an alert, and forward-reasoning determines if there are *consequences* of an alert. These two types of relationships between alerts are predefined in a configuration file. The main limitation of this approach is that it relies on the predefined duplicate and consequence relationships between alerts.

Goldman et al. [10] build a correlation system that produces a correlation graph, which indicates the security events that aim to compromise the same security goal, with IDS alerts as the supporting evidence of the security events. The reasoning process is based on the predefined goal-events associations. Therefore, this approach cannot discover attack scenarios if the attack strategy or objective is not known.

Some other researchers have proposed the framework of alert correlation and scenario analysis based on the pre-condition and post-condition of individual alerts [4, 5, 22]. The assumption is that when an attacker launches a scenario, prior attack steps are preparing for later ones, and therefore, the consequences of earlier attacks have a strong relationship with the prerequisites of later attacks. The correlation engine searches for alert pairs that have a consequences and prerequisites match and builds a correlation graph with such pairs. There are several limitations with this approach. First, a new attack may not be paired with any other attack because its prerequisites and consequences are not yet defined. Second, even for known attacks, it is infeasible to predefine all possible prerequisites and consequences. In fact, some relationships cannot be expressed naturally in rigid terms.

Our approach differs from prior work in that it focuses on discovering *new* and *unknown* attack strategies. Instead of depending on the prior knowledge of attack strategies or pre-defined alert pre/post-conditions, we correlate the alerts and construct attack scenarios based on statistical and temporal relationships among alerts. In this respect, our approach is analogous to *anomaly detection* techniques.

We also notice that alert correlation has been a research topic in network management for decades. There are several well-known approaches such as case-based reasoning system [19], code-book [18], and model-based reasoning systems [16, 23]. In network management system (NMS), event correlation focuses on alarms resulted from network faults, which often have fixed patterns. Whereas in security, the alerts are more diverse and unpredictable because the attackers are intelligent and can use flexible strategies. We nevertheless can borrow ideas in NMS event correlation for INFOSEC data analysis.

6   Conclusion and Future Work

In this paper, we presented an approach for correlating INFOSEC alerts and constructing attack scenarios. We developed a mechanism that aggregates and clusters raw alerts into high level hyper-alerts. Alert priority is calculated and ranked. The priority computation is conducted based on the relevance of the alert to the protected networks and systems. Alert correlation is conducted based on the Granger Causality Test, a time series-based causal analysis algorithm. Attack scenarios are analyzed by constructing a correlation graph based on the GCT results and on alert inspection. Our initial results have demonstrated the potential of our method in alert correlation and scenario analysis. Our approach can discover new attack relationships as long as the alerts of the attacks have statistical correlation. Our approach is complementary to other correlation approaches that depend on hard-coded prior knowledge for pattern matching.

We will continue to study statistical-based approaches for alert correlation, and develop algorithms to detect background alerts, develop techniques to integrate categorical variables such as patterns of TCP flags, and study how to reduce false causality rate. We will also develop other correlation algorithms, in particular, probabilistic reasoning approaches, to integrate multi-algorithms for alert correlation and scenario analysis. We will also study how to handle missing alerts of attack steps in scenario analysis. One approach may be to insert some hypothesis alerts and look for evidence to either support or degrade the hypothesis from other sensor systems. We will validate our correlation algorithms on alert streams collected in the real world.

Acknowledgments

This research is supported in part by a grant from DARPA (F30602-00-1-0603) and a grant from NSF (CCR-0133629). We thank João B.D. Cabrera of Scientific Systems Company for helpful discussions on time series analysis and Granger-Causality Test. We also thank Giovanni Vigna of University of California at Santa Barbara, Alfonso Valdes of SRI International and Stuart Staniford of Silicon Defense, as well as the anonymous reviewers for their valuable comments and suggestions.

References

1. J. B. D. Cabrera, L. Lewis, X. Qin, W. Lee, R. K. Prasanth, B. Ravichandran, and R. K. Mehra. Proactive detection of distributed denial of service attacks using mib traffic variables - a feasibility study. In *Proceedings of IFIP/IEEE International Symposium on Integrated Network Management (IM 2001)*, May 2001.
2. J. B. D. Cabrera and R. K. Mehra. Extracting precursor rules from time series - a classical statistical viewpoint. In *Proceedings of the Second SIAM International Conference on Data Mining*, pages 213–228, Arlington, VA, USA, April 2002.
3. J.B.D. Cabrera, L.Lewis, X. Qin, W. Lee, and R.K. Mehra. Proactive intrusion detection and distributed denial of service attacks - a case study in security management. *Journal of Network and Systems Management*, vol. 10(no. 2), June 2002.
4. S. Cheung, U. Lindqvist, and M. W. Fong. Modeling multistep cyber attacks for scenario recognition. In *Proceedings of the Third DARPA Information Survivability Conference and Exposition (DISCEX III)*, Washington, D.C., April 2003.
5. F. Cuppens and A. Miège. Alert correlation in a cooperative intrusion detection framework. In *Proceedings of the 2002 IEEE Symposium on Security and Privacy*, pages 202–215, Oakland, CA, May 2002.
6. DAPRA Cyber Panel Program. DARPA cyber panel program grand challenge problem (GCP). http://ia.dc.teknowledge.com/CyP/GCP/, 2003.
7. H. Debar and A. Wespi. The intrusion-detection console correlation mechanism. In *4th International Symposium on Recent Advances in Intrusion Detection (RAID)*, October 2001.
8. DEFCON. Def con capture the flag (ctf) contest. http://www.defcon.org. Archive accessible at http://wi2600.org/mediawhore/mirrors/shmoo/, 2000.
9. DEFCON. Def con capture the flag (ctf) contest. http://www.defcon.org. Archive accessible at http://smokeping.planetmirror.com/pub/cctf/defcon9/, 2001.
10. R.P. Goldman, W. Heimerdinger, and S. A. Harp. Information modleing for intrusion report aggregation. In *DARPA Information Survivability Conference and Exposition (DISCEX II)*, June 2001.
11. C.W.J. Granger. Investigating causal relations by econometric methods and cross-spectral methods. *Econometrica*, 34:424–428, 1969.
12. IETF Intrusion Detection Working Group. Intrusion detection message exchange format. http://www.ietf.org/internet-drafts/draft-ietf-idwg-idmef-xml-09.txt, 2002.
13. J. Haines, D. K. Ryder, L. Tinnel, and S. Taylor. Validation of sensor alert correlators. *IEEE Security & Privacy Magazine*, January/February, 2003.
14. J. Hamilton. *Time Series Analysis*. Princeton University Press, 1994.
15. A.J. Hayter. *Probability and Statistics for Engineers and Scientists*. Duxbury Press, 2002.
16. G. Jakobson and M. D. Weissman. Alarm correlation. *IEEE Network Magazine*, November 1993.
17. K. Julisch and M. Dacier. Mining intrusion detection alarms for actionable knowledge. In *The 8th ACM International Conference on Knowledge Discovery and Data Mining*, July 2002.
18. S. Kliger, S. Yemini, Y. Yemini, D. Oshie, and S. Stolfo. A coding approach to event correlations. In *Proceedings of the 6th IFIP/IEEE International Symposium on Integrated Network Management*, May 1995.
19. L. Lewis. A case-based reasoning approach to the management of faults in communication networks. In *Proceedings of the IEEE INFOCOM*, 1993.

20. G.M. Ljung and G.E.P. Box. On a measure of lack of fit in time series models. In *Biometrika 65*, pages 297–303, 1978.
21. P. Ning, Y. Cui, and D.S. Reeves. Analyzing intensive intrusion alerts via correlation. In *Proceedings of the 5th International Symposium on Recent Advances in Intrusion Detection (RAID)*, October 2002.
22. P. Ning, Y. Cui, and D.S. Reeves. Constructing attack scenarios through correlation of intrusion alerts. In *9th ACM Conference on Computer and Communications Security*, November 2002.
23. Y. A. Nygate. Event correlation using rule and object based techniques. In *Proceedings of the 6th IFIP/IEEE International Symposium on Integrated Network Management*, May 1995.
24. J. Pearl. *Probabilistic Reasoning in Intelligent Systems: Networks of Plausible Inference*. Morgan Kaufmann Publishers, Inc, 1988.
25. P. A. Porras, M. W. Fong, and A. Valdes. A Mission-Impact-Based approach to INFOSEC alarm correlation. In *Proceedings of the 5th International Symposium on Recent Advances in Intrusion Detection (RAID)*, October 2002.
26. W. Stallings. *SNMP, SNMPv2, SNMPv3, and RMON 1 and 2*. Addison-Wesley, 1999.
27. A. Valdes and K. Skinner. Probabilistic alert correlation. In *Proceedings of the 4th International Symposium on Recent Advances in Intrusion Detection (RAID)*, October 2001.

Correlation of Intrusion Symptoms: An Application of Chronicles

Benjamin Morin and Hervé Debar

France Télécom R&D, Caen, France
{benjamin.morin,herve.debar}@rd.francetelecom.com

Abstract. In this paper, we propose a multi-alarm misuse correlation component based on the chronicles formalism. Chronicles provide a high level declarative language and a recognition system that is used in other areas where dynamic systems are monitored. This formalism allows us to reduce the number of alarms shipped to the operator and enhances the quality of the diagnosis provided.

1 Introduction

The diagnosis provided by current intrusion detection systems is spread over numerous fine-grained alarms. As a result, the overall number of alarms is overwhelming. Moreover, their content is so poor that it requires the operator to go back to the original data source to assess the actual severity of the alarms.

Being able to express phenomena involving several alarms[1] is essential in diagnosis applications because using several observations i) strengthens the diagnosis, ii) reduces the overall number of alarms and iii) improves the content of the alarms. Strengthening the diagnosis enables to invalidate or confirm the alarms, which is very important in intrusion detection where false positives are prominent. The number of alarms is reduced because alarms (symptoms) are presented to the operator as labeled groups instead of being presented individually. The content is enhanced because the information of the symptoms are combined. Our approach implies a *multi-event* correlation component using as input IDS alerts.

The correlation component we propose is a *misuse* based. The definition of misuse correlation is similar to misuse intrusion detection: known malicious or undesired sequences of events are searched in the data stream. In our approach, the alarms are checked against a set of multi-events patterns (or signatures) expressed in a dedicated language. Several approaches have been proposed in the research field to provide signatures languages involving many events. In [2], Eckmann *et al* classify languages in six categories: event languages, response languages, reporting languages, correlation languages, exploit languages and detection languages. We are interested here in correlation languages. Correlation

---

[1] or *events* – in the remainder of this paper, we will either speak of events and alarms because alarms triggered by IDSes are input events of the correlation system

G. Vigna, E. Jonsson, and C. Kruegel (Eds.): RAID 2003, LNCS 2820, pp. 94–112, 2003.

languages rely on alarms provided by IDSes to recognize ongoing attack scenarios. Examples of existing correlation languages are Statl [2], P-Best [4] and Lambda [24].

We propose to use the chronicle formalism proposed by Dousson [11] to correlate alarms. Chronicles are used in many distinct areas [14]. They were primarily designed to analyze sequences of alarms issued by equipments in a telecommunication network and a voltage distribution network. They are now also used in some subtasks of a project aimed at representing car flows in road traffic. In the medical domain, they are being looked at for hepatitis symptoms tracking, intelligent patient monitoring or cardiac arrhythmia detection. We propose to use chronicles to correlate alarms issued by intrusion detection analyzers. Our correlation component uses Dousson's chronicle recognition system (CRS), available at `http://crs.elibel.tm.fr`.

In this paper, we first introduce the chronicles formalism. We then show how chronicles are applied to intrusion detection and illustrate how it solves some intrusion detection issues. We also describe in what extent chronicles integrate with an existing alarm correlation infrastructure. Before concluding and evoking future works, we compare our research with related work.

2   Chronicles

Chronicles provide a framework for modeling dynamic systems. They include an evolution monitoring mechanism to track changes in the modeled system. Recognition of chronicles is based on a formalism in which time is fundamental. This is in contrast with classical expert systems, which base their reasoning on rules, relegating time information to the background.

Chronicles are temporal patterns that represent *possible* evolutions of the observed system. A chronicle is a set of events, linked together by time constraints, whose occurrence may depend on the context. The available time information allows ordering and the specification of time spans between two occurrences of events. In the AI literature, chronicles are related to other approaches such as plan recognition and event calculus (see [12]).

In the remainder of this section, we present the essential features of the chronicles, and briefly sketch the recognition process. Detailed description can be found in [11, 13].

2.1   Representation

In the AI literature, a natural approach to the representation of temporal information consists in associating assertions with particular times. Chronicles representation relies on the *reified temporal logic* formalism [5, 7, 16]. In this formalism, propositional terms are related to times or other propositional terms through additional truth predicates, like *hold*. For example, in a reified logic, one may use *hold*(is(light, on), T) to represent the assertion "light is on over time T".

Time Representation For algorithm complexity reasons, time representation relies on the time points algebra and time is considered as a linearly ordered discrete set of instants whose resolution is sufficient for the environment dynamics.

It should be noticed that in the chronicle formalism, if several *identical* events occur at the same time point, only one is taken into account. As a consequence, the time resolution is very important because in domains like intrusion detection, many identical events may occur within a small time window.

A time interval I is expressed as pair $I = (t_1, t_2)$ corresponding to the lower and upper bound on the temporal distance between two time points t_1 and t_2.

Domain Attributes In the reified logic formalism, the environment is described through domain attributes. Domain attributes are the atemporal propositions of the modeled environment.

A domain attribute is a couple $P(a_1, \ldots, a_n) : v$, where P is the attribute name, $a_1, \ldots, a_n$ its arguments and v its value. For example, *Load(host)* can be a measure of a server load, and the possible values {low,medium,high}. Special attributes, called *messages*, are attributes without any associated value.

Reifying Predicates Reifying predicates are used to temporally qualify the set of domain attributes. Their syntax and informal semantics are sketched in Figure 1. The predicates used in chronicles are *hold*, *event*, *noevent* and *occurs*.

$hold(P : v, (t_1, t_2))$	The domain attribute P must keep the value v over the interval $[t_1, t_2[$.
$event(P : (v_1, v_2), t)$	The attribute P changed its value from v_1 to v_2 at t.
$event(P, t)$	Message P occurs at t.
$noevent(P, (t_1, t_2))$	The chronicle would not be recognized if any change of the value of the domain attribute P occurs between t_1 and t_2.
$occurs((n_1, n_2), P, (t_1, t_2))$ $(0 \leqslant n_1 \leqslant n_2)$	the event that matches the pattern P occurred exactly N times between the two time points t_1 and t_2, and $n_1 \leqslant N \leqslant n_2$. The value ∞ can be used for n_2.

$$occurs \text{ is unifying because } \begin{cases} noevent(P, (t_1, t_2)) \equiv occurs((0, 0), P, (t_1, t_2)) \\ event(P, t_1) \equiv occurs((1, \infty), P, (t_1, t_1 + 1)) \end{cases}$$

Fig. 1. Reifying Predicates

- The *hold* predicate models chronicle assertions (assertions for short). Assertions represent persistence of the value of a domain attribute over an interval, without knowing when this value was reached.
- The *event* predicate expresses a time stamped instance of a pattern. An event has no duration. Events denote a change of the value of a domain attribute.

- The *noevent* predicate expresses forbidden events, i.e. events whose occurrence leads to the invalidation of a chronicle instance during the recognition process.
- The *occurs* is a counting predicate.

Chronicle Model A chronicle model (or *chronicle*) represents a piece of evolution of the world. Chronicles are made of i) a set of time points, ii) a set of temporal constraints between the time points, iii) a set of event patterns which represent relevant changes of the world for this chronicle, iv) a set of assertions patterns which represent the context of the occurrences of events, and v) a set of external actions which will be performed by the system when a chronicle is recognized. Actions are not limited to report generation: the system can generate events and assertions. Both of them can later interact with other chronicles instances. Reinserting previously recognized chronicles in the flow of input events is referred to as "looping" functionality in the remainder (see section 3.4).

Chronicle models are expressed in the chronicle language. After a compilation stage during which the consistency of the chronicle constraints is tested, the chronicles are coded into efficient data structures used for the recognition process described thereafter.

2.2   Chronicle Recognition

After the chronicle models compilation, the recognition system is initialized by creating an empty chronicle instance for each chronicle model. A chronicle *instance* is a chronicle for which a complete match is not found yet. The chronicle recognition system then processes the stream of input events in one shot and on-line.

An event whose atemporal state unifies with a pattern of a chronicle is always considered for integration in a chronicle; the integration solely depends on the suitability of the chronicle temporal constraints, the previously integrated events and the event's timestamp. Events may be shared by many chronicles and the system is able to manage all the concurrent instances. The recognition process manages a set of partial instances of chronicles as a set of time windows (one for each forthcoming event) that is gradually constrained by each new matched event.

An event occurrence may also lead chronicle instances to be destroyed because an expected event's deadline is reached, and so all chronicles waiting for any event before this deadline are destroyed. Outdated assertions can also be suppressed after an event occurence.

If an assertion is violated or if a deadline expires, then a chronicle instance is destroyed.

When integrating an event occurence in a chronicle instance, the system cannot *a priori* be sure that the event will integrate well in the chronicle with regard to the forthcoming events. It is not possible to integrate an event inside a chronicle without maintaining the hypothesis that it is not necessarily *this* chronicle instance that will be recognized. As a result, every chronicle instance

```
1   chronicle example1 {
2      event(e1,t1);
3      event(e2,t2);
4      event(e3,t3);
5
6      t1<t2<t3
7      t3-t2 <= 4
8   }
```

Fig. 2. A Chronicle Example

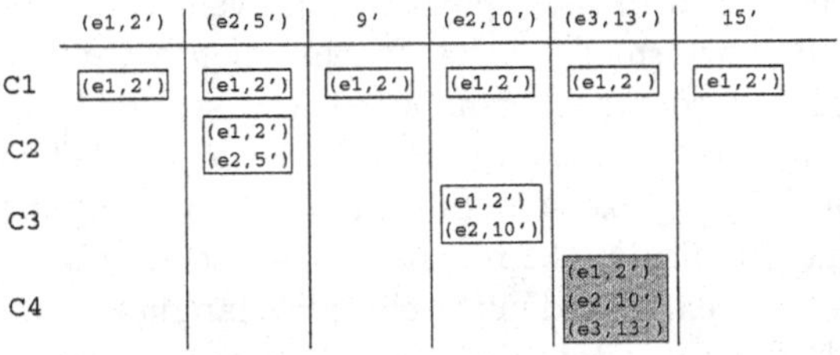

Fig. 3. Duplication example

is duplicated *before* the integration of an event. The systems maintains parallel hypothesis so that *all* event sequences satisfying the constraints are recognized.

We illustrate duplication of chronicles with the example in Figure 3. Let us consider the following chronicle:

$$event(e_1, t_1) \land event(e_2, t_2) \land event(e_3, t_3) \land (t_1 < t_2 < t_3) \land t_3 - t_2 \leqslant 4$$

which is equivalent to the one represented in the chronicle language in Figure 2.

The event stream is made of e_1 at 2', followed by e_2 at 5' followed by another e_2 at 10' and a e_3 at 13'. When e_1 arrives, a chronicle instance (C_1) of chronicle model C is created. When e_2 arrives, a duplicate of C_1 is created (C_2), and e_2 is integrated in C_2. At 9', C_2 dies because the constraint $t_{e_3} - t_{e_2} \leqslant 4$ is not true anymore. When the second e_2 arrives, a duplicate of C_1 (C_3) is created. When e_3 occurs, a duplicate of C_3 (C_4) is created and the chronicle is recognized (shaded box on figure). At 15', C_3 dies.

This mechanism imposes the chronicle recognition system to be exhaustive, i.e. all the possible instances of the defined chronicles are identified by the system.

For example, if we consider the chronicle

$$event(a, t_1) \land event(b, t_2) \land event(c, t_3) \land t_2 < t_3$$

and the event stream[2],

$$a_1, a_2, b_1, c_1, a_3$$

then the chronicle is recognized three times: $\{a_1, b_1, c_1\}$, $\{a_2, b_1, c_1\}$, $\{a_3, b_1, c_1\}$.

---

[2] indices are only used to distinguish event instances and we do not provide timestamps because we do not need them for the example

Chronicles duplication imposes chronicle models to be written with care. As a matter of fact, if no chronicle invalidation mechanism is specified in a chronicle model, the chronicle instances tree may grow up indefinitely because of chronicles living forever. Chronicles may be invalidated either with an assertion violation or a deadline being reached. As a result, in order to prevent chronicle instances to live forever, assertions (like *hold* or *noevent*) and/or quantitative time constraints (like $(t_2 - t_1) < 2$) should be specified inside chronicle models.

When a complete match is found, a chronicle is *recognized*, and the associated action is performed by the system.

3   Using Chronicles to Correlate Intrusion Alarms

The current three major issues in intrusion detection are alarm overload, poorness of the alarms semantics and false negatives. In our approach, we explicitly address the first two. The false negative issue is partly solved by making complementary sensors cooperate to provide an appropriate coverage of the monitoring of the environment. Cooperation is a kind of correlation that involves fusion of redundant alarms and synthesis of complementary alarms, and can be achieved by chronicles because we are not restricted to using a single input stream. Cooperation is indeed all the more essential as the multiplication of analyzers also multiplies the alarms. However, contrary to Cuppens in [24] whose correlation process infers unobserved alarms from attack scenarios, we solely rely on *available* alarms. We do not generate *almost recognized*[3] chronicles because this would imply that optional events are used inside chronicles models which could consequently be removed.

In the remainder of this section, we first briefly discuss the informal semantics of the chronicles used in intrusion detection. Then, we give examples to illustrate how chronicles can be used to enhance the content of the alarm and reduce the amount of alarms.

The domain attribute used in the following chronicle models is a triplet *alarm*(*name*, *src*, *trg*) where *name* is the attack identifier (*e.g* "cmd.exe access"), *src* is the attack source (*e.g* an IP address) and *trg* is the attack target (*e.g* an IP address). In fact, the *alarm* term may denote real attacks or benign events. Using the chronicle language, the *alarm* domain attribute is declared as follows:

```
message alarm[?name,?src,?trg]
{
}
```

Constraints on the parameter values can be specified inside the brackets. The ? is used to inform the system that attributes are variables that should be instantiated by the chronicle recognition system when an event occurs.

---

[3] i.e chronicles whose expected event set is not complete

3.1 Informal Semantics of the Chronicles Applied to Intrusion Detection

Chronicles model phenomena which involve more than one event. This definition does not presume the semantic of a chronicle. Actually, in the intrusion detection context, the modeled phenomena may either be *normal* or *malicious*. In this section, we describe these two kinds of chronicles.

Normal Phenomena. False alarms (false positives) are the primary cause of alarm overload. Although many false positives could be avoided by using more sophisticated signatures and detection mechanisms, it should be noted that some attacks can only be characterized by a single event. As a result, legitimate actions can be confused with attacks.

To solve this, it is possible to discriminate legitimate actions from attacks instead of discriminating attacks from legitimate actions. In this case, chronicles represent *normal* phenomena which involve an alarm as well as other peripheral and innocuous events which are indicative of normal activity. Paragraph 3.2 illustrates this situation. The recognition of such a chronicle invalidates the alarm; a chronicle invalidation (i.e a chronicle which is not recognized) means that the alarm is indicative of a real attack. In the former case, the alarm is not directly shown to the security operator (it is included in a recognized chronicle); in the latter case, the alarm is directly provided to the operator.

Notice that a chronicle instance can also be invalidated because only innocuous events are observed, but no alarms. In this case, the innocuous events shall not be shown to the operator. Examples of innocuous events are provided in Section 3.2.

Malicious Phenomena. Some attacks are characterized by several suspicious events. In this case, sensors trigger one alarm per event. Chronicles can be used to model these phenomena. Such a chronicle recognition contributes to alarm reduction because only one alarm (the recognized chronicle) is provided to the operator instead of each individual alarm. It also contributes to the semantic improvement because the recognized phenomena is more significant than each individual alarm. If partial chronicle are invalidated, their constitutive alarms are provided to the operator individually and may be used in other correlation mechanisms.

Innocuous events used in this kind of chronicles shall not be provided to the operator if the chronicle is invalidated. If a chronicle is recognized, then the involved innocuous events are available to the operator for investigation.

In the intrusion detection literature, alarm correlation often refers to *attack scenarios*. An attack scenario is a sequence of *explicit* attack steps which are logically linked and lead to an objective. A portscan followed by a buffer overflow against a given service is an example of attack scenario.

An attack scenario can be modeled by a chronicle. However, we do not intend to use chronicles to model attack scenarios. There are two reasons for this.

Firstly, the relevance of an attack scenario is questionable because many (unpredictable) paths may lead to a given attack objective. Secondly, it is hard to specify quantitative time constraints in chronicles because the time gaps between each step may vary a lot, depending on how hurried the attacker is. The attacker may even work on time gaps to evade detection.

As a result, malicious phenomena modeled with chronicles are phenomena whose occurrences are deterministic. Examples of such phenomena are given in sections 3.4 and 3.3.

3.2   Alarm Semantics Improvement

Description of the Phenomenon. False alarms are the main cause of alarm overload; Julisch reports that they represent up to 99% of the overall number of alarms [19].

We believe that the diagnosis provided by intrusion detection systems can be strengthened by taking into account contextual events to discriminate true from false positives. Contextual events can be benign events whose occurrence can reinforce or mitigate the confidence an operator has in an alarm. In that sense, chronicles can both represent known false positive cases and true positives.

To illustrate this, we propose a chronicle which is used identify a recurrent false positive triggered by a network IDS in our network, pretending that buffer overflow attacks occur. The shellcodes used in some buffer overflow attacks contain long 0x90 bytes strings. Many misuse network IDSes signatures are based on this property to detect buffer overflow attacks in a generic way. However, this kind of signature can provoke false positives because legitimate binary data going on the wire can match the signature. This is the case with ftp file transfers: binary file transfers can trigger alarms because the probability for a binary file to contain 0x90 bytes strings is potentially high[4]. Deactivating the signature is not a solution because true attacks against ftp servers would not be detected anymore.

One solution can consist in mitigating the alarm severity when it is triggered during a file transfer, *i.e* between a request from a client and the end of the file transfer. This implies that sensors generate events for each file retrieval request and the corresponding acknowledgement message. As a result, every file transfer provokes two innocuous events. Notice that the frequency of file transfer requests is moderate with regard to the events throughput managed by chronicles, so these innocuous events do not burden the recognition process. However, a security operator should keep this consideration in mind when writing chronicles.

Description of the Chronicle. The corresponding chronicle is in Figure 4. The goal of this chronicle is to generate a report informing the operator that a buffer overflow alarm was raised, but it occurred during a file transfer, so it is probably a false alarm. As a result, any buffer overflow alarm that is not inside a chronicle is really suspect.

---

[4] http://www.whitehats.com/info/IDS181

```
1  chronicle shellcode_mitigation[?source, ?target]
2  {
3      event(alarm[ftp_retr_request,?source,?target], t1)
4      event(alarm[shellcode,?source,?target], t2)
5      noevent(alarm[ftp_transfer_complete,?target,?source],
6                                            (t1+1,t3-1))
7      event(alarm[ftp_transfer_complete,?target,?source], t3)
8
9      t1<t2<t3
10
11     when recognized {
12        emit event(alarm[shellcode_mitigation, ?source, ?target], t2);
13     }
14 }
```

Fig. 4. A Chronicle Example: Alarm Mitigation

In this chronicle, ftp_retr_request and ftp_transfer_complete are the innocuous events which respectively indicate a FTP file transfer request made by the client and the end of file transfer. The shellcode alarm is the actual buffer overflow attempt. A sensor is required to trigger the first two events. Snort can be used for that purpose, with the adequate signatures to monitor control commands of the FTP protocol.

The order in which the reifying predicates are specified does not matter because the system relies on the temporal constraints.

The temporal symbols t1,t2 and t3 are variables which are instantiated by the system. Note that contrary to the domain attributes parameters, temporal symbols do not need to be prefixed by a "?", since temporal symbols only denote variables (absolute dates cannot be used as time symbols). The chronicle recognition system instantiates t1 (resp. t2 and t3) with the ftp_retr_request (resp. shellcode and ftp_transfer_complete) event timestamp.

The use of identical variable names as parameters of the domain attributes implicitly imposes the source and target involved in the chronicle to be identical.

The *noevent* predicate in line 5 is necessary to prevent chronicles to live forever in the system (see section 2.2). No quantitative temporal constraint is specified in this chronicle (we do not know how long a file transfer may last) and since the CRS recognition is exhaustive, the ftp_transfer_complete event could be used as the end of an earlier chronicle instance being recognized; as a result, we need to add a constraint saying that ftp_transfer_complete alarms should not occur twice within a chronicle.

When faced with a "normal" ftp transaction, (*i.e.* a ftp_retr_request followed by a ftp_transfer_complete event), the chronicle recognition system discards a chronicle instance when receiving the ftp_transfer_complete event, because the chronicle constraints (t2<t3) cannot be satisfied anymore.

```
1   chronicle portscan[?source, ?target]
2   {
3      event(alarm[sid_1,?source,?target], t1)
4      occurs((1,+oo),alarm[sid_2,?source,?target], (t1+1,t2))
5      noevent(alarm[sid_3,?source,?target], (t1,t2))
6      event(alarm[sid_3,?source,?target], t2+1)
7      t1<t2
8
9      when recognized {
10        emit event(alarm[portscan, ?source, ?target], t2);
11     }
12  }
```

Fig. 5. A Chronicle Example: portscan detected by Snort

3.3   Alarm Reduction

Description of the Phenomenon. Intrusion detection systems tend to spread their diagnosis over many alarms, mainly because the analysis is performed on single events; as a result, alarms are too fine-grained: a single phenomenon involving many events –be it benign or not– provokes many alarms. Let us take the example of portscan detection by Snort to illustrate this.

When detecting portscans, Snort generates three kinds of alarms: a portscan _begin alarm, several portscan_status during the scan, and finally a portscan _end when the portscan is supposedly finished.

Description of the Chronicle. A simple yet effective chronicle model to synthesize portscan alarms is provided in Figure 5. The sid_1, sid_2 and sid_3 alarms respectively correspond to the portscan_begin, portscan_status and portscan_end alarms. These alarms should have the same source and the same target. The first event (line 1) initiates the chronicle and instantiates t1; t2 is instantiated by the last event (line 6); between t1 and t2+1, an infinite number of portscan_status alarms may occur.

Portscans are recurrent phenomena. For the same reason as the previous chronicle example, we need to add a constraint saying that portscan end alarms should not occur twice within a chronicle.

3.4   Alarm Semantics Improvement and Alarm Reduction

Description of the Phenomenon. Recognizing known phenomena in which many events are involved both enables reduction of the number of alarms (we only have to consider the alarm set) and semantic enhancement (the identified phenomenon). More and more attacks are automated processes, making it possible to write interesting chronicles because the intrusion steps are always the same.

```
1   chronicle nimda[?source, ?target]
2   {
3       occurs((1,2),alarm[iis_code_red_ii_root_exe,?source,?target],
4                                                   (t,t+2000))
5       occurs((1,4),alarm[iis_decode_bug,?source,?target],(t,t+2000))
6       occurs((1,14),alarm[iis_cmd_exe,?source,?target],(t, t+2000))
7       occurs((1,3),alarm[web_dot_dot,?source,?target],(t,t+2000))
8       occurs((1,2),alarm[iis_unicode,?source,?target],(t,t+2000))
9       occurs((1,1),alarm[iis_unicode2,?source,?target],(t,t+2000))
10      occurs((1,1),alarm[iis_unicode3,?source,?target],(t,t+2000))
11      occurs((1,1),alarm[iis_decode_bug3,?source,?target],(t,t+2000))
12      occurs((1,1),alarm[iis_decode_bug2,?source,?target],(t,t+2000))
13      occurs((1,1),alarm[iis_decode_bug4,?source,?target],(t,t+2000))
14
15      when recognized {
16          emit event(alarm[nimda, ?source, ?target], t);
17      }
18  }
```

Fig. 6. A Chronicle Example: a Nimda worm attempt detected by Dragon

Example of such phenomena are worms. Worms attacks involve many events, each of which can trigger one or more alarm. As worms are recurrent attacks, reducing the number of alarms for each attempt has a strong impact on the overall alarm excess.

The Nimda worm attacks vulnerable IIS web servers. During each infection attempt, many suspect or malicious HTTP requests are sent to the target. Thus, each Nimda attempt triggers many alarms by conventional IDSes: Snort[5] generates about 20 alarms; Dragon[6] generates about 30 alarms.

Description of the Chronicle. In Figure 6 we show a chronicle suited for Dragon alarms. A Nimda attempt is characterized by a burst of 10 distinct alarms. Each alarm can occur several times (for instance, the `iis_cmd_exe` occurs 1 to 14 times at each attempt). All the alarms should have the same source and the same target, and they all occur within a 2s time window (the resolution here is 1 ms). When such an alarm burst occurs, a synthetic alarm `nimda_worm_attempt` is reported. Only one synthetic alarm represents the 30 original ones.

We provide an complementary chronicle example called `new_infection` in Figure 7. This example illustrate two important things: the chronicles *looping* functionality and the use of domain attributes which are not alarms. The goal of this chronicle is to recognize every new server infection by the Nimda worm. The first parameter of the `new_infection` chronicle is the newly infected server and the second parameter is the host causing the infection.

---

[5] http://www.snort.org
[6] http://dragon.enterasys.com

```
1   chronicle new_infection[?victim, ?attacker]
2   {
3     event(infected[?victim, somebody]:(true, false), t0)
4     noevent(infected[?victim, ?]:(false, true), (t0,t1))
5
6     event(alarm[nimda, ?attacker, ?victim], t1)
7     event(alarm[nimda, ?victim, ?], t2)
8
9     t2 - t1 in [1000,10000]
10    when recognized {
11        emit event(infected[?victim, ?attacker]:(false,true), t1)
12    }
13  }
```

Fig. 7. Identifying new Nimda infections

We can say that a host b is infected by a if a Nimda attempt from a to b is detected (line 6), followed by Nimda attempts from b to any host (line 7) 1 to 10 seconds later (line 8).

The problem is that a host still receives attack attempts although it is already infected. As a result, if we only use the previous two patterns to detect newly infected hosts, the chronicle would be recognized every time b is attacked. We want the chronicle to be recognized only once, so we need to *tag* infected hosts: b is newly infected only if it was not infected before the attack from a.

We use a *infected(?victim, ?attacker)* $\in \{true, false\}$ domain attribute. Note that *infected* is not an alarm. It is rather a topology-like relation. Note also that contrary to alarms which are messages, *infected* is a valued domain attribute.

Line 3 of the chronicle is the initialization of the state of the hosts: the chronicle recognition system should receive events saying that by default, no host is infected ("victim is infected by somebody" is false).

Line 4 should be read as "[For the chronicle to be recognized], victim must not have been previously infected by *any* host". When used solely, the "?" symbol represents a variable whose value should not be instantiated (*any*).

Line 6 and 7 are the manifestations of a successful infection. When the chronicle is recognized, the status of victim is updated (infected[?victim, ?attacker] becomes true when the attempt occurs – see line 11).

3.5   Sensor Cooperation

Description of the Phenomenon. The chronicle language is a high level declarative language. It does not presume the nature of the underlying input event stream. As a result, cooperation (*i.e.* correlation of alarms from heterogenous sources) is naturally modeled with chronicles. Of course, the input format must be compliant with the one expected by the chronicle recognition system (the domain attributes properties –arity, parameters domain values– have to be defined).

```
1  chronicle successful_codeExec[?source, ?target]
2  {
3    event(alarm[?bufov_snort_alarm, ?source, ?target], t1);
4    event(alarm[shell_exec, ?, ?target], t2);
5    noevent(alarm[login, ?, ?target], (t1,t2));
6    ?bufov_snort_alarm in {sid_203, sid_34}
7
8    t2 - t1 in [0,100]
9
10   when recognized {
11     emit event(alarm[successful_buffer_overflow, ?source, ?target],
12                                                            t2);
13   }
14 }
```

Fig. 8. A Chronicle example: example of IDS cooperation

The upstream sensors that generate alarms must have their clocks synchronized, and the gap between two clocks should be coherent with the time resolution used in the chronicle models. If these conditions hold, then chronicles are able to manage delays due to sensors processing or transport durations. Whether an event is delayed or not, its integration in a chronicle is done in the same way because the chronicle temporal reasoning is solely performed over the events timestamp, not on the running clock.

Description of the Chronicle. In the example provided in Figure 8, three sensors are used: Snort, Snare and Syslog. The Snort sensor sends the alarm ?bufov_snort_alarm, shell_exec is triggered by a system-based monitoring tool (Snare) and the login alarm is sent by Syslog. The chronicle monitors successful attacks resulting in the execution of a shell on a host.

In line 3, we wait for any alarm about a buffer overflow attack. In line 6, the Snort alarm names (sid_xxx) that refer to buffer overflow attacks are enumerated. If such an attack is followed by a shell execution on the same target, and no login execution occurred between the two (which could justify the shell execution), then the chronicle is recognized.

3.6   Experimental Results

The chronicle models proposed in this paper have not been tested on a live system yet. We plan to do this in the near future. They have only been validated on alarm logs collected in our network.

However, concerning the ability of the chronicle recognition system to cope with intrusion alarm flow, one should notice that chronicles were primarily designed to diagnose failures in telecommunication network by analyzing alarms issued by equipments. In this context, the recognition system must be efficient because it has to deal with alarm bursts and high alarm rates.

The alarm rates observed in the intrusion detection field are of the same order as the ones observed in other fields where the chronicles have already successfully been applied.

The performance issue may arise if no chronicle invalidation mechanism is specified by the chronicle writer in a chronicle model. In this case, the chronicle instances tree may grow up indefinitely because of chronicles living forever (see section 2.2).

Performance also depends on the number of chronicle models used in parallel. The time required to process an event grows linearly with the number of chronicle models. In [11], efficiency experiments are performed with 80 chronicle models, containing about 10 event patterns among 50 domain attributes, 20 temporal constraints and 4 assertions. In this configuration, the integration of an event required about 10 ms. Detailed efficiency arguments about chronicles can be found in [11] (pages 78–81).

4   M2D2: An Intrusion Alarm Correlation Infrastructure

Except the chronicle model proposed in Figure 7, $alarm(name, src, trg)$ is the only domain attribute used in the chronicle models discussed in the previous section.

In [1], we argue that current alarm correlation approaches do not take advantage of all the available information, especially environmental information. For example, false alarms are often abusively attributed to poor intrusion detection systems techniques: in many cases, false alarms are caused by the environment properties not being taken into account.

To address this, we proposed a formal data model called M2D2. M2D2 federates the information that is required for alarm correlation. In this section, we sketch how the chronicle recognition system can cooperate with the M2D2 framework.

4.1   Overview of M2D2

M2D2 can be seen as an infrastructure upon which alarm correlation systems can rely for events and structural information. M2D2 provides concepts and relations modeled with standard propositions of the classical first-order logic.

The concepts of M2D2 can be categorized in four groups: i) characteristics of the information system, ii) vulnerabilities, iii) security tools and iv) events.

Characteristics of the information system include information about the cartography[7] and the security policy. Vulnerabilities include information about the characteristics of known vulnerabilities: prerequisites, effect, products affected. Security tools include information about the nature and the configuration of the tools used to monitor entities of the information system for signs of attacks.

---

[7] cartography both refers to the topology of the network and the softwares running on the hosts

Events include basic events (signs of the attacks) and alarms provided by IDSes, but also by the correlation systems.

A more detailed description of M2D2 can be found in [1].

4.2   M2D2 and the Chronicles

There is a two-way relationship between M2D2 and the chronicles: as a correlation system, the chronicles take advantage of the data provided by M2D2 and also act as an alarm provider for M2D2.

M2D2 data are modeled with first-order logic predicates, so they can be used as the atemporal information of the reified logic on which the chronicles are based. In other words, the M2D2's concepts are used as domain attributes of the chronicles. In our current approach, only M2D2's alarm concepts are used as domain attributes of chronicles (see section 3). However, the other available concepts would enhance the chronicle models.

The `infected` domain attribute in the example 3.4 is an example of the use of a domain attribute corresponding to M2D2's cartography class of information. We illustrate the use of topological information with another example: video conferences require the firewall to be open. Every participant is notified of the port number he/she shall use, and connections bursts on the server are observed. Thus, over these periods, portscans shall be described as false positives. By tracking the topological modification (the firewall opening), a chronicle could qualify the portscans as false positives during video-conference sessions.

In M2D2, the high level alarms triggered by correlation systems are related to lower level alarms with the *part_of* relation. Thus, alarms are structured in a hierarchy, where leaf nodes are the lowest level alarms provided by basic IDSes and root nodes are the highest level alarms, built with intermediate events. Only the hierarchies root alarms are directly shown to the operator. If detailed information about the alarms is required, the operator can browse the alarm hierarchy. There is a straightforward mapping between the IDWG [15] alarm structures and the event concept of M2D2.

Using previously recognized chronicles into other chronicle models is a functionality already included in the chronicle recognition system (see the looping functionality in section 2.1). By making M2D2 and the chronicle recognition system cooperate, the recognized chronicles are transformed into M2D2 high level alarms linked with the events with the *part_of* relation. The new alarms provided by the chronicle recognition system are *de facto* made available to other correlation systems relying on M2D2. This is illustrated in Figure 9. There are two alarm generators, a Snort sensor and CRS. When a nimda attack occurs, Snort generates the three `iis-decode-bug`, `iis-cmd-exe` and `iis-unicode` alarms. These alarms are made available to CRS, which recognizes a nimda attack. A `nimda` alarm is triggered, and related to the previous alarms with the *part_of* relationship. Only the nimda alarm is provided to the operator. On the contrary, the `shellcode` alarm is not related to any recognized chronicle so it is directly provided to the operator. The `nimda` alarm could be involved in another alarm via the *part_of* relation. For instance, we can use the vulnerabilities information

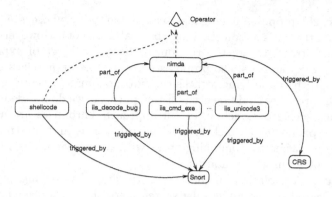

Fig. 9. Relations between alarms

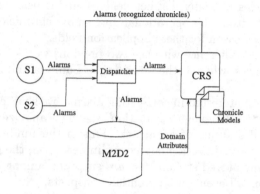

Fig. 10. Interactions between the chronicles and M2D2

contained in M2D2 to check whether the target server is really vulnerable or not (see [1]).

The architecture of the global system is summarized in Figure 10. On this figure, we see that alarms provided by sensors (S_1 and S_2) are sent to a dispatcher. The dispatcher assigns unique identifiers to events and dispatches them to the M2D2 database and to the correlation systems performing asynchronous (i.e. event-driven) analysis. Chronicle recognition is one of these asynchronous processes. Other environmental information contained in M2D2 are exploited as domain attributes of the chronicles.

5   Related Work

Among the six categories of languages proposed by Eckmann *et al* [2], two are of relevance here: detection languages and correlation languages. Our approach aims at correlating alarms, so we shall first compare to other correlation languages.

Cuppens [23] proposes a language, called Lambda, whose scenarios steps represent the attacker's action (be they observable or not). However, we believe that attackers strategies are too random to be the subject of explicit attack scenarios. In [24], Cuppens also proposes more flexible approaches to correlate alarms through the underlying attacks consequences and prerequisites.

Although chronicles could be used for this purpose, we do not dedicate chronicles to attack scenario modeling. In our approach, chronicles are used to represent known phenomena which involve several alarms and to strengthen and enhance single alarms by combining them with other events, as well as other information not found in the alarms.

The Statl [2] correlation language is a transition-based language, which is strongly dedicated to the underlying search algorithm, whereas the chronicles language is a high level declarative language. This language enabled to successfully apply chronicles to many distinct fields. Our intrusion alarm correlation component benefits from the operational and stable chronicle recognition system developed by Dousson for these application fields.

Another essential difference with the two previous works is that time is fundamental in chronicles, whereas the reasoning of Lambda and Statl is not based on time.

Although we are interested in correlating alarms, we shall compare our work with existing *detection* languages. Detection languages analyze raw events, some of which are manifestations of an attack. This is the fundamental difference between correlation and detection languages: in detection, the goal is to identify the events in the monitored stream that *are* suspects, among all the legitimate ones. In correlation, all events are potentially suspects.

However, from the point of view of the operators used in such languages, the distinction between detection and correlation languages is rather small. Thus, operators used in high-level declarative detection languages like Sutekh from Pouzol [21], LogWeaver from Goubault-Larrecq [3] are closer from our work than previously cited correlation languages. These languages could most likely be transposed to correlation languages (i.e take alerts as input instead of raw events).

Pouzol and Goubault-Larreq use non-reified temporal approaches; they take as input a trail, i.e a totally ordered set of events. From the point of view of expressiveness, since reified logics accord a special status to time and allow one to predicate and quantify over propositional terms, they are more expressive for classifying different types of temporal occurrence and in representing both non-temporal and temporal aspects of causal relationships.

As much as we know, Pouzol does not provide the counting predicate, but the chronicles would benefit of his work concerning the problem of the recognition being exhaustive, evoked in section 2.2 [22].

We way also compare our work with an existing alarm correlation system, called Risk Manager [8]. Risk Manager uses time information to aggregate alarms but is not *based* on a temporal reasoning. Moreover, it does not provide any mean to express explicit alarm sequences.

6   Conclusion and Future Work

In this paper, we proposed to apply chronicles to alarm correlation in intrusion detection. Chronicles benefit of strong theoretical background. They provide a high level declarative language which does not presume the nature of the underlying input events. An operational and stable implementation of the recognition system exists. Chronicles are indeed being successfully used in many distinct areas to monitor dynamic systems where the time information is relevant.

We have illustrated how chronicles might solve some of current intrusion detection issues like alarm overload, false positives and poor alarm semantics.

The proposed chronicles currently only use alarms as domain attributes. We plan to integrate the chronicle recognition system with an alarm correlation infrastructure, M2D2, in order to extend domain attributes to other relevant concepts, like topology, which is more and more dynamic.

Chronicle models are currently written by experts of the domain. A chronicle learning tool called *Face* is currently being developed by Dousson to discover frequent chronicles. In intrusion detection, many alarm groups are caused by recurrent phenomena, especially worms. We plan to apply the chronicle learning tool to discover such phenomena.

Acknowledgments

We are very greatful to Christophe Dousson for his help to use the Chronicle Recognition System. We would also want to thank Ludovic Mé and Mireille Ducassé for their comments.

References

1. B. Morin, L. Mé, H. Debar and M. Ducassé, "M2D2: a formal data model for intrusion alarm correlation", *Proceedings of the 5th Recent Advances in Intrusion Detection 2002 (RAID2002)*, 2002.
2. S.T. Eckmann, G. Vigna, R.A. Kemmerer, "STATL: An Attack Language for State-based Intrusion Detection", *Dept. of Computer Science, University of California, Santa Barbara*, 2000.
3. M. Roger, J. Goubault-Larrecq, "Log Auditing Through Model-Checking", *Proceedings of the 14th IEEE Computer Security Foundations Workshop (CSFW01)*, 2001.
4. U. Lindqvist, P.A. Porras, "Detecting Computer and Network Misuse Through the Production-Based Expert System Toolset (P-BEST)", *Proceedings of the IEEE Symposium on Security and Privacy*, 1999.
5. D.V. McDermott, "A Temporal Logic for Reasoning about Processes and Plans", *Cognitive Science*, pp.101–155, 1982.
6. F. Bacchus, J. Tenenberg, J.A. Koomen, "A non-reified Temporal Logic", *Artificial Intelligence*, pp.87–108, 1991.
7. J. Allen, "Towards a General Theory of Action and Time", *Artificial Intelligence*, pp.123–154, 1984.

8. H. Debar, A. Wespi, "Aggregation and Correlation of Intrusion Detection Alerts", *Proceedings of the 4th Recent Advances in Intrusion Detection (RAID2001)*, October 2000.

9. S. Manganaris, M. Christensen, D. Zerkle, K. Hermiz, "A Data Mining Analysis of RTID Alarms", *Computer Networks: The International Journal of Computer and Telecommunications Networking*, Volume 34, Issue 34, October 2000.

10. C. Dousson, P. Gaborit, and M. Ghallab, "Situation Recognition: Representation and Algorithms", *in proceedings of the 13th IJCAI*, pp.166–172, August 1993.

11. C. Dousson, "Suivi d'évolutions et reconnaissance de chroniques", *PhD Thesis*, http://dli.rd.francetelecom.fr/abc/diagnostic/, 1994.

12. C. Dousson, "Alarm Driven Supervision for Telecommunication Networks: Online Chronicle Recognition", *Annales des Telecommunications*, pp.501–508, 1996.

13. C. Dousson, "Extending and Unifying Chronicles Representation with Event Counters", *in proceedings of the 15th European Conference on Artificial Intelligence (ECAI 2002)*, August 2002.

14. M. O. Cordier, C. Dousson, "Alarm Driven Monitoring Based on Chronicles", *in proceedings of the 4th Symposium on Fault Detection Supervision and Safety for Technical Processes (Safeprocess 2000)*, pp. 286–291, June 2000.

15. H. Debar, M.Y. Huang, D.J. Donahoo, "Intrusion Detection Exchange Format Data Model", *IETF Draft*, 2002.

16. Y. Shoham, "Temporal Logics in AI: Semantical and Ontological Considerations", *Journal of Artificial Intelligence*, pp.89–104, 1987.

17. R. Dechter, I. Meiri, J. Pearl, "Temporal Constraint Networks", *Artificial Intelligence*, pp.61–95, 1991.

18. G. Jakobson and M. D. Weissman, "Alarm correlation", *IEEE Network Magazine*, pp. 52–60, 1993.

19. K. Julisch, "Mining Alarm Clusters to Improve Alarm Handling Efficiency", *Proceedings of the 17th ACSAC*, December 2001.

20. S. Manganaris, *et al*, "A Data Mining Analysis of RTID Alarms", *First International Workshop on the Recent Advances in Intrusion Detection (RAID98)*, September 1998.

21. J.P. Pouzol, M. Ducassé, "From Declarative Signatures to Misuse IDS", *Proceedings of the 4th Recent Advances in Intrusion Detection (RAID)*, 2001.

22. J.P. Pouzol, M. Ducassé, "Formal Specification of Intrusion Signatures and Detection Rules", *Proceedings of the 15th IEEE Computer Security Foundations Workshop (CSFW)*, 2002.

23. F. Cuppens, "Managing Alerts in Multi-Intrusion Detection Environment", *Proceedings of the 17th Annual Computer Security Applications Conference (ACSAC 01)*, 2001.

24. F. Cuppens, A. Miege, "Alert Correlation in a Cooperative Intrusion Detection Framework", *Proceedings of the IEEE Symposium on Security and Privacy*", 2002.

Modeling Computer Attacks:
An Ontology for Intrusion Detection

Jeffrey Undercoffer, Anupam Joshi, and John Pinkston

University of Maryland, Baltimore County
Department of Computer Science and Electrical Engineering
1000 Hilltop Circle, Baltimore, MD 21250
{undercoffer,joshi,pinkston}@umbc.edu

Abstract. We state the benefits of transitioning from taxonomies to ontologies and ontology specification languages, which are able to simultaneously serve as recognition, reporting and correlation languages. We have produced an ontology specifying a model of computer attack using the DARPA Agent Markup Language+Ontology Inference Layer, a descriptive logic language. The ontology's logic is implemented using DAMLJessKB. We compare and contrast the IETF's IDMEF, an emerging standard that uses XML to define its data model, with a data model constructed using DAML+OIL. In our research we focus on low level kernel attributes at the process, system and network levels, to serve as those taxonomic characteristics. We illustrate the benefits of utilizing an ontology by presenting use case scenarios within a distributed intrusion detection system.

1 Introduction

A central component of an IDS is the taxonomy employed to characterize and classify the attack or intrusion, and a language that describes instances of that taxonomy. The language is paramount to the effectiveness of the IDS because information regarding an attack or intrusion needs to be intelligibly conveyed, especially in distributed environments, and acted upon. Several taxonomies have been proposed by the research community. Some include a descriptive language; however, most do not. Likewise, several attack languages have been proposed, but most are not grounded in any particular taxonomy, hence their associated classification schemes are *ad hoc* and localized. The inherent problem with this approach is threefold:

i. In order to operate over instances of the data model characterized by a particular taxonomy, the data model must be encoded within a software system. Any changes or updates to the data model necessitate a change to the software system.

ii. Taxonomies only provide schemata for classification. They lack the necessary and sufficient constructs needed to enable a software system to reason over an instance of the taxonomy, which is representative of the domain under observation.

iii. Most attack and signature languages are particular to specific domains, environments and systems; consequently, they are not extensible, are not communicable between non-homogeneous systems, and their semantics are often vague and lack grounding in any formal logic.

G. Vigna, E. Jonsson, and C. Kruegel (Eds.): RAID 2003, LNCS 2820, pp. 113–135, 2003.
© Springer-Verlag Berlin Heidelberg 2003

To mitigate the effects of theses problems, we suggest transitioning from taxonomies to ontologies. We construct a data model that characterizes the domain of computer attacks and intrusions as an ontology and implement that data model with an ontology representation language. Ontologies, unlike taxonomies, provide powerful constructs that include machine interpretable definitions of the concepts within a domain and the relations between them. Ontologies, therefore, provide software systems with the ability to share a common understanding of the information at issue, in turn empowering software systems with a greater ability to reason over and analyze this information. Gruber [17] defines an ontology as an explicit specification of a conceptualization. The term, which is borrowed from philosophy, is used to provide a formal specification of the concepts and relationships that can exist between entities within a domain. Accordingly, ontologies are designed for the purpose of enabling knowledge sharing and reuse between the entities within a domain. In our case, those entities are Intrusion Detection Systems (IDS) and IDS sensors.

Ontology representation languages may be mapped into first-order relational sentences and a set of first-order logic axioms. This mapping restricts the allowable interpretations of the non-logical symbols (i.e., relations, functions, and constants) [11], enabling instances of the ontology to be operated over using formal and complete theorem provers.

Commenting on the Internet Engineering Task Force's emerging standard – the *Intrusion Detection Message Exchange Format Data Model and Extensible Markup Language (XML) Document Type Definition* (IDMEF)[6], and its ability to enable interoperability between non-homogeneous IDS sensors, Kemmerer and Vigna [25] state that the IDMEF is a first step and that additional effort is needed to provide a common ontology that lets IDS sensors agree on what they observe.

We illustrate the benefits of using ontologies by presenting an implementation of one being utilized by a distributed intrusion detection system. We have constructed our ontology using the Darpa Agent Markup Language + Ontology Inference Layer (DAML+OIL) [22] and have implemented its logic using DAMLJessKB [28], an extension to the Java Expert System Shell [13].

Although our IDS model is not the focus of this paper, we briefly describe it in order to provide context to the reader. Our IDS [23] is a two-phased, host based system. The first phase is an anomaly detector which detects aberrant behavior at the system level. We have instrumented the Linux kernel and gather 190 distinct attributes at the process, system and network levels, several times per second. We use *Principal Component Analysis* (PCA) [15] to reduce the dimensionality of the data set and then use *Fuzzy Clustering* [29] on the reduced data set in order to obtain clusters that model the quiescent state of the system. Once the baseline has been established, we use the Mahalanobis metric [5] as a dissimilarity measure in order to determine if subsequent data samples fall within the bounds of the normative state. The second phase of our IDS *reasons* over the subsequent samples of the feature set that fall outside of the bounds of the normative state, and possibly represent anomalous behavior. The sample, constrained by the ontology, is asserted into a *knowledge base* which is continually queried for evidence of an intrusion or an attack. Figure 1 illustrates a single component of our distributed system.

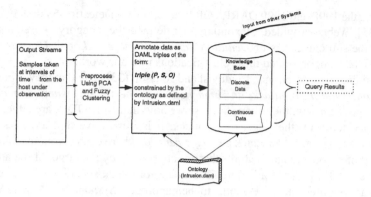

Fig. 1. Distributed IDS Framework

The goal of this work is to demonstrate the utility of ontologies and the overwhelming benefits that may be derived by the IDS research community by transitioning from taxonomies and their linguistic and symbolic representations, to ontologies and ontology representation languages.

The remainder of this paper is organized as follows: Section 2 presents related work in the area of attack taxonomies, attack languages and ontologies for intrusion detection. Section 3 details the motivation for transitioning from taxonomies to ontologies. Our ontology is presented in Section 4. Section 5 details our implementation and Section 6 provides a use case scenario illustrating the utility of using an ontology in detecting instances of a *Denial of Service, Mitnick* and *Buffer Overflow* attacks. We conclude with Section 7.

2   Related Work

There is little, if any, published research formally defining ontologies for use in Intrusion Detection. Raskin et al. [40] introduce and advocate the use of ontologies for information security. In stating the case for using ontologies, they claim that an ontology organizes and systematizes all of the phenomena (intrusive behavior) at any level of detail, consequently reducing a large diversity of items to a smaller list of properties.

The preponderance of existing research in the area of the classification of computer attacks is limited to taxonomies and the taxonomies that are implicit in attack languages. The following subsections address taxonomies and attack languages.

2.1   Related Work: Taxonomies

There are numerous attack taxonomies proposed for use in intrusion detection research.

Landwehr et al. [31] present a taxonomy categorized according to genesis (how), time of introduction (when) and location (where). They include sub-categories of: *validation errors, boundary condition errors* and *serialization errors*, as a means of effecting an intrusion. We have incorporated these sub-categories into our ontology.

During the 1998 and 1999 DARPA Off Line Intrusion Detection System Evaluations [20, 26, 35], Weber provided a taxonomy that defined the category *consequence*. This includes the sub-categories of *Denial of Service, Remote to Local, User to Root* and *Probe*. We have incorporated these classifications into our work.

In defining their taxonomy, Lindqvist and Jonsson [33] state that they *"focus on the external observations of attacks and breaches which the system owner can make"*. Our effort is consistent with their focus because we hold that, since IDSs are either adjacent to or co-located with the target of an attack, it is imperative that any classification scheme used to represent an attack be *target-centric*, where each taxonomic character is comprised of properties and features that are observable by the target of the attack.

Ning et al.[37] propose a hierarchical model for attack specification and event abstraction using three concepts essential to their approach: *System View, Misuse Signature* and *View Definition*. Their model is based upon a thorough examination of attack characteristics and attributes and is encoded within the logic of their proposed system. We include a global system view in our ontology.

As detailed by Allen et al. [1] and McHugh [36], the taxonomic characterization of intrusive behavior has typically been from the attacker's point of view, each suggesting that alternative taxonomies need to be developed. Allen et al. state that intrusion detection is an immature discipline and has yet to establish a commonly accepted framework. McHugh suggests classifying attacks according to protocol layer or, as an alternative, whether or not a completed protocol handshake is required. Likewise, Guha [18] suggests an analysis of each layer of the TCP/IP protocol stack to serve as the foundation for an attack taxonomy. Consequently, we have endeavored to make our ontology as *target centric* as possible.

Aslam et al. [3] observe that many potential faults and vulnerabilities are intrinsic to the software development process. Their observations are consistent with our own. Our ontology defines the class *"Means of Attack"* and is comprised of many of the attributes identified by Aslam et al.

Our intent is to not criticize the use of taxonomies. To the contrary, they have served their purpose well, particularly in identifying and classifying the characteristics of computer attacks and intrusions. We do, however, advocate leveraging their work by building upon existing taxonomies and transitioning to ontologies. We feel that this is necessary and warranted because, according to Staab and Maedche [43], taxonomies do not contain the necessary *meta-knowledge* required to convey modeling primitives such as concepts, relations and axioms that are required to make sense of and operate on specific objects. Ontologies do. It should be pointed out that a complete and well formed ontology subsumes a taxonomy.

2.2   Related Work: Attack Languages

There are several *attack languages* proposed in the literature. These languages are often categorized as Event, Response, Reporting, Correlation, and Recognition Languages [8, 9]. We concentrate on correlation, reporting and recognition languages because an ontology representation language is able to simultaneously provide the functionality of all three.

A. P-Best

The P-BEST Toolset [34] (Production-Based Expert System Toolset) is a correlation language from which users may specify the inference formula for reasoning and acting upon facts asserted into its fact base and from facts derived from external events. P-BEST supports the writing of rules for signature detectors. According to Doyle et al. [8], the P-BEST language lacks concepts that are specific to event recognition and consists solely of a formalism for expressing probabilistic and linguistic rules.

B. STATL

STATL [9] is an extensible state/ transition-based attack detection language designed to support intrusion detection. STATL allows one to describe computer penetrations as sequences of actions that an attacker performs in order to compromise a computer system. In STATL, scenarios are *attacker centric*. This language provides constructs to represent an attack as a composition of states and transitions. The constructs are similar to those used in programming languages, which describing conditional, sequential and iterative events. STATL lacks constructs for combining sub-events into larger events. Reporting on the efficacy of various attack recognition languages, Doyle et al. [8] state: "STATL constitutes the most clearly defined language for use in attack recognition".

C. LogWeaver

LogWeaver [16] is a log auditing tool that takes a system log as input and processes it according to a signature (rule) file. The signature file defines the type of events that are to be monitored and reported on. LogWeaver is able to match regular expressions and make correlations between events, provided that they are executed by the same user. LogWeaver employs logic that is based upon *model checking* [42]. Essentially, LogWeaver is a specification for a detection language, which defines a syntax and grammar for the end-user to use when writing signatures.

D. CISL

The Common Intrusion Detection Framework (CIDF) [24] started as a DARPA initiative in 1998. CIDF was an effort to develop protocols and application programming interfaces to give IDS research projects the ability to share information and resources and to enable IDS component reuse by multiple systems. The CIDF framework is comprised of components which exchange data in the form of a *GIDO* (generalized intrusion detection object) which are represented in a standard format. This standard format is specified in the Common Intrusion Specification Language (CISL) [10], a reporting language. The CIDF effort appears to have lost inertia, with many of its developers now working on the IETF's IDMEF.

E. BRO

Bro [39] is a real-time, network based IDS that utilizes the specialized "Bro Language", a detection language. The goal of the "Bro Language" is to express security policies in terms of scripts written within that language. In turn, the scripts consist of event handlers that specify what to do whenever a particular event occurs. According to Paxson, the scripts require environment specific tailoring.

F. Snort Rules

SNORT [41] is a network intrusion detection system that performs real time analysis and packet logging on IP networks. SNORT uses a detection language to define rules. The rules are two part: header and options. The header contains the rule's action and addressing information. The options section contains the alert message as well as specifying packet inspection criteria.

G. IDMEF

The Internet Engineering Task Force's proposed Intrusion Detection Message Exchange Format Data Model and Extensible Markup Language (XML) Document Type Definition [6] is a profound effort to establish an industry wide data model which defines computer intrusions. It defines a data model that is representative of data exported by an IDS. It also defines data formats and exchange procedures for inter/intra IDS exchanges. The data model is defined in an XML *Document Type Definition* and implemented in the Extensible Markup Language (XML) [47].

The IDMEF assumes a hierarchal configuration of three IDS components: *sensors, analyzers, and managers*. Sensors are located at the bottom most level of the hierarchy. Sensors output data to analyzers, which in turn report up to a manager, located at the topmost level of the hierarchy.

Because the IDMEF data model, encoded in XML, is an emerging standard, we compare and contrast it to the notion of using ontologies to represent the data model and the subsequent encoding of the data model in an ontology representation language.

2.3   XML in Comparison to DAML+OIL

The IDMEF's principal shortcoming is its use of XML, which is limited to a syntactic representation of the data model. This limitation requires that each individual IDS interpret and implement the data model programmaticaly. This shortcoming may be mitigated by using an ontology representation language such as DAML+OIL.

The ontology specification language DAML+OIL, is a descriptive logic language and is grounded in both model-theoretic[1] and axiomatic semantics[2] and has been "cooked" specifically for the Internet. Consequently it is able to:

i. Model the attributes and characteristics of a domain.
ii. Report the existence of an instance of the domain (model) in a manner that is "comprehensible" by any entity that possess the specific ontology.
iii. Aggregate specific instances of the domain in a knowledge base and enable the conclusion that some larger, or more comprehensive, instance of the ontology exists.

The following best explains the inadequacies of XML vis-á-vis DAML+OIL.

Humans are able to combine new facts with existing knowledge to derive new knowledge, computers are not. When a computer acquires new data in XML, it may be able

---

[1] model-theoretic semantics is the process of constructing mathematical models of logical consequence and establishing when the model satisfies a formula
[2] axiomatic semantics is the process of defining a language using axioms and proof rules

Table 1. Language Feature Comparison: DAML+OIL versus XML

Feature	Description	DAML +OIL	XML
bounded lists	Uses a first/rest structure to represent unordered bounded lists, with nil representing the end of the list.	Yes	No
cardinality constraints	minCardinality and maxCardinality	Yes	Yes
class expressions	Wherever a Class is referenced allows an expression involving *unionOf, disjointUnionOf,intersectionOf* or *complementOf.*	Yes	No
data types	e.g: numerical, temporal and string data types	Yes	Yes
defined classes	Allows new classes to be defined based on property values or other restrictions of an existing class.	Yes	No
enumerations	Allows specification of a restricted set of values for a given attribute to include *oneOf*	Yes	No
equivalence	Supports *equivalentTo* for classes, properties, and instances to support reasoning across ontologies and knowledge bases	Yes	No
extensibility	Allows new properties to used with existing classes.	Yes	No
formal semantics	Semantics have been expressed in both model-theoretic and axiomatic forms.	Yes	No
inheritance	Fully supports *subClassOf* and *subPropertyOf*	Yes	No
inference	Has constructs such as *TransitiveProperty, UnambiguousProperty, inverseOf*, and *disjointWith* for reasoning engines.	Yes	No
local restrictions	Allows restrictions to be associated with a Class/Property pairs.	Yes	No
qualified constraints	Allows expressions such as "all children of X are of type Y".	Yes	No
reification	Provides a standard mechanism for recording data sources, timestamps, etc., without intruding on the data model.	Yes	No

to respond, but only because of some other software which is not part of the XML specification. Although conforming to the XML specification, different systems may very well respond differently, given the same XML encoded data. If a computer acquires new data in DAML+OIL, it can generate entirely new information, solely based on the DAML+OIL standard. Given the same data, any system that conforms to the DAML+OIL specification will generate the same new information and conclusions. A set of DAML+OIL statements, in conjunction with the DAML+OIL specification, enables the conclusion of yet another DAML+OIL statement, whereas a set of XML statements, in conjunction with the XML specification, does not allow the conclusion of any other XML statements. To employ XML to generate new data, knowledge needs to be embedded in some procedural code, which is in stark contrast to DAML+OIL where the knowledge is explicitly stated in DAML+OIL statements.

Although XML supports sub types which are restrictions of extensions on a type, there are no classes. Consequently, there is no notion of inheritance. The following exemplifies the benefits of inheritance. Suppose that you wished to define an event of type X, that is an aggregation of two other events of types Y and Z. Furthermore, suppose that Y and Z are comprised of subclasses Y_1 and Y_2 and Z_1 and Z_2, respectively. If this information were encoded in XML, we would need application logic that iteratively checked for all possible combinations of Y and Z to satisfy a query. If the same information were to be encoded in DAML+OIL, we would only need to query for the existence of X. Table 1 provides a feature by feature comparison between DAML+OIL and XML.

3   From Taxonomies to Ontologies: *The Case for Ontologies*

An ontology subsumes a taxonomy, therefore, before explaining ontologies, a clear understanding of the definition, purpose and objective of a taxonomy is in order.

3.1   Characteristics of a Sufficient Taxonomy

A *taxonomy* is a *classification* system where the classification scheme conforms to a systematic arrangement into groups or categories according to established criteria [48]. Glass and Vessey [14] contend that taxonomies provide a set of unifying constructs so that the area of interest can be systematically described and aspects of relevance may be interpreted. The overarching goal of any taxonomy, therefore, is to supply some predictive value during the analysis of an unknown specimen, while the classifications within the taxonomy offer an explanatory value.

According to Simpson [44], classifications may be created either *a priori* or *a posteriori*. An *a priori* classification is created non-empirically whereas an *a posteriori* classification is created by empirical evidence derived from some data set. Simpson defines a taxonomic character as a feature, attribute or characteristic that is divisible into at least two contrasting states and used for constructing classifications. He further states that taxonomic characters should be observable from the object in question.

Amoroso [2], Lindqvist et al. [33], Krusl [30] and others have identified what they believe to be the requisite properties of a sufficient and acceptable taxonomy for computer security. Collectively, they have identified the following properties as essential to a taxonomy:

Mutually Exclusive. A classification in one category excludes all others because categories do not overlap.

Exhaustive. The categories, taken together, include all possibilities.

Unambiguous. The category is clear and precise so that classification is not uncertain, regardless of who is classifying.

Repeatable. Repeated applications result in the same classification, regardless of who is classifying.

Accepted. The taxonomy should be logical and intuitive so that it can become generally approved.

Useful. The taxonomy can be used to gain insight into the field of inquiry.

Comprehensible. The taxonomy should be useful to those with less than expert knowledge.

Conforming. The terminology of the taxonomy should comply with established security terminology.

Objectivity. The features must be identified from the object under observation where the attribute being measured should be clearly observable.

Deterministic. There must be a clear procedure that can be followed to extract the feature.

Specific. The value for the feature must be unique and unambiguous.

Upon review of the above list, we believe that, for our purposes, a sufficient and acceptable taxonomy must be: **Mutually Exclusive, Exhaustive, Unambiguous, Useful, Objective, Deterministic, Repeatable** and **Specific**. Hence, these requirements form the underpinnings of our ontology and were selected because they have been identified by the IDS community as essential. We did not adopt the property "Comprehensible" because the requirement that a taxonomic property be comprehensible dictates that those with less than expert knowledge should find the ontology and its taxonomy useful. We felt that this requirement has the potential to oversimplify and relax the structure of the ontology. We did not adopt the property "Accepted", due to the requirement that it be intuitive. The knowledge engineering process employed to build a viable ontology is often more than simple intuition and, at times, appears counter-intuitive.

3.2   Ontologies

According to Davis et al. [7], knowledge representation is a surrogate or substitute for an object under study. In turn, the surrogate enables an entity, such as a software system, to reason about the object. Knowledge representation is also a set of *ontological* commitments specifying the terms that describe the essence of the object. In other words, *meta-data* or data about data describing their relationships.

Frame Based Systems are an important thread in knowledge representation. According to Koller et al. [27], Frame Based Systems provide an excellent representation for the organizational structure of complex domains. Frame Based Languages, which support Frame Based Systems, include RDF [32], and are used to represent ontologies. According to Welty et al. [49], an ontology, at its deepest level, subsumes a taxonomy. Similarly, Noy and McGuinness [38] state that the process of developing an ontology includes arranging classes in a taxonomic hierarchy.

The relationship among data objects may be highly complex; however, at the the finest level of granularity, the *Knowledge Representation* of any object may be represented by an *RDF-S* (Resource Description Framework Schema) statement [4] which formally defines the RDF model as:

i. A set called *Resources*.
ii. A set called *Literals*.
iii. A subset of Resources called *Properties*.
iv. A set called *Statements*, where each element is a triple of the form: {*subject, predicate, object* }. Where *predicate* is a member of Properties, *subject* is a member of Resources, and *object* is either a member of Resources or a member of Literals.

Primarily, RDF-S is about defining class hierarchies (i.e.: taxonomies) and introduces the notions of *Class, Property, Domain* and *Range*. RDF and DAML+OIL extend RDF-S with richer modeling primitives. Figure 2 graphically illustrates the basic RDF-S model, where *(subject, predicate, object),* which is the same as *(resource, property,*

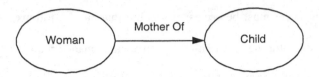

Fig. 2. RDF-S Relationship Graph

```
<?xml version='1.0' encoding='ISO-8859-1'?>
<!DOCTYPE rdf:RDF [
    <!ENTITY rdf 'http://www.w3.org/1999/02/22-rdf-syntax-ns#'>
    <!ENTITY rdfs 'http://www.w3.org/TR/1999/PR-rdf-schema-19990303#'>
    <!ENTITY daml_oil 'http://www.daml.org/2001/03/daml+oil#'>]>

<rdf:RDF
  xmlns:rdf ="&rdf;"
  xmlns:daml_oil ="&daml_oil;"
  xmlns:rdfs ="&rdfs;">

<daml_oil:ObjectProperty rdf:ID="Mother_Of">
  <daml_oil:range rdf:resource="#Child"/>
  <daml_oil:domain rdf:resource="#Woman"/>
</daml_oil:ObjectProperty>

<daml_oil:Class rdf:ID="Woman">
  <rdfs:subClassOf rdf:resource="&daml_oil;#Thing"/>
</daml_oil:Class>

<daml_oil:Class rdf:ID="Child">
  <rdfs:subClassOf rdf:resource="&daml_oil;#Thing"/>
</daml_oil:Class>

</rdf:RDF>
```

Fig. 3. DAML+OIL Specification for the Mother Child Relationship

resource[or literal value]), is illustrated by the *(Woman, Mother Of, Child)* relationship, where *Mother* is the subject, *Child* is the object and *Mother Of* is the predicate. Figure 3 illustrates the Mother Child relationship specified in DAML+OIL. It should be noted that a set of *N-triples*, an RDF-S graph, and a DAML+OIL specification are equivalent if they each describe the same ontology.

In applying ontologies to the problem of intrusion detection, the power and utility of the ontology is not realized by the simple taxonomic representation of the attributes of the attack. Instead, **the power and utility of the ontology is realized by the fact that we can express the relationships between collected data and use those relationships to deduce that the particular data represents an attack of a particular type**. Because ontologies provide powerful constructs that include machine interpretable definitions of the concepts within a specific domain and the relations between them, they may be utilized not only to provide an IDS with the ability to share a common understanding of the information at issue, but also to further enable the IDS, with an improved capacity, to reason over and analyze instances of data representing an intrusion.

Moreover, specifying an ontological representation decouples the data model from the logic of the intrusion detection system. The decoupling of the data model enables non-homogeneous IDSs to share data without a prior agreement as to the semantics of the data. To effect this sharing, an instance of the ontology is shared between IDSs in the form of a set of DAML+OIL statements. Non-homogeneous IDSs do not need to run the same type of software and the sensors of a distributed IDS may monitor different aspects of an enterprise. A shared ontology enables these disparate components to operate as a coalition, sharing, correlating and aggregating each other's data.

4   Our IDS Ontology: *Attributes of the Class Intrusion*

In constructing our ontology, we conducted an empirical analysis [46] of the features and attributes, and their interrelationships, of over 4,000 classes of computer attacks and intrusions that are contained in the CERT/CC Advisories and the "Internet Catalog of Assailable Technologies" (ICAT) maintained by NIST. Our analysis indicates that the overwhelming majority of attacks are the result of malformed input exploiting a software vulnerability of a network attached process. According to *CERT*, root access is the most common consequence, while according to *ICAT*, a denial of service is the most common consequence.

Figure 4 presents a high level view of our ontology. The attributes of each class and subclass are not depicted because it would make the illustration unwieldy. As stated in Section 1, we have instrumented the Linux kernel, using it to gather 190 distinct attributes (i.e.: address from which system calls are made, total virtual memory size, etc) at the system, process and network levels. Consequently, our ontology, and the taxonomy that it subsumes, is defined solely in terms of the causal relationships of the observables and measurables at the target of the attack.

It should be noted that an RDF graph does not depict flow. In an RDF graph, ellipses are used to denote a class, which may have several properties. When two vertices (classes) are connected by a directed edge, the edge represents a property whose domain is denoted by the start of the edge, and whose range is denoted by the end of the edge. An undirected edge between two vertices (classes) indicates that one class is an instance of another class.

At the top most level of Figure 4 we define the class *Host*. Host has the predicates *Current State* and *Victim of*. *Current State* ranges over *System Component* and *Victim of* ranges over the class *Attack*. As earlier stated, the predicate defines the relationship between a subject and an object.

The System Component class is comprised of the following subclasses:

i. Network. This class is inclusive of the network layers of the protocol stack. We have focused on TCP/IP; therefore, we only consider the IP, TCP, and UDP subclasses. For example, and as will be later demonstrated, the TCP subclass includes the properties *TCP_MAX, WAIT_STATE, THRESHOLD* and *EXCEED_T*. *TCP_MAX* defines the maximum number of TCP connections. *WAIT_STATE* defines the number of connections waiting on the final *ack* of the three-way handshake to establish a TCP connection. *THRESHOLD* specifies the allowable ratio between maximum connections and partially established connections. *EXCEED_T* is a boolean value indicating that the allowable ratio has been exceeded. It should be noted that these are only four of several network properties.

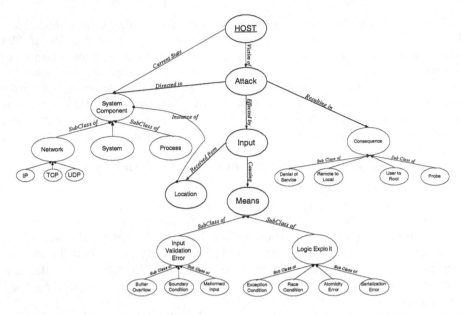

Fig. 4. Our IDS Ontology

ii. System. This includes attributes representing the operating system of the host. It includes attributes representing overall memory usage (*MEM_TOTAL, MEM_FREE, MEM_SWAP*) and CPU usage (*LOAD_AVG*). The class also contains attributes reflective of the number of current users, disk usage, the number of installed kernel modules, and change in state of the interrupt descriptor and system call tables.

iii. Process. This class contains attributes representing particular processes that are to be monitored. These attributes include the current value of the instruction pointer (*INS_P*), the current top of the stack (*T_STACK*), a scalar value computed from the stream of system calls (*CALL_V*), and the number of child processes (*N_CHILD*).

The class *Attack* has the properties *Directed to*, *Effected by*, and *Resulting in*. This construction is predicated upon the notion that an attack consists of some input which is directed to some system component and results in some consequence. Accordingly, the classes *System Component*, *Input*, and *Consequence* are the corresponding objects. The class Consequence is comprised of several subclasses which include:

i. Denial of Service. The attack results in a Denial of Service to the users of the system. The denial of service may be because the system was placed into an unstable state or all of the system resources may be consumed by meaningless functions.

ii. User Access. The attack results in the attacker having access to services on the target system at an unprivileged level.

iii. Root Access. The attack results in the attacker being granted privileged access to the system, consequently having complete control of the system.

iv. Probe. This type of an attack is the result of scanning or other activity wherein a profile of the system is disclosed.

Finally, the class *Input* has the predicates *Received from* and *Causing* where *Causing* defines the relationship between the *Means* of attack and some input and *Received from* defines the relationship between *Input* and *Location*. The class *Location* is an instance of *System Component* and is restricted to instances of the Network and Process classes. We define the following subclasses for *Means* of attack:

i. Input Validation Error. An input validation error exists if some malformed input is received by a hardware or software component and is not properly bounded or checked. This class is further sub-classed as:

   (a) Buffer Overflow. The classic buffer overflow results from an overflow of a static-sized data structure.
   (b) Boundary Condition Error. A process attempts to read or write beyond a valid address boundary or a system resource is exhausted.
   (c) Malformed Input. A process accepts syntactically incorrect input, extraneous input fields, or the process lacks the ability to handle field-value correlation errors.

ii. Logic Exploits. Logic exploits are exploited software and hardware vulnerabilities such as race conditions or undefined states that lead to performance degradation and/or system compromise. Logic exploits are further subclasssed as follows:

   (a) Exception Condition. An error resulting from the failure to handle an exception condition generated by a functional module or device.
   (b) Race Condition. An error occurring during a timing window between two operations.
   (c) Serialization Error. An error that results from the improper serialization of operations.
   (d) Atomicity Error. An error occurring when a partially-modified data structure is used by another process; An error occurring because some process terminated with partially modified data where the modification should have been atomic.

As previously stated, the properties of Mutual Exclusion, Exhaustive, Non-ambiguity, Usefulness, Objectivity, Determinism, Repeatability and Specificity are the overarching requirements that determine the taxonomic characteristics of our ontology. We believe that we have met these requirements predicated upon the following:

i. Mutual Exclusion. Each class in the ontology is disjoint from the other classes because none share an identical set of properties.
ii. Exhaustive. Our analysis of the available data indicates that computer attacks and intrusions are effected by some input, that is directed to some system component, causing some heretofore unintended system response (means), and results in some adverse system consequence. Our ontology captures these notions.
iii. Non-ambiguity. Each class in the ontology has a definite set of properties and restrictions.
iv. Usefulness. As will be exemplified in Section 5, Implementation, our ontology enables the conclusion (entailment) of new knowledge from seemingly disassociated facts.

v. Objectivity. The properties of the classes of our ontology are directly derivable from 190 distinct system features. This feature set characterizes system state at any particular time.

vi. Deterministic. The properties of each class obtainable from metrics associated with the Linux kernel.

vii. Repeatability. An instantiated object within our ontology will always be evaluated to the identical conclusion. Moreover, the same object will be evaluated to the same conclusions by any entity using the ontology.

viii. Specific. The property values for classes that define aberrant system behavior are unique and are limited to a set of 190 attributes.

5   Implementation

There are several *reasoning systems* that are compatible with DAML+OIL[12, 19, 28, 21], which according to their functionality, may be classified as backward-chaining or forward-chaining. Backward-chaining reasoners process queries and return proofs for the answers they provide. Forward-chaining reasoners process assertions substantiated by proofs, and draw conclusions.

We have prototyped the logic portion of our system using the *DAMLJessKB* [28] reasoning system. DAMLJessKB is employed to reason over instances of our data model that are considered to be suspicious. These suspicious instances are constrained according to our ontology and asserted into the knowledge base.

Upon initialization of DAMLJessKB, we parse the DAML+OIL statements representing the ontology, converting them into *N-Triples*, and assert them into a knowledge base as rules. The assertions are of the form:

```
(assert
(PropertyValue (predicate) (subject) (object)))
```

Once asserted, DAMLJessKB generates additional rules which include all of the chains of implication derived from the ontology.

As will be illustrated shortly, additional information in the form of instances of the ontology is asserted into the knowledge base as facts.

5.1   Querying the Knowledge Base

Once the ontology is asserted into the knowledge base and all of the derived rules resulting from the chains of implication are generated, the knowledge base is ready to receive instances of the ontology. Instances are asserted and de-asserted into/from the knowledge base as temporal events dictate. The query language is of the form *((predicate) (subject) (object))* where at least one of the three elements of the triple must be contain a value. The other one or two elements may be left uninstantiated (signified by prefacing them with a "?"). If there are any triples in the knowledge base that match the query either as the result of an assertion of a fact or derived rules resulting from the chain of implication, the value of those triples will be returned.

To query the knowledge base for the existence of an attack or intrusion, the query could be so granular that it requests an attack of a specific type, such as a Syn Flood:

```
(defrule isSynFlood

(PropertyValue
(p http://www.w3.org/1999/02/22-rdf-syntax-ns#type)
(s ?var)
(o http://security.umbc.edu/IntrOnt#SynFlood))
=>
(printout t ''A SynFlood attack has occurred.''  crlf
            ''with event number: '' ?var))
```

The query could be of a medium level of granularity, asking for all attacks of a specific class, such as denial of service. Accordingly, the following query will return all instances of an attack of the class Denial of Service.

```
(defrule isDOS

(PropertyValue
(p http://www.w3.org/1999/02/22-rdf-syntax-ns#type)
(s ?var)
(o http://security.umbc.edu/IntrOnt#DoS))
=>
(printout t ''A DoS attack has occurred.''  crlf
            ''with ID number: '' ?var))
```

Finally, the following rule will return instances of any attack, where the event numbers that are returned by the query need to be iterated over in order to discern the specific type of attack:

```
(defrule isConseq

(PropertyValue
(p http://www.w3.org/1999/02/22-rdf-syntax-ns#type)
(s ?var)
(o http://security.umbc.edu/IntrOnt#Conseq))
=>
(printout t ''An attack has occurred.''  crlf
            ''with ID number: '' ?var))
```

These varying levels of granularity are possible because of DAML+OIL's notion of classes, subclasses, and the relationships that hold between them. The query variable *?var*, which corresponds to the subject, contained in each of the queries, is instantiated with the subject whenever a predicate and object from a matching triple is located in the knowledge base.

6   Using the Ontology to Detect Attacks: *Use Case Scenarios*

To test our implementation and experiment with it, we created instances of our ontology in DAML+OIL notation, and asserted them into the knowledge base. We then ran our queries against the knowledge base.

6.1   Denial of Service – Syn Flood

The DAML+OIL representation of an instance of a *Syn_Flood* attack is illustrated in Figure 5. The first statement indicates that an event numbered 00035 has occurred, which has the *resulting_in* property instantiated to an instance of a Syn Flood that is uniquely identified as event number 00038.

```
<Intrusion:Host rdf:about="&IntrOnt;00035"
        Intrusion:IP_Address="130.85.112.231"
        rdfs:label="00035">
        <Intrusion:resulting_in rdf:resource=
                "&IntrOnt;00038"/>
</Intrusion:Host>

<Intrusion:Syn_Flood rdf:about="&IntrOnt;00038"
        Intrusion:Exceed_T="true"
        Intrusion:time="15:43:12"
        Intrusion:date="02/22/2003"
        rdfs:label="00038"/>
```

Fig. 5. DAML+OIL Notation for an Instance of a Syn Flood Attack

When the knowledge base was queried for instances of Denial of Service (DoS) attacks, the following was returned:

```
The event number of the intrusion is:
http://security.umbc.edu/Intrusion#00038
The type of intrusion is:
http://security.umbc.edu/Intrusion#Syn_Flood
The victim's IP address is:
130.85.112.231
The time and date of the event:
15:43:12 hours on 02/22/2003
```

It is important to note that we only queried for the existence of a Denial of Service attack, we did not specifically ask for Syn Flood attacks. The instance of the Syn Flood attack was returned because it is a subclass of Denial of Service.

6.2   The Classic Mitnick Type Attack

This subsection provides an example of using our ontology as it operates within a coalition of distributed IDSs to detect the *Mitnick* attack. This particular attack is a distributed attack consisting of a Denial of Service attack, TCP sequence number prediction and IP spoofing.

The following example of a distributed attack illustrates the utility of our ontology.

The Mitnick attack is multi-phased; consisting of a Denial of Service attack, TCP sequence number prediction and IP spoofing. When this attack first occurred in 1994, a Syn Flood was used to effect the denial of service; however, any denial of service attack would have sufficed.

In the following example, which is illustrated in figure 6, **Host B** is the ultimate target and **Host A** is trusted by **Host B**.

The attack is structured as follows:

i. The attacker initiates a Syn/Flood attack against **Host A** to prevent **Host A** from responding to **Host B**.
ii. The attacker sends multiple TCP packets to the target, **Host B**, in order to be able to predict the values of TCP sequence numbers generated by **Host B**.

iii. The attacker then pretends to be **Host A** by spoofing **Host A**'s IP address, and sends a Syn packet to **Host B** in order to establish a TCP session between **Host A** and **Host B**.

iv. **Host B** responds with a SYN/ACK to **Host A**. The attacker does not see this packet. **Host A**, since its input queue is full due to number of half open connections caused by the Syn/Flood attack, cannot send a *RST* message to **Host B** in response to the spurious Syn message.

v. Using the calculated TCP sequence number of **Host B** (recall that the attacker did not see the Syn/ACK message sent from **Host B** to **Host A**) the attacker sends an *Ack* with the predicted TCP sequence number packet in response to the *Syn/Ack* packet sent to **Host A**.

vi. **Host B** is now in a state of belief that a TCP session has been established with a trusted host **Host A**. The attacker now has a one way session with the target, **Host B**, and can issue commands to the target.

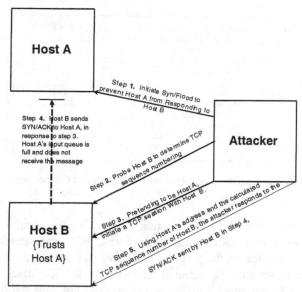

Fig. 6. Illustration of the Mitnick Attack

It should be noted that an intrusion detection system running exclusively at either host will not detect this multi-phased and distributed attack. At best, Host A's IDS would see a relatively short lived Syn Flood attack, and Host B's IDS might observe an attempt to infer TCP sequence numbers, although this may not stand out from other non-intrusive but ill-formed TCP connection attempts.

The following example illustrates the utility of our ontology, as well as the importance of forming coalitions of IDSs. In our model, all of the IDSs share a common ontology and utilize a secure communications infrastructure that has been optimized for IDSs. We present such a communications infrastructure in [45].

Consider the case of the instance of the Syn Flood attack presented in Section 6.1, and that it was directed against **Host A** in our example scenario. Since the IDS responsible for

Host A is continually monitoring for anomalous behavior, asserting and de-asserting data as necessary, it detects the occurrence of an inordinate number of partially established TCP connections, and transmits the instance of the Syn Flood illustrated in Figure 5 to the other IDSs in its coalition.

This instance is converted into a set of *N-Triples* and asserted into the knowledge base of each IDS in the coalition. (Note: those same *N-Triples* will be de-asserted when the responsible IDS transmits a message stating that the particular host is no longer the victim of a Syn Flood attack.) Since this situation, especially in conjunction with **Host B** being subjected to a series of probes meant to determine its TCP sequencing, is anomalous and may be the prelude to a distributed attack the, current and pending connections are also asserted into the knowledge base.

Figure 7 lists the set of DAML+OIL statements describing those connections that were used in our experiments:

```
<IntrOnt:Connection rdf:about="&IntrOnt;00043"
        IntrOnt:IP_Address="130.85.112.231"
        IntrOnt:conn_time="15:42:59"
        IntrOnt:conn_date="02/22/2003"
        rdfs:label="00041"/>

<IntrOnt:Connection rdf:about="&IntrOnt;00043"
        IntrOnt:IP_Address="130.85.112.231"
        IntrOnt:conn_time="15:44:17"
        IntrOnt:conn_date="02/22/2003"
        rdfs:label="00043"/>
```

Fig. 7. DAML+OIL Notation for an Instances of Connections

Figure 8 illustrates the DAML+OIL notation specifying the Mitnick attack. Notice that it is a subclass of both the class defining a Denial of Service attack and the TCP subclass, with a restriction on the property indicating that the target of the attack has established a connection with the victim of the Denial of Service Attack.

DAML+OIL, like any other notation language, does not have the functionality to perform mathematical operations. Consequently, when querying for the existence of a Mitnick type of attack, we must define a rule that tests for concomitance between the DoS attack and the establishment of the connection with the target of the DoS attack. The following query performs that test:

```
(defrule isMitnick

(PropertyValue
(p http://security.umbc.edu/IntrOnt#Mitnick )(s ?eventNumber)(o "true"))

(PropertyValue
(p http://security.umbc.edu/IntrOnt#Int_time)(s ?eventNumber)(o ?Int_Time))

(PropertyValue
(p http://security.umbc.edu/IntrOnt#Conn_time)(s ?eventNumber)(o ?Conn_Time))
=>
(if (>= ?Conn_Time ?Int_Time) then
(printout t ``event number: `` ?eventnumber `` is a Mitnick Attack: crlf)))
```

```
<daml:Class rdf:about="&Intrusion;Mitnick"
    rdfs:label="P\_Mitnick">
  <rdfs:subClassOf>
    <daml:Restriction>
      <daml:onProperty rdf:resource=
          "&IntrOnt;Victim"/>
      <daml:hasValue rdf:resource="#true"/>
      <daml:toClass rdf:resource=
          "&IntrOnt;DoS"/>
    </daml:Restriction>
  </rdfs:subClassOf>
  <rdfs:subClassOf>
    <daml:Restriction>
      <daml:onProperty rdf:resource=
          "&IntrOnt;est_connections"/>
      <daml:hasValue rdf:resource=
          "#IP_Address"/>
      <daml:toClass rdf:resource=
          "&IntrOnt;TCP"/>
    </daml:Restriction>
  </rdfs:subClassOf>
</daml:Class>
```

Fig. 8. DAML+OIL Specification of the Mitnick Attack

This query makes the correlation between event Number 00043, the connection occurring at 15:44:17, with the host at IP address 130.85.112.23, and event number 00038, the Denial of Service attack. The query, in conjunction with the other queries, produced the following response:

```
The synflood attack is:
http://security.umbc.edu/Intrusion#00038
The dos  attack is:
http://security.umbc.edu/Intrusion#00038
The event number of the connection is:
http://security.umbc.edu/Intrusion#00043
The mitnick attack is:
http://security.umbc.edu/Intrusion#genid21
A connection with 130.85.112.231 was
made at 15:44:17 on 02/22/2003
```

where event number *genid21* was generated through a chain of implication based upon events 00038 and 00043 and the specification of the Mitnick attack in the ontology.

At this point, it is important to review the sequence of events leading up to the discovery of the Mitnick attack. Recall that the IDS responsible for the victim of the Syn Flood attack queried its knowledge base for an instance of a *DoS* denial of service attack. The query returned an instance of a Syn Flood, which was instantiated solely on the condition that a Syn Flood is a subclass of both the *DoS* and *Network* classes restricted to the value of *Exced_T* being true.

The instance (its properties) of the Syn Flood attack was transmitted in the form of a set of DAML+OIL statements to the other IDSs in the coalition. In turn, these IDSs converted the DAML+OIL notated instance into a set of *N-Triples* and asserted them into their respective knowledge bases. As a Syn Flood is a precursor to a more insidious attack, instances of established and pending connections were asserted into the knowledge base. As the state of the knowledge base is dynamic, due to the assertions and de-assertions, the rule set of each IDS is continually applied to the knowledge base.

Finally, the instance of the Mitnick attack was instantiated by the knowledge base, based upon the existence of both the instance of the TCP connection and the instance of the DoS attack.

6.3   Buffer Overflow Attack

The "C" strcpy() function is one of several functions that needs to be bounded in order to prevent a buffer overflow attack. A buffer overflow attack occurs when deliberately constructed code is placed onto the stack frame, overwriting the return address from the current function. When a function is called, input parameters to the function, the frame pointer(ebp register) and the return address (the current eip + the length of the call instruction) are pushed onto the stack. Like all instructions, they are located in the *Text* address space of memory.

As previously stated, we have instrumented the Linux kernel and are able to intercept any given process at each system call, and examine the contents of its registers and stack frame. Consequently, we are able to define the characteristics of a buffer overflow attack such that the instruction pointer references a memory location that is outside of the boundaries of the Text segment. Figure 9 presents the DAML+OIL notation for the class *Buffer Overflow* and one of its properties.

```
<daml:Class rdf:about="&IntrOnt;Buff_OF"
    rdfs:label="Buff_OF">
  <rdfs:subClassOf rdf:resource=
        "&IntrOnt;R_to_L"/>
    <rdfs:subClassOf rdf:resource=
          "&IntrOnt;U_to_R">
      <rdfs:subClassOf rdf:resource=
            "&IntrOnt;Process">
        <daml:Restriction>
        <daml:onProperty rdf:resource=
              "&IntrOnt;EIP_out_Txt"/>
          <daml:hasValue rdf:resource="#true"/>
        </daml:Restriction>
      </rdfs:subClassOf>
</daml:Class>

<rdf:Property rdf:about="&IntrOnt;EIP_out_Txt"
          rdfs:label="EIP_out_Txt">
      <rdfs:domain rdf:resource="&IntrOnt;
          Buff_OF"/>
        <rdfs:range rdf:resource="&IntrOnt;
          BooleanValue"/>
</rdf:Property>
```

Fig. 9. DAML+OIL Notation Specifying the Buffer Overflow SubClass

Similar to the previous two examples, querying the knowledge base with the following will yield all instances of a buffer overflow.

```
(defrule isBufferOverflow

(PropertyValue
(p http://www.w3.org/1999/02/22-rdf-syntax-ns#type)
(s ?var)
(o http://security.umbc.edu/IntrOnt#Buff_OF))
=>
(printout t ''A Buffer Overflow has occurred.''  crlf
              ''with ID number: '' ?var))
```

7   Conclusion and Future Work

We have stated the case for transitioning from taxonomies and the languages (event, correlation and recognition) employed by them to ontologies and ontology representation languages for use in Intrusion Detection Systems. We have constructed and have presented an initial ontology, which is available at: http://security.cs.umbc.edu/Intrusion .daml.

We have used the ontology specification language DAML+OIL to implement our ontology and to distribute information regarding system state within a distributed coalition. In the Mitnick example, the ontology (DAML+OIL) and an inference engine was initially employed as an event recognition language, by discerning that a type of Denial of Service attack was taking place. Secondly, DAML+OIL was used as a reporting language to communicate that fact to other systems. Finally, the ontology (DAML+OIL) and the inference engine were used as an event aggregation language to fuse the existence of the Denial of Service attack, a network connection, and session establishment to deduce that a Mitnick type attack had occurred.

Moreover, the only prerequisite for the disparate systems with the distributed coalition is that they share the same ontology.

We are continuing our research, initiating attacks in a controlled environment in order to capture their low level kernel attributes at the system, process and network levels in order to further specify our ontology.

References

1. J. Allen, A. Christie, W. Fithen, J. McHugh, J. Pickel, and E. Stoner. State of the Practice of Intrusion Detection Technologies. Technical Report 99tr028, Carnegie Mellon - Software Engineering Institute, 2000.
2. E. G. Amoroso. *Fundamentals of Computer Security Technology*. Prentice-Hall PTR, 1994.
3. T. Aslam, I. Krusl, and E. Spafford. Use of a Taxonomy of Security Faults. In *Proceedings of the 19th National Information Systems Security Conference*, October 1996.
4. D. Brickley and R. Guha. RDF Vocabulary Description Language 1.0: RDF Schema. http://www.w3c.org/TR/rdf-schema/, 2003.
5. P. C.Mahalanobis. *On Tests and Meassures of Groups Divergence*. International Journal of the Asiatic Society of Bengal, 1930.
6. D. Curry and H. Debar. "intrusion detection message exchange format data model and extensible markup language (xml) document type definition. http://www.ietf.org/internet-drafts/draft-ietf-idwg-idmef-xml-10.txt, January 2003.
7. R. Davis, H. Shrobe, and P. Szolovits. What is Knowledge Representation? *AI Magazine*, 14(1):17 − 33, 1993.

8. J. Doyle, I. Kohane, W. Long, H. Shrobe, and P. Szolovits. Event Recognition Beyond Signature and Anomaly. In *2nd IEEE-SMC Information Assurance Workshop*, June 2001.
9. S. Eckmann, G. Vigna, and R. Kemmerer. STATL: An Attack Language for State-based Intrusion Detection. *Journal of Computer Security*, 10(1/2):71 – 104, 2002.
10. R. Feiertag, C. Kahn, P. Porras, D. Schackenberg, S. Staniford-Chen, and B. Tung. A Common Intrusion Specification Language. http://www.isi.edu/ brian/cidf/drafts/language.txt, June 1999.
11. R. Fikes and D. L. McGuinness. An Axiomatic Semantics for RDF, RDF-S, and DAML+OIL. http://www.w3.org/TR/daml+oil-axioms, December 2001.
12. G. Frank, J. Jenkins, and R. Fikes. JTP: An Object Oriented Modular Reasoning System. http://kst.stanford.edu/software/jtp.
13. E. J. Friedman-Hill. Jess, The Java Expert System Shell. http://herzberg.ca.sandia.gov/jess/docs/52/, November 1977.
14. R. L. Glass and I. Vessey. Contemporary Application-Domain Taxonomies. *IEEE Software*, pages 63 – 76, July 1995.
15. G. Golub and C. Loan. *Matrix Computations*. The Johns Hopkins University Press, 1989.
16. J. Goubault-Larrecq. An Introduction to LogWeaver (v2.8). http://www.lsv.ens-cachan.fr/ goubault/DICO/tutorial.pdf, September 2001.
17. T. F. Gruber. A Translation Approach to Portable Ontologies. *Knowledge Acquisition*, 5(2):199–220, 1993.
18. B. Guha and B. Mukherjee. Network Security via Reverse Engineering of TCP Code: Vulnerability Analysis and Proposed Solutions. In *IEEE Networks*, pages 40 – 48. IEEE, July/August 1997.
19. V. Haarslev and R. Moller. RACER: Renamed ABox and Concept Expression Reasoner. http://www.cs.concordia.ca/ faculty/haarslev/racer/index.html, June 2001.
20. J. W. Haines, L. M. Rossey, R. P. Lippman, and R. K. Cunningham. Extending the DARPA Off-Line Intrusion Detection Evaluations. In *DARPA Information Survivability Conference and Exposition II*, volume 1, pages 77 – 88. IEEE, 2001.
21. I. Horrocks, U. Sattler, and S. Tobies. Reasoning with Individuals for the Description Logic SHIQ. In *Proceedings of the 17th International Conference on Automated Deduction*, number 1831. Springer-Verlag, 2000.
22. J. Hendler. DARPA Agent Markup Language+Ontology Interface Layer. http://www.daml.org/2001/03/daml+oil-index, 2001.
23. A. Joshi and J. Undercoffer. On web semantics and data mining: Intrusion detection as a case study. In *Proceedings of the National Science Foundation Workshop on Next Generation Data Mining*, 2002.
24. C. Kahn, D. Bolinger, and D. Schackenberg. Communication in the Common Intrusion Detection Framework v 0.7. http://www.isi.edu/ brian/cidf/drafts/communication.txt, June 1998.
25. R. A. Kemmerer and G. Vigna. Intrusion Detection: A Brief History and Overview. *Security and Privacy a Supplement to IEEE Computer Magazine*, pages 27 – 30, April 2002.
26. K. Kendall. A Database of Computer Attacks for the Evaluation of Intrusion Detection Systems. Master's thesis, MIT, 1999.
27. D. Koller and A. Pfeffer. Probabilistic Frame-Based Systems. In *Proceedings of the Fifteenth National Conference on Artifical Intelligence*, pages 580 – 587, Madison, Wisconsin, July 1998. AAAI.
28. J. Kopena. DAMLJessKB. http://edge.mcs.drexel.edu/ assemblies/software/damljesskb/ articles/DAMLJessKB-2002.pdf, October 2002.
29. R. Krishnapuram, A. Joshi, O. Nasraoui, and L. Yi. Low-Complexity Fuzzy Relational Clustering Algorithms for Web Mining. In *IEEE transactions on Fuzzy Systems*, volume 9, August 2001.

30. I. Krusl. *Software Vulnerability Analysis.* PhD thesis, Purdue, 1998.
31. C. E. Landwehr, A. R. Bull, J. P. McDermott, and W. S. Choi. A Taxonomy of Computer Program Security Flaws. *ACM Computing Surveys,* 26(3):211 – 254, September 1994.
32. O. Lassila and R. R. Swick. Resource Description Framework (RDF) Model and Syntax Specification. http://www.w3.org/TR/1999/REC-rdf-syntax-19990222/, February 1999.
33. U. Lindqvist and E. Jonsson. How to Systematically Classify Computer Security Intrusions. In *Proceedings of the 1997 IEEE Symposium on Security and Privacy,* pages 154 – 163, May 1997.
34. U. Lindqvist and P. A. Porras. Detecting computer and network misuse through the production-based system toolset (p-best). In *Proceedings of the 1999 IEEE Symposium on Security and Privacy,* pages 146 – 161. IEEE, May 1999.
35. R. Lippmann, D. Fried, I. Graf, J. Haines, K. Kendall, D. McClung, D. Weber, S. Webster, D. Wyschogrod, R. Cunningham, and M. Zissman. Evaluating Intrusion Detection Systems: The 1998 DARPA Off-line Intrusion Detection Evaluation. In *Proceedings of the DARPA Information Survivability Conference and Exposition, 2000,* pages 12 – 26.
36. J. McHugh. Testing Intrusion Detection Systems: A Critique of the 1998 and 1999 DARPA Intrusion Detection System Evaluations as Performed by Lincoln Laboratory. *ACM Transactions on Information and System Security,* November 2000.
37. P. Ning, S. Jajodia, and X. S. Wang. Abstraction-Based Intrusion in Distributed Environments. *ACM Transactions on Information and Systems Security,* 4(4):407 – 452, November 2001.
38. N. F. Noy and D. L. McGuinnes. Ontology development 101: A guide to creating your fisrt ontology. Stanford University.
39. V. Paxson. Bro: A system for Detecting Network Intruders in Real Time. In *Proceedings of the 7th Symposium on USENIX Security,* 1998.
40. V. Raskin, C. F. Hempelmann, K. E. Triezenberg, and S. Nirenburg. Ontology in Information Security: A Useful Theoretical Foundation and Methodological Tool. In *Proceedings of NSPW-2001,* pages 53 – 59. ACM.
41. M. Roesch. Snort, version 1.8.3. availble via www.snort.org, August 2001. an open source NIDS.
42. M. Roger and J. Goubault-Larrecq. Log Auditing through Model Checking. In *Proceedings of 14th the IEEE Computer Security Foundations Workshop (CSFW'01),* pages 220 – 236, 2001.
43. S. Staab and A. Maedche. Ontology Engineering Beyond the Modeling of Concepts and Relations. In *Proceedings of the 14th European Congress on Artificial Intelligence,* 2000.
44. G. G. Sumpson. *Principals of Animal Taxonomy.* Columbia University Press, 1961.
45. J. Undercoffer, F. Perich, A. Cedilnik, L. Kagal, and A. Joshi. A Secure Infrastructure for Service Discovery and Access in Pervasive Computing. *Mobile Networks and Applications: Special Issue on Security,* 8(2):113 – 126, 2003.
46. J. Undercoffer and J. Pinkston. An Empirical Analysis of Computer Attacks and Intrusions. Technical Report TR-CS-03-11, University of Maryland, Baltimore County, 2002.
47. W3C. Extensible Markup Language. http://www.w3c.org/XML/, 2003.
48. WEBSTERS, editor. *Merriam-Webster's Collegiate Dictionary.* Merriam-Webster, Inc., tenth edition, 1993.
49. C. Welty. Towards a Semantics for the Web. www.cs.vassar.edu/faculty/welty/papers/dagstuhl-2000.pdf, 2000.

Using Specification-Based Intrusion Detection
for Automated Response

Ivan Balepin[1], Sergei Maltsev[2], Jeff Rowe[1], and Karl Levitt[1]

[1] Computer Security Laboratory, University of California, Davis
Davis, CA, 95616, USA
{Balepin,Rowe,Levitt}@cs.ucdavis.edu
[2] IU8, Bauman Moscow State Technical University,
Moscow, 105005, Russia
SVMaltsev@iu8.bmstu.ru

Abstract. One of the most controversial issues in intrusion detection is auto-mating responses to intrusions, which can provide a more efficient, quicker, and precise way to react to an attack in progress than a human. However, it comes with several disadvantages that can lead to a waste of resources, which has so far prevented wide acceptance of automated response-enabled systems. We feel that a structured approach to the problem is needed that will account for the above mentioned disadvantages. In this work, we briefly describe what has been done in the area before. Then we start addressing the problem by coupling automated response with specification-based, host-based intrusion detection. We describe the system map, and the map-based action cost model that give us the basis for deciding on response strategy. We also show the process of sus-pending the attack, and designing the optimal response strategy, even in the presence of uncertainty. Finally, we discuss the implementation issues, our ex-perience with the early automated response agent prototype, the Automated Re-sponse Broker (ARB), and suggest topics for further research.

1 Introduction

Automated response to intrusions is an exciting area of research in intrusion detection. Development of a system that resists attacks carried out or programmed by another human being can be approached in many ways, including the one in which we teach the machine to beat an attacker in the game of intrusion and response.

Let us begin by formulating the objectives of our work.

1.1 Objectives

With the growing speed and intensity of computer attacks [13] comes the need for quick and well-planned responses. Currently, some of the most intense intrusions are automated. A reliable automated response system, with the right approach, could certainly provide an efficient protection, or a degree of tolerance for all kinds of at-tacks. However, automated response remains mostly an area of research due to the following issues:

G. Vigna, E. Jonsson, and C. Kruegel (Eds.): RAID 2003, LNCS 2820, pp. 136–154, 2003.

- Primitive response systems that ignore the cost of intrusion and response apply response actions that cause more harm than the intrusion itself
- A large part of commercially available Intrusion Detection Systems (IDS) produces an extensive number of false positive alerts, potentially causing numerous, unnecessary, and costly response actions [12]

Both cases lead to a denial of service to legitimate users of the system.

The objective of this work is to develop a consistent, organized, cost-based approach to automated response that would address these issues. An optimal response would stop the progressing intrusion at early stages, and clean up after it as much as feasible. The scheme described in this work is geared to produce such responses.

We start addressing the problem by considering host-based automated responses. The key parts of our approach are the basis for response decisions (the system map and the cost model), and the process (response selection even in the presence of uncertainty).

Let us briefly summarize the work previously done in the area.

1.2 Related Work

Primitive automated response actions are implemented in some Intrusion Detection Systems (IDS) commercially available today (i.e., re-setting suspicious network connections or "shunning" a certain network address – not accepting any traffic to or from it). [12] However, these actions are rather simple and reflexive by their nature. Even with a limited response arsenal, many practitioners report that they disable the systems' intrusion prevention/response capabilities due to a high number of false positives from IDS's which give an incorrect basis for response, and also a denial of service caused by non-sophisticated response strategies.

An interesting research work on Survivable Autonomic Response Architecture (SARA) [8] uses the term *autonomic response* by drawing an analogy with the autonomic nervous system, which automatically controls certain functions of an organism without any conscious input. The authors propose having two separate "loops" of response: a local autonomic response and a global response carried out by the hosts in a system in co-operation. The primary focus of the work is a network with multiple hosts.

Alphatech's Light Autonomic Defense System (αLADS) relies on control theory when selecting a response [1]. The authors describe it as a part of Autonomic Computing, which, according to them, is an emerging area of study of design and construction of self-managed computing systems with a minimum of human inteAfphateeh's work is not applicable to general-purpose computer systems. The work is focused on developing a full-scale solution that has its own profile-based intrusion detection components and is intended to defend a very specific range of systems. The issue of compatibility with existing intrusion detection systems has not received much attention in published descriptions of αLADS. However, Alphatech's work is of interest to further automated response research, since it is one of the early organized approaches to the problem of quick automated responses.

Another study of network-oriented automated response that relies on Control Theory is currently done at UC Davis [15].

A study by Toth, et.al., [16] proposes yet another promising model for automating intrusion response. The authors suggest approaching the problem of response to network intrusions by constructing dependency trees that model configuration of the network, and they give an outline of a cost model for estimating the effect of a response.

Other significant response works include a thorough consideration of some intrusion detection and response cost modeling aspects by Lee, et.al. [7], a response taxonomy by C. Carver and U. Pooch [3], and Fred Cohen's work on deception [4], which is another interesting perspective on countering malicious activity.

The analysis of related work leads us to the conclusion that the primary area of interest so far has been a computer network that consists of multiple hosts. The idea of responding at a level of a single host has received relatively little attention. Also, we note that despite the efforts to produce a working cost model for a set of protected resources, no well-developed and well-tested model currently exists that guarantees a consistent and fair representation of protected resources, and their true value.

1.3 This Work

This paper has the following remaining sections: Section 2, in which we describe the basis for constructing a response chain; Section 3, in which we discuss an implementation of our model; Section 4, which lists possible directions for future work; and, finally, conclusions in Section 5. The reason for separating the basis for response decisions from implementation notes on our prototype is to attempt to describe a model for host-based response in Section 2 that would not be tied to any particular operating system, and, potentially, could be used for applications other than host-based response.

2 Basis for Automated Response

Several pieces of information are necessary in order to plan a sequence of response actions. For the system we are protecting, we need a clear representation of the most valuable resources and also the underlying resources that provide the basic functionality. The true value of some resources (for example, the TCP/IP network service) is heavily influenced by other resources that depend on them (network is needed by *httpd*, etc.), and we need a clear way to reflect these dependencies before we can decide how to deal with a compromised entity. We also need an organized way to store information about malicious and compromised entities, and to decide how they relate to our key resources. Part of this representation will be highly dynamic, since some entities reflected (processes, etc.) are dynamic; however, a large part of it, such as file structure, program configuration (dependence on files, sockets, etc.), and system configuration, can be determined statically.

We narrow the scope of the problem by noting that transferring an entire computer system to a safe state is a challenging task, and limiting the scope of the problem to returning a set of critical system resources to a reasonably safe and working state.

Resources we will model are anything of value in our system — system subjects and objects, files and running processes, sockets, file systems, etc. We arrange them in two different ways – the resource type hierarchy and the system map.

2.1 Resource Type Hierarchy

It is convenient to group resources by their type, since every such group most likely will have common response actions associated with it. Also, resource types can be arranged in a hierarchy similar to the one on Fig. 1.

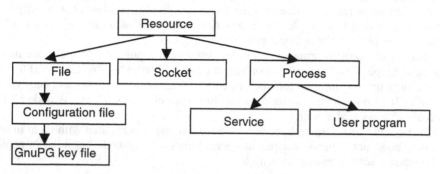

Fig. 1. An example of a response type hierarchy

On a Linux system, for instance, we can subdivide resources into files, sockets, processes, etc., in advance. However, in certain situations a more specific category would be appropriate. Consider a file that contains keys for automatic encryption/decryption of emails using the GNU Privacy Guard software (GPG, [5]). In addition to response action that applies to a more general node in the hierarchy (configuration files, "restore the configuration file from backup and restart the corresponding service"), we define a response action specific to this sub-category ("also revoke and re-issue the keys").

Since these more specific categories, and their corresponding response actions, depend highly on the system configuration, we cannot define all of them in advance for all systems. We should provide a way for the users of the response system to define new custom categories with response actions tailored to specific resources on the target systems.

2.2 System Map

Although the response type hierarchy is useful for storing general response actions that might apply to a resource, it carries no information about the specific instances of resources on a system, merely their types. Therefore, we need an additional data structure to satisfy the requirements for a decision basis as mentioned above.

We suggest representing the necessary information as a directed graph, which we will refer to as the system map. The vertices of the graph (which we will refer to as map nodes) represent the resources in our system. Besides nodes, our map has node templates and edges.

2.2.1 Map Nodes

The system map contains important nodes of all types — the system's priorities. By "important nodes" we mean "all nodes with a non-zero cost", with cost assigned according to our cost model described in the corresponding sub-section. In addition to the priorities, our map also reflects the underlying basic resources that these priorities need for proper operation. For example, most applications need a working mounted file system with read/write access right in order to operate properly. Therefore, if we have applications A, B, and C that are our priorities, we place them on the map along with the node that represents the file system. We also note that the file system, as an underlying basic resource, does not need to be explicitly specified as a priority itself, since in this simple example it does not have any value of its own. It costs only as much as the priority nodes that depend on it.

Each node holds information about the resource it represents. Namely, we need to know the type of the resource according to our type hierarchy. We also need to know some type-specific information such as path and filename for types and sub-types of "file"; PID, name and owner for type and sub-types of "process", etc. A node also has a cost value associated with it.

Some static nodes might have several node templates associated with them in order to later construct dynamic dependent nodes. Finally, every node has a list of applicable response actions associated with it.

2.2.2 Node Responses

Every node has a list of *basic response actions* that restore its functionality. Currently, we require that this list contain only the actions that completely restore the node to a working state.

The node's list of responses is constructed from response actions that are listed for this type of node and its parent types in the type hierarchy. Each such response action has an *activation condition* associated with it. Referring to the example we have used before, type "configuration file" would inherit a response "restore from backup" from the parent type "file". The activation condition would be, "the node of this type was a target of an illegal *write* system call" or "the node of this type was a target of an illegal *unlink* system call."

Another important property of a simple response action is *what nodes it affects*. Currently, we assume that an action either damages several resources, or does not. If the chosen intrusion detection technique relies on system calls, activation conditions for each response action will be also expressed in terms of system calls. The number of system calls is finite (approx. 200 in a Linux system), and the number of node types is finite (6 in the prototype). Furthermore, there are only a few system calls that are applicable to one type of a resource. Thus, it is feasible to pre-define response lists for every valid combination.

We also complement the node's response list with a response "take no action". That is an essential response alternative that has a certain cost, just like other responses, and by including it, we will ensure that any response action we take is not more expensive than the intrusion itself.

Therefore, an entry in a node's response list has three fields:

- the action itself (a Linux command, etc.)
- the activation criteria
- the list of nodes the action damages

2.2.3 Map Edges

Edges on our map represent dependencies between the resources. If an edge is directed from node A to node B, it means that A provides some service to B, B depends on A, and, most likely, A produces information that B consumes.

However, it does not seem feasible to attempt to trace information flow through our map, since it contains nodes that are often times not comparable (for example, file systems and sockets), and also nodes that obscure information flow (if node A reads from node "file system", node B writes to node "file system", there is not necessarily an information flow from B to A). Therefore, we do not use our map for intrusion detection. For all information about the intrusion we rely on some detection technique.

The true value of the map edges is that they allow us to properly carry out single response actions that involve several nodes ("restart the service that corresponds to this configuration file", i.e., the service that consumes information from the file). Also, the edges allow us to collect information about the nodes that depend on a certain node, therefore allowing us to calculate the dynamic cost of the node in our system.

Relationships between the nodes can be specified with greater detail, such as "node A writes to node B that often", or "node A writes to node B with probability N." However, for our purposes, it is sufficient to only reflect the fact that one node provides services to another node, and therefore, the latter depends on the former. Also, some authors model dependency alternatives (node A depends on node B *or* node C) [16]. From a standpoint of resources of a single host, this is a relatively rare situation, so we will not consider it here.

2.2.4 Constructing the Map

As we have mentioned before, the map will have a static part, which will consist of nodes that can be produced by static analysis of our priority resources when no processes are running. The static part of the map will have information about objects of the system, but not subjects. Operation begins just with the static part of the map. As the system runs, dynamic nodes are added.

In our design, there are five ways we can add a node to the map. Static nodes are added to the map upon upgrades/reconfigurations of the protected system.

For the dynamic part, we propose to add new nodes for every subject or object mentioned in the incident alert from the IDS that was not previously on the map. Such nodes would be assigned cost 0, since they were not included in the list of priorities, and they get assigned the most specific type from the type hierarchy that we are able to automatically determine. Consequently, the node will have a response list that corresponds to its assigned type.

Also, as we will describe in later sections, sometimes we will be able to classify a whole group of subjects as malicious, whereas only a few of them might have been explicitly mentioned in alerts. Such situations can occur, for example, when a malicious process caused an alert, and immediately produced a number of child processes that have not yet done anything illegal themselves. We will put the whole related group of subjects on the map and treat them just like the nodes mentioned in the alerts, despite the fact that only a few were mentioned in the alert. Then the whole group gets marked as suspicious, or "contaminated".

Finally, we will have some dynamic nodes that will represent our priority resources. Often times, a resource in general can be mapped to several nodes. For example, a "web server" resource encompasses the executable file, a number of running processes, and dependent resources (configuration files, sockets, etc.). At the time of static analysis, we will not have a running instance of a web server; however, we can get most of information about the web server process node at that time. Therefore, with every important executable we create a set of templates that will characterize the subjects and objects later to be produced by running the executable file. A node template is a prototype for building nodes that has all the information in place except for the type-specific information (like PID or filename) that gets filled in upon use of the template.

2.2.5 Properties and Benefits of the Map

The map has only a few static and dynamic nodes that are critical to the system's operation. They are not updated periodically; rather, we update them only when significant events happen (alerts for dynamic nodes and system re-configuration for static ones). Therefore, if our system runs for a long time without getting attacked, the map will not be updated in order to minimize the overhead.

The nodes on the map can be of very different nature, so they cannot always be compared directly (for example, file systems and processes).

Let us illustrate some properties of the map with a small example. Suppose, we have a Linux system equipped with System Health and Intrusion Monitoring IDS (SHIM, [6]) that has been compromised, and now has an active malicious process A that was produced by a program B which is not supposed to make system calls from the *exec* family. Process A has its parent's specifications imposed on it by SHIM. Suppose then that process A produces process C, and process C writes to a file. Since SHIM would promptly alert our response system about A, B and C being involved in several illegal *exec* system calls, the whole family would appear on the map, and would be marked as malicious. As far as the file that C has written to, if specifications for A allowed such behavior, then we would not get an alert about the file write, and, therefore, would not reflect that fact on the map. However, if it was not legal according to A's specifications and the system policy, we would get an alert about a possibly contaminated file, place the corresponding node on the map, and plan our response strategy with that alert in mind.

As we have shown above, our map contains all necessary information about our priorities, and resources they need to operate. The map also will reflect information about malicious entities, and their relation to our priorities. The map, as we have described it, gives us a solid basis for designing an intrusion response strategy.

2.3 Cost Model

In most cases, when deciding on response to a malicious action, there will be several response actions with activation criteria matching the current situation. We solve the problem of comparing these alternatives and selecting the optimal one by introducing an action cost model. The cost model helps us pick the best response and also ensure that we don't cause denial of service to ourselves by performing responses that are more harmful (i.e., more costly to us) than the intrusion itself.

Our cost model is based on numerical cost values associated with every map node. Designing a cost model that allows us to quickly associate a number with a resource and to precisely reflect the value of that resource is a difficult task. Most of the attempts to produce such a model left it up to the system administrators to determine cost values for their resources. Although it is true that only the system's owner, familiar with its configuration and primary functions, can point out the true value of the resources, it is very hard to assign the cost values in a consistent manner that would always guarantee optimal response without exhaustive testing of the system. In our implementation, we rely on ordering the resources by their importance to help produce a cost configuration that would yield an optimal response.

There are only a few priority nodes that have an actual cost value in our model. For example, let us consider a system with only one such priority – the web server. In the static part of the map it is represented with the executable file of the web server. There will be a static node for the file itself, and it will have a cost of 0. The static node for the executable file will, however, have a template for web server processes to be created, and that template will have a cost value associated with it. In our model, all process nodes that get created according to that template, will share an equal fraction of the template's cost with existing processes. For example, suppose the system's owner has estimated that the web server has cost x. When there is no web server running, the executable file will have no cost value. If one instance of *httpd* gets started, its node will get assigned a cost value x. If y nodes of *httpd* get created, each will get a cost value of x/y.

A static node can also get an explicit cost value assigned to itself, and not to its templates; or it might not even have any templates. For example, some files might be indicated as a priority, even though they are not used by any subjects of that system.

Cost-wise, another category of nodes on our map is the underlying service nodes. Most likely, these nodes will have a zero cost of their own. However, any harmful action on these nodes will also affect the costly resources that rely on them, and by reflecting these dependencies on the map we will take into account the true value of the underlying services.

Finally, we have all the resources that were not put on our map as a priority resource or its dependency. We assign all such resources cost 0; if they become malicious or get involved in an incident, they are put on the map, and a response action that affects these 0-cost nodes even in the most dramatic way will not be harmful for the system in general.

Once we determine the cost values for our map nodes based on these factors, we then can associate a cost value with any *action* that an intruder or the response system takes.

We define *the cost of an intrusion action* as the sum of costs of map nodes, previously in a safe state, that get negatively affected by the action. We define the *benefit of a response action* as the sum of costs of nodes, previously in the set of affected nodes, that this response action restores to a working state. Finally, we define the *cost of a response action* in terms of costs of the nodes that get negatively affected by the response action ("lost to the intruder," or not functioning properly). The goal of a response system is to carry out the response sequence that yields the maximum benefit at the minimum cost. We note that such an approach does not emphasize transferring the system to the ultimate safe state, or completely recovering from an intrusion, since there are situations in which these goals would be much more costly than the intrusion itself. With our approach, we are, however, guaranteed to come up with a response strategy that is optimal for the current situation.

2.4 Response Selection

Once we have the whole picture of the intrusion, our goal is then to "win" the resources on the "contaminated" side back. We start by listing all response alternatives at every contaminated node whose activation condition matches the intrusion. The goal of response selection is to build a response action sequence that will have one action out of a list of every contaminated node. That way, we ensure that every contaminated node is addressed. As mentioned before, an optimal response action is the one that yields the maximum benefit at the minimum cost. We then assume that a response sequence (response strategy) is optimal if it consists of response actions that are optimal for every node. Therefore, if we have the complete picture of the intrusion, we can build the response chain from optimal responses at every node, and then carry it out.

2.4.1 Managing Uncertainty

Sometimes we might encounter situations where we do not know for certain what the intruder has exactly done. For example, suppose the capabilities allowed the intruder to perform a *write* call on a file, which is illegal according to the current system policy. The file could have been overwritten, appended to, or erased completely (overwritten with an empty string). In certain situations, response actions, and their cost, may vary depending on what has really happened. Then we turn to decision theory, which provides well-defined ways to construct the response plan, for different requirements in presence of uncertainty.

The possible results of a *write* call would be over-written data in the file, data appended to the file, or data completely erased from the file (the latter being a special case of the first one). This allows us to list the possible system states. Every one of these states will have a potential damage value and a probability associated with it. Now, using the decision theory convention [10], we can describe the situation with the following "gain matrix":

	Π_1	Π_2	Π_3	Π_4	Π_5
A_1	a_{11}	a_{12}	a_{13}	a_{14}	a_{15}
...			...		
A_N	a_{N1}	a_{N2}	a_{N3}	a_{N4}	a_{N5}
Q	q_1	q_2	q_3	q_4	q_5

where Π_i are the possible states, q_i are the probabilities, and A_i represent the response alternatives. a_{ij} in this matrix, again, represents the usefulness, or benefit, of using the ith decision in case of a jth sub-state. This value can be estimated as:

$$a_{ij} = -c_i - \left(-\varepsilon_{ij}\right)^{\gamma} B_j. \tag{1}$$

where B_j is the potential damage of a sub-state,

c_i – response cost,

ε_{ij} – efficiency(benefit) of response i in sub-state j, and

γ is 0 if $\varepsilon_{ij}{=}0$, 1 otherwise.

Considering the above parameters, we observe that the greater the value of a_{ij} the more useful the corresponding response alternative will be in the corresponding state.

We define the risk of losing in a particular game situation (r_{ij}) as the difference between the player's gain for strategy A_i for conditions of Π_j, and the player's gain for the strategy he would have chosen, had he known the conditions of Π_j. It is clear that had the player known the system state and its conditions in advance, he would have chosen the strategy that yields the maximum gain in its matrix column (m_j). According to our definition,

$$r_{ij} = m_j - a_{ij}, \text{ where } m_j = \max_i a_{ij}. \tag{2}$$

Defined in this way, the concept of risk also reflects how favorable a given state is to us. Consequently, a risk matrix constructed similarly to the gain matrix, gives us a more complete picture than the gain matrix.

Relying on probability significantly simplifies the decision making process, especially if we can produce relatively accurate probability estimates using the system history, general knowledge, anomaly analysis tools, etc.

A promising way to eliminate the uncertainty, or, at least estimate the values of probability of a certain intrusion sequence, is monitoring the system for a long period of time and building a profile for important resources. For that, machine learning techniques can be used; also, much can be drawn from the anomaly-based and misuse-based intrusion detection techniques [2]. We discuss these suggestions in more detail in Section 4.

Let us take mathematical expectation of probability-based gain $\overline{a_i}$ to be the effectiveness criterion W that we obviously would like to maximize.

$$\overline{a_i} = q_1 a_{i1} + q_2 a_{i2} + ... + q_n a_{in}. \tag{3}$$

The optimal strategy is the one that yields the maximum $\overline{a_i}$ in the gain matrix. It would also yield a minimum average risk based on the risk matrix.

Special care must be taken to accurately estimate probability. Pure probability, as a statistics-based value, might not always be available. In that case, it can be subjectively estimated. Certain events might be more likely than others according to the system logs. There are several techniques available that help us quantify these subjective estimates.

For cases in which we have no statistical information for the system states, we can assign equal probabilities to each possible state, i.e.:

$$q_1 = q_2 = ... = q_n = 1/n. \tag{4}$$

This approach is called Laplace insufficient reason criterion ([10]).

For another approach, we assume that we can order possible system states by their likeliness. In order to represent the probabilities in this case, we can use a converging arithmetic series:

$$q_1 : q_2 : ... : q_n = n : (n-1) : ... : 1. \tag{5}$$

where:

$$q_i = \frac{2(n-i+1)}{n(n+1)} \tag{6}$$

We can also rely on expert estimates.

If we manage to completely eliminate uncertainty in some situations, the probability values for the determined system state becomes 1, probabilities of all other states become 0, the matrix turns into a single column, and decision making becomes trivial.

2.4.2 The Optimal Decision Criteria

There are several methods for selecting the decision criteria in the decision theory ([10]). In the Minimax risk criterion (Savage criterion) we select the strategy from the risk matrix that provides us with the minimal risk value under the most unfavorable conditions. The efficiency W is then estimated as $W = \min_i \max_j r_{ij}$. The Minimax risk approach allows us to avoid making the high-risk decisions. The Maximin criterion favors strategies with the largest minimal gain (with W defined differently, see [10]). The Hurwicz criterion is neither pessimistic nor optimistic. Risk-based criterion is analogous to Hurwicz

Selection of criterion and its parameters is subjective. It is useful to analyze the situation using various approaches. If majority of criterions indicate that a certain strategy is optimal, it should certainly be selected. Should several different criterions suggest different strategies, it is up to the system owner to select (or pre-select) the right strategy based on the fact that some criterion might be preferred over the others.

3   Implementation

We have implemented several concepts mentioned in the previous section in a prototype response system, the Automated Response Broker (ARB). ARB is developed for Linux, and it relies on SHIM for detection. Let us briefly mention why we chose SHIM for that role.

3.1   Intrusion Detection: SHIM

SHIM is specification-based. It relies on the Generic Software Wrapper Toolkit (GSWTK,[9]) for all information about the system calls. SHIM does not try to recognize an attack as a whole. Instead, it relies on a set of specifications (for programs, or protocols, etc.) that reflect the system policy.

SHIM addresses a large part of intrusions by enforcing specifications for privileged Linux programs. System calls of interest are reported by the GSWTK, and then classified as legal or illegal according to the specifications, with an alert being issued for the latter.

SHIM is a great vehicle for testing our automated response scheme. Such a fine event granularity allows us to catch the exact system call that started the intrusion. Also, the fact that SHIM does not need the whole intrusion to recognize its signature, allows it to catch unknown intrusions, and intrusions that are still in progress. The last feature also gives us a chance to stop an intrusion in progress by responding to the first few steps of it that have been detected.

The underlying assumption about SHIM that we make is that it always promptly detects and reports all intrusions. Also, SHIM and GSWTK give us a capability to check if a system call is legal before it is executed. However, such a mode of operation causes a large overhead for every system call, and does not seem feasible.

3.2 Map Implementation

We build the map starting with a set of nodes we want to protect. It is the set of all programs that are constrained by SHIM (regardless of whether they are among our priorities; the cost will reflect that fact), and several nodes for resources that might not be constrained by SHIM, but the system owner wants to protect as well.

The type hierarchy is constructed upon installation of a system. It does not have a dynamic part and it does not change, since it simply contains information about the types of nodes, not the nodes themselves.

In ARB, the type hierarchy is constructed in C++. While it might be sufficient for experiments and testing, obviously a more convenient interface for configuring the type hierarchy is needed. Currently, we experiment with XML for type hierarchy definitions. XML so far has proved to be powerful enough to express all the information necessary, and there is an abundance of tools for parsing the type hierarchy defined in XML into our program.

Below is an example of a response list of a configuration file node. Event name and target constitute the activation condition for the action. The victim tag marks the damaged nodes.

```
<actions>
     <event name="chown" target="self">
          <action>restore_attributes;</action>
          <action>kill_offender;</action>
          <victims>offender</victims>
     </event>
     <event name="chown" target="self">
          <action>delete_self;</action>
          <action>kill_offender;</action>
          <victims>self</victims>
          <victims>dependents</victims>
          <victims>offender</victims>
     </event>
     <event name="write" target="self">
          <action>
                    restore_from_backup;
                    fire_event("httpd","restart",true);
          </action>
     </event>
     ...
</actions>
```

Should XML fail to be descriptive enough for the task, a new domain-specific language (DSL) will be designed for describing the type hierarchy.

Similarly to the type hierarchy, the map itself is constructed manually as a collection of C++ data structures. We are currently experimenting with more flexible ways to define a map, such as, again, XML or a new DSL.

As mentioned above, all components of a system in our prototype are determined manually. However, some of them can be pre-defined for most systems; some can be determined by automated analysis upon installation or re-configuration. The ultimate goal is to let the ARB user specify just the custom types, responses to custom types, and the system's priorities. The remainder of the map (such as the basic types, under-lying service nodes, all dependencies and templates) can be determined automatically. We list the requirements for automating the map construction and problems associ-ated with it in the future work section.

Node response lists are constructed from the type hierarchy. The set of response actions that are implemented, or will be implemented in the prototype include: *delete a file, restore a file from backup, restart a service, change permissions, kill proc-ess(es), reboot the system, block a connection, re-configure a firewall rule, unmount a file system, change the owner of the process(es), start checkpointing, slow down the process(es), roll back to a checkpoint, return a random result, perform a random action, operate on a fake file, tunnel the process(es) to a sandbox, operate on a fake socket.*

3.3 Node Costs

The most difficult task of any implementation of a response system is performing a consistent cost assignment that reflects the true value of resources. This part of map construction cannot be completed in advance, or even automated, since it needs input from the owner of the system. Currently, we approach the problem by first manually ordering the key resources of the system, so that the resources (R_i) are listed in the following form:

$$R_0 < R_1 = R_2 = R_{3...} < R_{i-1} < R_i \tag{7}$$

The least important resource gets assigned priority 1, and the priorities of all other (more important) resources are approximated as N times the priority of the next less important one:

$$\text{Priority}(R_j) = N * \text{Priority}(R_{j-1}), \tag{8}$$

where N is an approximate value and is determined experimentally. Finally, for con-venience, we obtain a cost value C_i for a resource R_j from priority values according to the following formula:

$$C_i = 100*\text{Priority}(R_i)/\Sigma\text{Priority}(R_i), \tag{9}$$

where *ΣPriority(R_i)* is a sum of the priorities of all resources.

Currently, the process of assignment is completely manual. The cost assignment method described above is only an approximation of the real resource costs. Work is being done on improving the method to ensure consistency of the cost assignment.

3.4 Damage Assessment and Response Selection

Let us say ARB received an alert about some malicious actions involving several nodes on our map. Currently, ARB reads alerts from a socket that SHIM writes to. A closer form of integration with SHIM is being developed, since the current implemen-tation is sufficient for evaluation of response, but is vulnerable to attacks.

First, we need to stop the intrusion, if it is still in progress. The map is partitioned into a set of nodes that are affected (or might have been affected) by the incident, and a set of nodes that are not dependent on any in the first set, and therefore, not affected by the incident.

Upon an alert that, say, mentions only one subject, the damage assessment procedure of ARB puts all ancestors and offspring this subject may have on the map independent of further alerts. That allows us to freeze the intrusion in progress before the children attempt to perform further malicious action, since having a suspicious process as a parent already gives us a right to mark a child process as suspicious as well, without waiting for further alerts. We freeze the intrusion by temporarily suspending the contaminated processes (by sending them a *kill -19* message).

ARB operates with a concept of an incident. Alerts are grouped to form a single incident if they report subjects from the same family as suspicious. ARB considers the damage assessment procedure completed when it constructed and froze the entire family of suspicious processes. All new alerts are treated as parts of a new incident. The testing of ARB that we have done so far indicates that such approach allows us to clearly separate individual incidents, freeze an incident, assess the damage, and carry out response actions.

Upon completion of the damage assessment procedure, we have the suspended intrusion, the frozen suspicious processes, and the complete picture of an intrusion in form of the partitioned map.

Finally, the response strategy is built and carried out, as described in the previous sections.

3.5 Example

Let us demonstrate how ARB carries out the entire process of response selection with an actual example. We will consider a classic vulnerability in the RedHat Linux 6.2 *dump* utility [11], which examines the files on a file system, and determines the ones that need to be backed up. These files are copied to a disk, tape, or other storage medium. The dump utility depends on the environment variables *TAPE* and *RSH*.

The goal of the dump exploit is to set the *RSH* environment variable to an executable file that will be executed with suid root privileges. File */bin/bash* is copied to */tmp/rootshell*, and the root shell is executed.

Specifications for the *dump* utility are provided by SHIM. According to them, *dump* is allowed to make few system calls: *open* and *read* certain files, *fork*, and *connect*. Consequently, when this intrusion happens on a system that runs SHIM, but is not protected with ARB, the system administrator will get several alerts. There will be an alert about *dump* copying the shell executable to the */tmp* directory. Another key alert is issued when *dump* executes file */tmp/rootshell*. The last alert will be issued when the attacker uses the obtained root shell to issue the *open* and *write* system calls to the target. The target in our example will be the file *secring.gpg*, which contains the keys the GPG software uses for encryption/decryption.

Let us first show the relevant parts of the map before the intrusion begins (Fig. 2).

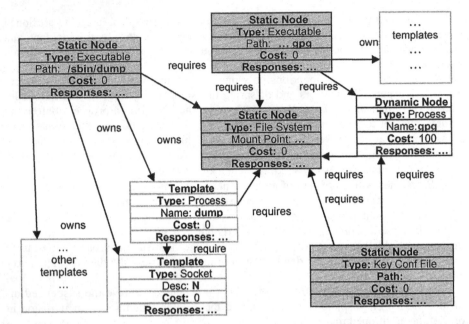

Fig. 2. The map of a part of a computer system before an intrusion. Only a few essential nodes are shown.

The map was built according to the type hierarchy on Fig. 1. According to the map, our only priority in the entire system is the *gpg* program that encrypts and decrypts email messages. However, we also put *dump* node on the map, since it has SHIM specifications.

Experiments with the ARB prototype showed that it takes a variable period of time for SHIM to issue an alert, and for ARB to receive it and process it. For certain test cases with favorable conditions, that period was short enough for ARB to freeze the entire attack right after the first alert. For test cases under the least favorable conditions, however, ARB completed the damage assessment procedure only after the attacker already had access to the root shell.

Regardless of the current conditions, our goal is to stop the intrusion and clean up after the actions that already happened. The system map for the worst case that has been observed is shown in Fig. 3.

According to the new map, four nodes are contaminated as the result of the intrusion. A node for */tmp/rootsh* appeared on the map because the file was involved in an illegal file copy by *cp*. However, the *cp* process itself is gone by the time ARB completed damage assessment, so it is not reflected on the map.

ARB starts building the response sequence addressing node by node, in arbitrary order. The *dump* process node is an issuer of an illegal *exec* system call, so ARB chooses the most efficient response – killing the process – since the value of nodes affected by the response is 0. The */tmp/rootsh* node was created as a result of an illegal *creat* system call, and it does not have any cost or dependencies. The matching response would be to remove the file. Finally, the response for the secring.gpg file is selected as follows. Several response alternatives apply to the file, including deleting it or restoring it from the backup. Deleting the file would certainly damage it. By using the map, we detect that the *gpg* process depends on the file; therefore, deleting the key file would damage the file and the process, and the cost of such response would equal to the sum of affected nodes – namely, 100 points. Another alternative with an activation criterion that matches a *write* system call is restoring the file from backup, with a cost of 0. We select the second alternative as the least expensive one. Another matching response action is "restart the corresponding service(s)," and it was inherited by the custom type "key configuration file" from general type "configuration file." By using the map, we determine the corresponding service to be the *gpg* in this case, and we restart it with a restored key file.

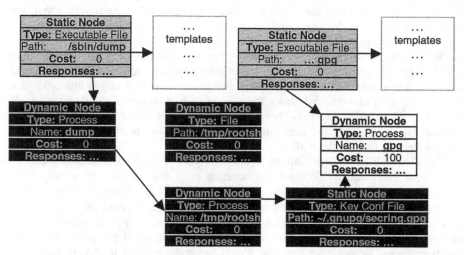

Fig. 3. The map of a part of a computer system after ARB has stopped an attack.

In this case, SHIM has not indicated that the content of the file has been read. Therefore, the response alternative "reissue all keys" does not apply, and we do not re-issue the keys.

3.6 Experience with ARB

The ARB prototype was tested for several well-known attack scripts. Work is in progress to extend it and test it with the broadest range of other intrusions. ARB can only be run on Linux kernel 2.2.14, since the current version of GSWTK relies on that kernel version, and the current version of SHIM relies heavily on GSWTK. As we mentioned before, the map in ARB is built manually for only a subset of all resources that really should be on the map.

The current version of ARB does not handle uncertainty in intrusions. It does, however, successfully freeze the set of test attacks, stop them, and respond to them. The attacks we handle include the two examples from this paper.

The prototype so far has forced us to re-design our original approach to automated response greatly, and posed several new problems, which were not obvious before. One such problem was the fact that at first we did not define when the damage assessment procedure is complete, and we can actually start deciding and carrying out a response. In order to resolve the issue, the concept of an incident was introduced in the prototype.

We currently continue to work on the prototype, and we expect promising results from the future work with ARB.

4 Future Work

4.1 Automating the Map Construction

First, since with SHIM all malicious actions that involve a map node can be expressed as Linux system calls, and the number of Linux system calls is relatively small, we can partially automate the generation of nodes' response lists. For a new type of a node, we list all applicable system calls that this node can make as an activation criteria. Then, we either borrow the corresponding response actions from the type above in the hierarchy, or ask the system user to define a response action and the damaged nodes. Then we construct a list of applicable system calls that target this type of a node as activation criteria, and obtain the corresponding response and damaged node information in a similar manner. Therefore, we can simplify the task of constructing response lists by guiding the user through the process and producing the output in some convenient format like XML.

Also, construction of the map itself and analysis of node dependencies can be mostly done automatically. When constructing a map, we can rely, for example, on the program installation package (i.e., Linux RedHat Package Manager information); the program's source code (when available); documentation (*man* pages); etc., for dependency information about opened files, sockets, pipes, inter-process communication, etc. We are also currently working on learning program dependency data from execution traces. Designing a tool that would assist a system's user with map construction presents an interesting implementation task.

4.2 Learning the Configuration

The problem of assigning the true costs, determining the actual relationships between the nodes, and testing the efficiency of ARB can be determined experimentally. As the next step of this work, the following experiment will be carried out.

One Linux system (*defender*) will be equipped with SHIM, ARB and several protected valuable services. Another system (*attacker*) will continuously generate attacks targeting every node of the *defender*. A third system (*referee*) will record the outcomes and help restoring the *defender* after successful attacks.

At first, the attacks will be run under supervision. As a measure of efficiency, uptime and performance of a certain service under attack will be measured with ARB protection, and compared to its uptime and performance under the same attack without the protection.

Once such a setup is implemented, it can be used to analyze the flaws in ARB response strategies to determine the "blame" for successful attacks. Furthermore, node costs and degrees/probabilities of relationships can be represented as weights in a neural network, and some machine learning algorithm (backpropagation, other gradient descent methods, etc.) can be applied to continuously improve the ARB setup, possibly with much of the supervision done by the *referee* system.

4.3 Other Directions

Introducing nodes of type CPU, or memory, or user may allow us to model and respond to denial-of-service attacks. We did not consider the topic in this work, but it seems promising; especially when the intrusion detection technology will provide us with ways to clearly identify denial-of-service attacks.

Storing information about past intrusions and incorporating that knowledge in response is also promising. For example, a large number of attacks in a small period of time might cause the system to take extra response measures targeted at preventing future intrusions rather than responding to ones already in effect. Also, we might design a set of more strict specifications for the privileged programs that would reflect a stricter system policy in response to a large number of intrusions. Another option would be to implement a "pre-emptive" mode as a wrapper in GSWTK: all system calls would be checked in advance, and not carried out if illegal. This mode of operation would cause a large overhead for every single system call; however, it might be useful when trying to counter particularly severe types of intrusions. Again, the cost of switching to such mode has to be carefully weighed.

Currently, our response model does not consider actions that partially restore a node, and it assumes that an action either damages resources, or does not. Considering actions that only partially restore resources and introducing a degree of damage also deserve consideration for further work.

Another interesting research direction would be to attempt to combine our host-based approach and network-oriented response mentioned in Section 1, to design a network-wide response system that possibly might be based on single host components, such as ARB, cooperating with each other to protect the entire network.

Finally, in our opinion, the most exciting future work option is combining a specification-based IDS, features of anomaly- and misuse-based IDS's and the requires/provides model of intrusions [14] to form basis for response decisions. With SHIM being a "low-level", system-call oriented IDS that ignores the intrusion as a whole, and focuses on individual constraint violations instead, it is able to catch violations that have never been seen before, and cannot be detected with signature-based detection systems; whereas signature-based systems can see farther ahead than SHIM, since they have a signature of the entire intrusion.

In a situation where we receive several SHIM alerts (which represent the first few steps of an intrusion), we can use our system map to calculate the capabilities of the attacker, describing them in JIGSAW [14], and also browse the signature database for all signatures that, at least partially, match the current intrusion. By using some historical data from an anomaly-based system we can determine probability of each intrusion path (signature), and initiate a game with the intruder. By winning such a game, we will be able to prevent complex intrusions instead of responding to the ones that are already in full progress.

5 Conclusion

In this work, we stated the problems associated with automated intrusion response, and began addressing them.

The system map and the resource hierarchy provide a basis for response. The damage assessment procedure and response selection that accounts for uncertainty produce the optimal response strategy.

The current implementation of these ideas – ARB – successfully responded to several host attacks. Work is being done to improve ARB and measure its efficiency and performance.

References

1. Alphatech: ALPHATECH Light Autonomic Defense System,
   http://www.alphatech.com/secondary/techpro/alads.html (last accessed June 30, 2003)
2. Amoroso, E: Intrusion Detection: an introduction to Internet surveillance, correlation, trace back, traps, and response, Intrusion.net Books, New Jersey. (1999)
3. Carver, C.A, Jr. and Pooch, U.W.: An Intrusion Response Taxonomy and its Role in Automatic Intrusion Response, Proceedings of the 2000 IEEE Workshop on Information Assurance and Security, United States Military Academy, West Point, NY. (6-7 June, 2000)
4. Fred Cohen & Associates, Deception for Protection,
   http://all.net/journal/deception/index.html (last accessed June 30, 2003)
5. Free Software Foundation, Inc., The GNU Privacy Guard, http://www.gnupg.org (last accessed June 30, 2003)
6. Ko, C.C.W.: Execution Monitoring of Security-Critical Programs in a Distributed System: A Specification-Based Approach, Ph.D. Thesis, Davis, CA. (August 1996)
7. Lee, W., Fan, W., Miller, M., Stolfo, S., Zadok, E.:Toward Cost-Sensitive Modeling for Intrusion Detection and Response, Journal of Computer Security, Vol. 10, Numbers 1,2 (2002)
8. Lewandowski, S., Van Hook, D., O'Leary, G., Haines, J., Rosse, L., SARA: Survivable Autonomic Response Architecture, DISCEX II'01, Anaheim, CA. (June 2001)
9. Network Associates Laboratories: Secure Execution Environments/Generic Software Wrappers for Security and Reliability,
   http://www.networkassociates.com/us/nailabs/research_projects/secure_execution/wrappers.asp (last accessed June 30, 2003)
10. Raiffa, H.: Decision Analysis: Introductory Lectures on Choices under Uncertainty, Addison-Wesley, Reading, MA. (1968)
11. RedHat, Inc.: Red Hat Security Advisory RHSA-2000:100-02,
    http://rhn.redhat.com/errata/RHSA-2000-100.html (last accessed June 30, 2003)
12. SecurityFocus, Mailing List: FOCUS-IDS,
    http://www.securityfocus.com/archive/96/310579/2003-02-03/2003-02-09/1 (last accessed June 30, 2003)
13. Staniford, S., Paxson, V., Weaver, N.: How to Own the Internet in Your Spare Time, Proceedings of the 11th USENIX Security Symposium (2002)
14. Templeton, S., Levitt, K.: A requires/provides model for computer attacks. In Proceedings of the New Security Paradigms Workshop, Cork, Ireland. (September 2000)
15. Tylutki, M.: Optimal Intrusion Recovery and Response Through Resource and Attack Modeling, Ph.D. Thesis, Davis, CA. (September 2003)
16. Toth, T., Kruegel, C.: Evaluating the impact of automated intrusion response mechanisms, 18th Annual Computer Security Applications Conference, Las Vegas, Nevada. (December 9-13, 2002)

Characterizing the Performance
of Network Intrusion Detection Sensors

Lambert Schaelicke, Thomas Slabach, Branden Moore, and Curt Freeland

Department of Computer Science and Engineering, University of Notre Dame,
384 Fitzpatrick Hall, Notre Dame, Indiana 46556, USA
Tel. +01 574-631-8320. Fax +01-574-631-9260.
{lambert,tslabach,bmoore,curt}@cse.nd.edu

Abstract. Network intrusion detection systems (NIDS) are becoming an important tool for protecting critical information and infrastructure. The quality of a NIDS is described by the percentage of true attacks detected combined with the number of false alerts. However, even a high-quality NIDS algorithm is not effective if its processing cost is too high, since the resulting loss of packets increases the probability that an attack is not detected. This study measures and compares two major components of the NIDS processing cost on a number of diverse systems to pinpoint performance bottlenecks and to determine the impact of operating system and architecture differences. Results show that even on moderate-speed networks, many systems are inadequate as NIDS platforms. Performance depends not only on the processor performance, but to a large extent also on the memory system. Recent trends in processor microarchitecture towards deep pipelines have a negative impact on the systems NIDS capabilities, and multiprocessor architectures usually do not lead to significant performance improvements. Overall, these results provide valuable guidelines for NIDS developers and adopters for choosing a suitable platform, and highlight the need to consider processing cost when developing and evaluating NIDS techniques.

1 Introduction

Network intrusion detection is becoming an increasingly important tool to detect and analyze security threats on an organization's network. It complements other network security techniques, such as firewalls, by providing information about the frequency and nature of attacks. A *network intrusion detection system* (NIDS) often consists of a sensor that analyzes every network packet on the segment under observation, and forwards packets deemed interesting together with an alert message to a backend system that stores them for further analysis and correlation with other events. The sensor is often implemented as a general-purpose computer system running network intrusion detection software. A separate system may host a database or similar software to provide long-term storage and additional analysis capabilities [2][5]. By relying on off-the-shelf hardware and software, this approach produces a cost-effective and flexible network intrusion detection system.

Commonly, the performance of a network intrusion detection system is characterized by the probability that an attack is detected in combination with the number of false alerts. However, equally important is the system's ability to process

G. Vigna, E. Jonsson, and C. Kruegel (Eds.): RAID 2003, LNCS 2820, pp. 155–172, 2003.

traffic at the maximum rate offered by the network with minimal packet loss. Significant packet loss can leave a number of attacks undetected and degrades the overall effectiveness of the system. A high-performance sensor is not only able to process packets at a higher rate, but can also apply more sophisticated detection techniques to reduce the number of false alerts. Unlike other networking components, NIDS hosts cannot rely on flow control mechanisms and acknowledgments to control the incoming data rate. Instead, the NIDS must be able to process packets at the maximum rate offered by the network segment. The work presented here focuses on the performance of the NIDS sensor, especially the hardware platform, since it is one of the most critical component in a network intrusion detection system and its deficiencies can propagate through the entire system.

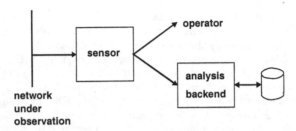

Fig. 1. Common NIDS Architecture

This paper presents a methodology to quantify the network intrusion detection capabilities of general-purpose computer systems. It is based on a set of experiments that test a platform's capabilities under different traffic characteristics while separating the NIDS processing load into distinct components. Combined, the observed behavior can be used to predict the performance of a NIDS on a network link. The results also provide valuable guidelines for researchers, designers and adopters of network intrusion detection systems.

A comparative analysis of a variety of systems running the Snort [18] rule-based NIDS sensor reveals that most general-purpose computer systems are inadequate as NIDS sensor platforms even for moderate-speed networks. The analysis also shows that no single factor alone determines the performance of a system, instead a number of architectural and system parameters such as operating system structure, main memory bandwidth and latency as well as the processor microarchitecture contribute to a system's suitability as a NIDS sensor platform. Furthermore, recent trends towards deep processor pipelines to maximize the CPU clock frequency, and towards small-scale multiprocessors do not significantly improve NIDS performance and may even have detrimental effects. Since in the past DRAM performance improvements have not kept pace with advances in processor and network speeds, NIDS sensors are likely to become an increasingly significant bottleneck in the future.

The following section describes the design and rationale of the experimental methodology in more detail. Section 3 first describes the measured platforms and then presents and discusses the results. Section 4 contrasts this work with related work in the areas of performance characterization, high-speed network intrusion detection and high-performance networking. Finally, section 5 draws conclusions and outlines future work.

2   Experimental Methodology

2.1   A Network IDS Performance Model

A network intrusion detection sensor inspects every packet on the network under observation in an effort to identify suspicious packets that are likely related to intrusion attempts. One common approach is based on user-defined rules that describe or fingerprint potentially harmful or interesting packets to the NIDS software. The intrusion detection algorithm then applies these rules or patterns to every packet and forwards any packet with a positive match, together with an alert message, to the analysis backend [18].

The processing load exerted by this algorithm depends on the characteristics of the rules as well as on the network traffic. Rules generally fall into one of two categories, depending on whether they apply to the packet header or the payload. *Header rules* inspect the packet header in an attempt to detect specific combinations of features, such as the source and destination address, port numbers, checksums or sequence numbers. *Payload rules* attempt to match a specific byte sequence in a packet's payload. NIDS rules may also combine header and payload specific match conditions. Since header size is generally fixed, the processing cost of applying header rules is nearly constant for each packet regardless of actual packet size, while the cost of payload rules scales with the packet size.

Real network traffic, on the other hand, is comprised of packets of different sizes. Small packets involve a larger relative overhead, as they carry less payload per header than larger packets. While applications wishing to maximize effective bandwidth generally utilize large packets, an effective NIDS must be able to handle packets of any size.

The two different classes of NIDS rules lead to two separate trends in the sustained performance of an NIDS platform. The analysis of traffic consisting of small packets is dominated by the constant cost of header rules, while for larger packets the cost of payload analysis begins to dominate. On a network segment of a fixed capacity, the number of packets transferred per second is inversely proportional to the packet size. For this reason header rules exhibit the highest processing load for small packets. On the other hand, the relative header overhead decreases with larger packet sizes, and thus the cost of payload rules scales with packet size.

In addition to the NIDS processing cost, regardless of the type of rule applied, each packet incurs processing cost due to interrupt and system call handling and related protocol processing, as well as the memory copy involved when reading packets into user space. Similar to the two classes of NIDS rules, interrupt and protocol cost is largely constant across packets, while the memory copy cost scales with the packet size. It should be noted however, that packets on most NIDS platforms do not traverse the complete network protocol stack. Since the NIDS software inspects packet headers as well as the payload, packets are usually read from the raw network device before they would normally enter the TCP/IP protocol stack. Internally however, the NIDS software may replicate some of the protocol stack functionality, as it inspects both the IP header and the encapsulated higher-level protocol header.

2.2 Measurements

To comprehensively describe the performance envelope of a network IDS platform, measurements are performed for four different packet payload sizes: 64 bytes, 512 bytes, 1000 bytes, and 1452 bytes, thus covering the range from minimum to maximum size packets on Ethernet networks. Separate experiments are performed for header rules and payload rules. This separation allows one to attribute observed bottlenecks to the particular type of rules.

Network traffic is generated between a pair of hosts by the public-domain TTCP utility. TTCP transmits a specified amount of data between a server and client over a TCP connection. The traffic generation hosts are connected by a 100 Mbit per second full-duplex Ethernet segment with a half-duplex tap to send a copy of every data packet of the TTCP conversation to a sensor platform running the Snort network intrusion detection software. The sending hosts are able to nearly saturate the 100 Mbit per second network link with an effective bandwidth of over 92 Mbit per second.

To precisely determine the processing cost of NIDS rules, the number of NIDS rules is increased until the number of packets reported by the intrusion detection software is less than the actual number of packets sent, thus indicating that packets are being dropped by the NIDS platform. Each header rule is unique to eliminate the possibility of any optimization of the pattern matching engine, but all rules are of identical overall structure and incur identical cost. The payload rules used here scan the entire packet payload for a matching string. All rules are designed such that no rule matches the observed packet stream and that no alerts are generated, since in most NIDS deployments attacks are the exception rather than the norm. This design ensures that all rules are applied to every packet. If a rule triggers an alert, an intrusion detection system may skip the remaining rules, but generating and forwarding the alert incurs additional cost that is in many cases comparable to or exceed the cost of the remaining rules.

Experiments are run for 15 seconds on otherwise idle systems and are repeated multiple times to minimize the impact of measurement error. The total number of rules that a platform is able to support is a measure of the platform's NIDS capabilities.

The approach of varying the number of rules instead of the network traffic rate was chosen because it more closely corresponds to the usage of intrusion detection systems in the field, where administrators have little control over the packet rate and bandwidth on a network, but can adjust the number of rules. Overall, these experiments are modeled after realistic NIDS setups and thus provide meaningful insights and recommendations for users of intrusion detection systems.

While these experiments use one specific network intrusion detection system, the approach of decomposing NIDS cost into constant and payload-dependent components makes most conclusions also applicable to other NIDS software that relies on pattern matching techniques. Nearly any system receiving network traffic incurs a constant per-packet cost from interrupt handling and protocol processing, whether it is done inside the kernel or by the NIDS software. In addition, in most cases inspection of the packet payload incurs cost that scales with the packet size. Advances in pattern matching algorithms and other optimization techniques can reduce the cost of signature-based intrusion detection and may also change the relationship between the number of rules and the per-packet and per-byte cost. On the other hand, in the experiments presented here over 45 percent of the CPU time was spent inside the operating system handling interrupts and system calls. This portion of the NIDS processing cost is independent of the particular NIDS algorithm employed by the system. Consequently, conclusions drawn from these experiment concerning a system's sutability as an NIDS platform are applicable to other NIDS systems and provide meaningful insights for designers and users of network intrusion detection systems.

Figure 2 shows a plot of the percentage of dropped packets as a function of the number of payload rules for a 1.2 Ghz Pentium-3 system running Snort 1.9.1. As of this writing, Snort is distributed with a set of over 1000 rules of different classes [22].

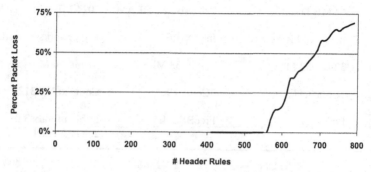

Fig. 2: Dropped Packets versus Number of Header Rules (Pentium-3 / 1200 Mhz, 512 byte packets)

This example demonstrates that for small numbers of rules, nearly no packets are lost, but when the number of rules exceeds the maximum processing capability of the system the number of dropped packets increases drastically. The magnitude of the increase in lost packets underlines the need to understand performance limitations of general-purpose systems when used as NIDS platforms. The results shown in the following section are based on the maximum number of rules supported by a platform with a packet loss of less than 2.5 percent.

2.3   Experimental Systems

The set of experiments described above is performed on six IA-32-based systems of diverse processing capabilities and configurations. Table 1 summarizes the relevant configuration parameters.

These platforms cover a wide range of system architectures and capabilities and can thus provide insight into the contribution of various system characteristics towards the observed NIDS performance. While a number of parameters vary considerably between test platforms, the NIDS software and instruction set remain fixed to allow a meaningful comparison. All systems run Snort 1.9 with libpcap 0.7.1.

The results presented in the following sections compare different subsets of these systems to provide insight into the contribution of system architecture and configurations on the NIDS capabilities of a platform.

Table 1. Test System Configuration

	PP-180	**P3-600**	**P3-800**
Processor	PentiumPro/MMX 180 Mhz	Pentium III 600 Mhz	Pentium III 800 Mhz single or dual processor
L-1 Cache	8 kByte	16 kByte	16 kByte
L-2 Cache	256 kByte	256 kByte	256 kByte
System Bus	60 Mhz	100 Mhz	133 Mhz
Memory	64 MB DRAM	128 MByte SDRAM	1024 MByte SDRAM
Chipset	Intel 440 FX PCIset	Intel 810E	Serverworks ServerSet III LE
PCI Bus	32-bit, 33 Mhz	32-bit, 33 Mhz	64-bit, 66 Mhz
NIC	3Com 3c905	3Com 3c905	Compaq NC 3123
OS	FreeBSD 4.5	FreeBSD 4.5	Debian Linux 3.0 2.4.19 Kernel

	P3-1200	**P4-1800**	**P4-2400**
Processor	Celeron 1.2 Ghz	Pentium 4 1.8 Ghz	Dual Pentium 4 Xeon 2.4 Ghz with Hyperthreading
L-1 Cache	16 kByte	12/8 kByte	12/8 kByte
L-2 Cache	256 kByte	256 kByte	512 kByte
System Bus	100 Mhz	400 Mhz	400 Mhz
Memory	128 MByte SDRAM	128 MByte SDRAM	1024 MByte DDR SDRAM
Chipset	Serverworks ServerSet III LE	Intel 845	Serverworks ServerSet GC-HE
PCI Bus	64-bit, 66 Mhz	32-bit, 33 Mhz	64-bit, 66 Mhz
NIC	Compaq NC 7760	3Com 3c905	Compaq NC3163
OS	FreeBSD 4.5 or Debian Linux 3.0 2.4.19 Kernel	FreeBSD 4.5	Debian Linux 3.0 2.4.19 Kernel

3   Results

3.1   Overall Comparison

Table 2 summarizes the maximum number of header rules supported by each of the platforms tested. Increasing the number of rules beyond these values leads to significant packet loss which negatively impacts an intrusion detection system's ability to detect attacks.

Table 2. Maximum Number of Header Rules Supported by each System

System	Packet Payload Size (bytes)			
	64	512	1000	1452
PPro / 180	0	0	43	109
P-3 / 600	0	209	321	362
P-3 / 800	0	378	590	693
P-3 / 1200	101	560	667	722
P-4 / 1800	0	251	291	328
P-4 / 2400	189	472	507	543

Overall, the results lead to two significant conclusions. First, most of the general-purpose systems tested appear inadequate to serve as a NIDS platform, especially when considering that the Snort 1.9.1 distribution includes over 1000 rules of various classes. Only two systems are able to process network traffic consisting of minimum-size packets on a saturated 100 Mbit per second network. While this scenario is unlikely under normal network conditions, occasional bursts of short packets can still overwhelm the intrusion detection system. Potential intruders can exploit such weakness by hiding attacks in a large number of short packets. Since these experiments keep the network bandwidth constant, small packets result in a significantly higher packet rate and thus fewer rules can be applied on the same platform.

Second, a platform's NIDS capabilities are not directly related to the microprocessor alone, but are also affected by other system parameters. Hence, further evaluation and comparison is performed in the later sections to uncover the sources of performance bottlenecks and deficiencies.

Table 3 summarizes the maximum number of payload rules supported by the same set of test platforms. The total number of payload rules is notably smaller than the maximum number of header rules that the same platform can support. Unlike header rules, payload rules search the entire data portion of a packet for a matching pattern. This sequential scan is significantly more expensive than a test of the fixed-size packet header. In addition, header rules check for a match at exactly one known location in the packet header, while payload rules may be required to search for a sequence of bytes anywhere in the packet body.

Table 3. Maximum Number of Payload Rules Supported by each System

System	Packet Payload Size (bytes)			
	64	512	1000	1452
PPro / 180	0	0	3	5
P-3 / 600	0	21	33	37
P-3 / 800	0	38	50	57
P-3 / 1200	27	71	88	95
P-4 / 1800	0	64	87	97
P-4 / 2400	94	140	191	217

However, generally the same conclusions hold for these experiments. General-purpose systems are in many cases not able to perform any significant processing of packets on a fully-saturated network link. Furthermore, CPU performance alone is not a sufficient indicator of a systems NIDS capabilities. To gain a better understanding of various bottlenecks in these platforms, the later sections compare different subsets of systems.

3.2   Normalized Performance

In the experiments described above, the total network bandwidth is constant across the different packet sizes. Consequently, tests with small packets produce a higher packet rate than tests with larger packets. On the other hand, header rules are expected to incur a constant cost regardless of the packet size, and even payload rules should incur interrupt costs that are independent of the total packet size. To investigate the processing costs independently of the packet rate, the graphs in Figure 3 show the product of rules and packets per second for constant-cost header processing, and the product of the number of rules and the data rate for payload processing.

The first graph plots the product of the number of header rules and the packet rate over the four different packet sizes for all systems tested. Given that header rules exert a constant processing load, the product of the packet rate and rule count is expected to be approximately constant. The graph shows however that for most systems 512-byte packets are the least expensive to process. For smaller packets, performance often drops sharply due to the excessive interrupt rates. In these tests, the fully-saturated 100 Mbit per second Ethernet link transfers approximately 64000 64-byte packets per second.

Given an interrupt cost of several tens of microseconds, CPU utilization from interrupt handling alone can approach a significant percentage of total CPU time. Furthermore, interrupt handling interferes with application processing by evicting cache and translation lookaside buffer (TLB) entries, and more frequent interrupts increase the pressure on the caches and TLBs.

Header Rule Cost

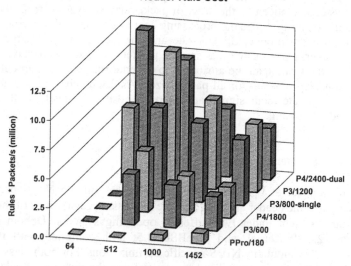

Payload Rule Cost

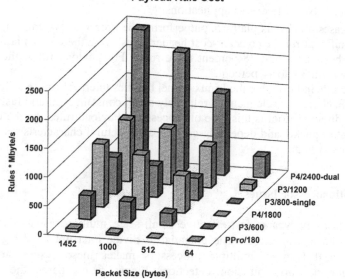

Fig. 3: Normalized Rule Processing Cost

Larger packets are also slightly more expensive, due to the packet copy operation in the read() system call. Even though header rules do not inspect the packet payload, the entire packet is copied from kernel into user space. For larger packets, this operation becomes more expensive.

The second graph shows the product of payload rules and data rate over packet size for all systems. Notice that the order of packet size is reversed from the previous graph to improve clarity. Since the processing cost of payload rules is proportional to the payload size, the product of data rate and number of rules is expected to be constant. However, results show that smaller packets are more expensive than large packets. This effect can again be attributed to the interrupt and system call handling cost which is nearly constant for all packet sizes. As discussed earlier, small packets arriving at a high rate incur significant interrupt costs, leaving less CPU time for actual payload processing.

3.3   Operating System Sensitivity

To gauge the impact of operating system differences on the NIDS performance, Figure 4 compares the header and payload rule processing capabilities of the same 1.2 Ghz Pentium-3 system under two different operating systems: Debian Linux 3.0 based on the 2.4.19 Kernel, and FreeBSD 4.5, both compiled with the default configuration and without any NIDS-specific optimizations. For both classes of rules, processing capabilities are normalized by multiplying the number of rules with the packet rate and data rate respectively, as shown in the previous section. The Linux and FreeBSD operating systems were chosen because both are widely used as NIDS platforms since they are freely available, well understood and are proven stable platforms for network-intensive applications.

In both cases, the Linux platform outperforms the FreeBSD system. The difference is most significant for the constant-cost header rules, were the Linux platform is able to support between 5 and 38 percent more rules. For payload rules, the difference ranges only from 3.4 to 14 percent.

These results indicate that the Linux kernel handles interrupts more efficiently than FreeBSD. Each header rule incurs a relatively small constant cost, and faster interrupt processing directly benefits this type of processing. Payload rules, on the other hand, scan the entire packet and depend largely on architectural characteristics rather than the operating system.

3.4   Multiprocessor Issues

Over the past few years, cost-effective small-scale multiprocessors have become available from many sources. The potential to divide interrupt handling and NIDS processing cost between multiple processors makes these system an attractive platform for network intrusion detection. Figure 5 compares the normalized processing capabilities of the same system with one and two processors. The 800 Mhz platform was selected because it supports a choice of one or two processors. Furthermore, its NIDS capabilities are close to that of the best-performing system, hence the conclusions apply to other current high-end systems.

For header processing, the dual-CPU system performs significantly better than a single-CPU system on minimum-size packets. Even though the Linux process scheduler does not support the assignment of a process to a particular CPU, it appears that the interrupt handling is effectively off-loaded to the second processor. In fact, the dual-processor system is able to apply 51 header rules to this traffic whereas the single-CPU system is completely saturated and does not support any rules at all. For 512-byte packets, the dual-processor system outperforms the single-CPU host by approximately 16 percent.

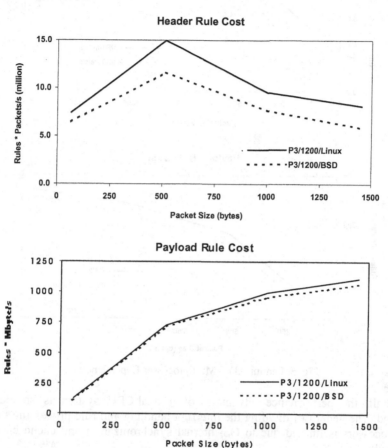

Fig. 4. Pentium-3 / 1200 OS Dependencies

For large packets, on the other hand, the additional processor offers a smaller performance improvement of 7.6 percent. For this type of traffic, packets arrive at a slow enough rate that interrupt handling is not a significant source of processing load. However, if interrupts are handled by one CPU and the NIDS software executes on the other, the sharing of packet buffers leads to cache-coherency traffic between the CPUs, slowing down memory requests. In addition, synchronization inside the kernel between the interrupt and system call handler imposes limits on the speedup.

For payload processing, a similar trend can be observed, with the benefit of a second CPU ranging from 5 to 15 percent. Again, for small packets the interrupt rate is sufficiently high that offloading it to the second processor improves performance, but for larger packets the coherency traffic counteracts this effect.

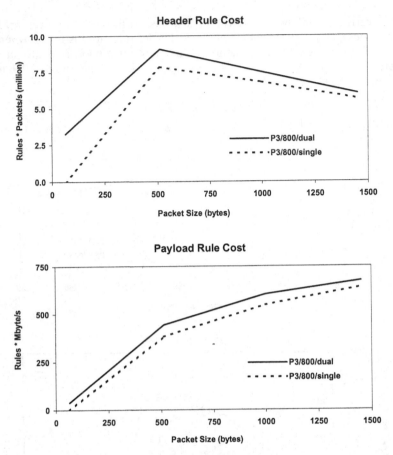

Fig. 5. Pentium-3 / 8 Multiprocessor Dependencies

Overall, the performance advantage of a dual-CPU system is smaller than expected. The benefit of dividing the interrupt handling and rule processing between two processors is limited due to OS-internal synchronization and cache coherency overhead.

3.5   Sensitivity to Architectural Parameters

This section presents comparative results for the Pentium-3/600, Pentium-3/1200, Pentium-4/1800 and dual-Pentium-4/2400 systems. By eliminating operating system dependencies, this comparison provides insight into the contribution of various architectural parameters on overall NIDS performance.

In addition to the configuration parameters available from public documentation, several system parameters are measured using LMbench [24]. Table 4 summarizes processor clock speed, memory hierarchy performance, system call latencies and peak I/O bus performance, and also lists the observed NIDS sensor performance of each platform. In addition, the three rightmost columns show the relative improvement of each parameter compared to the baseline Pentium-3/600 system.

Memory latency is measured by LMbench through a sequence of dependent load instructions, reported results are thus true load-to-use latencies observed by programs. Bandwidth is measured using the system's native 'memcpy' routine. It is reported here because part of the NIDS cost stems from a memory copy operation between kernel and user space.

System call latency is measured via the 'getpid' system call. In the measured systems, the code path involved in system calls and external interrupts is identical except for the actual handler function, and microprocessors use the same mechanisms to handle interrupts and software traps, hence system call latencies are a good indication of a system's interrupt performance as well. Generally, reading a network packet from the raw device involves one system call and at least one network interrupt. Unfortunately, LMbench does not measure I/O bus performance. To give an indication of the systems PCI bus capabilities, peak performance is reported here.

For both header and payload processing, the Pentium-3/1.2 Ghz system shows a speedup over the baseline 600 Mhz Pentium-3 platform that exceeds the CPU clock frequency improvement alone. This effect can be attributed to advances in the memory and I/O subsystem. Cache latency and copy bandwidth as well as I/O bus bandwidth show disproportional improvements. The system call latency measurement indicates that the faster memory system leads to significantly faster system call and interrupt handling. The 1.8 Ghz Pentium-4 system shows only moderate improvements over the baseline system, despite the fact that it runs at a three times higher processor clock rate and is based on a more modern microarchitecture. Only the level-1 cache and main memory bandwidth and the level-1 cache latency are improved, while other memory systems aspects exhibit lower performance than the baseline system. Most interestingly, system call latencies are 33 percent higher than on the baseline system. The Pentium-4 system features a very deep pipeline to achieve high clock rates [10]. While this microarchitecture benefits compute-intensive codes with regular structures, interrupt handling and other operating system codes perform poorly on such systems due to expensive pipeline flushes on branch mispredictions and other serialization conditions. These disadvantages lead to poor performance on header processing for this Pentium-4 system. Only for payload processing can the high clock frequency and slightly higher memory bandwidth compensate for the effects of the deep pipeline.

The 2.4 Ghz Pentium-4 Xeon system shows similarly small improvements for header processing, but outperforms all other systems for payload processing. While the irregular and branch-intensive header processing is penalized by the deep processor pipeline, the significantly improved memory subsystem results in high payload processing performance. The network adapter transfers incoming packets into main memory via DMA, invalidating previously cached copies of the receive buffers in the CPU cache. Subsequently, most references to the packet contents incur cache misses and are satisfied from main memory. Consequently, the high-bandwidth main memory system in combination with the processors high clock frequency lead to these significant payload processing improvements. As shown previously, the dual-processor architecture has a relatively small impact on NIDS performance.

The 2.4 Ghz Pentium-4 Xeon processor in the dual-CPU system implements hyperthreading, a form of simultaneous multithreading [13]. This architectural technique implements two logical processors on one chip to improve system throughout at a small cost increase. To the operating system, the logical processors appear as independent CPUs that can execute different processes and handle interrupts. However, since the logical processors share most execution resources including the caches and the system interface, the performance improvement from the second logical processor is significantly smaller than that of a traditional multiprocessor. Consequently, the contribution of hyperthreading to the NIDS capabilities of the 2.4 Ghz Pentium-4 Xeon system is relatively minor.

Table 4 Architectural Parameters and Observed Performance

	Absolute values				Improvement over P3/600		
	P3/600	P3/1.2	P4/1.8	P4/2.4	P3/1.2	P4/1.8	P4/2.4
Processor clock (Mhz)	600	1200	1800	2400	2.0	3.0	4.0
L1 cache latency (ns)	5	2	1.18	0.83	2.50	4.24	6.02
L2 cache latency (ns)	11	6	10.9	7.65	1.83	1.01	1.44
DRAM latency (ns)	150	104	180	165	1.44	0.83	0.91
L1 cache copy BW (MB/s)	5000	10490	5142	7100	2.10	1.03	1.42
L2 cache copy BW (MB/s)	1192	3550	1050	1150	2.98	0.88	0.96
DRAM copy BW (MB/s)	150	189	240	560	1.26	1.60	3.73
System call latency (ns)	719	268	953	747	2.68	0.75	0.96
I/O bus BW (MB/s)	132	528	132	528	4.00	1.00	4.00
Header rules (512 byte)	209	560	251	472	2.68	1.20	2.26
Header rules (1452 byte)	362	722	328	543	1.99	0.91	1.50
Payload rules (512 byte)	21	71	64	140	3.38	3.05	6.67
Payload rules (1452 byte)	37	95	97	217	2.57	2.62	5.86

Unfortunately, the impact of the I/O bus on overall NIDS performance is not clear from these experiments. While the two fastest systems tested both feature a 66 Mhz 64-bit PCI bus, even a slower 33 Mhz 32-bit bus can easily sustain the moderate data rate of the testbed network. A fully saturated 100 Mbit per second Ethernet link transfers at most 12.5 Mbytes per second, including packet headers. Most standard I/O buses do not pose a bottleneck for this transfer rate. However, in addition to writing network packets into main memory, the I/O bus is also used by the processor to access control registers during interrupt handling. The faster clock rate on the high-end I/O bus leads to a slightly improved control-register read latency that benefits interrupt costs somewhat.

4   Related Work

The work presented in this paper is one of the first efforts to systematically study the performance requirements of network IDS sensors across a variety of platforms, and to attribute bottlenecks to specific system features.

Previous work on evaluating intrusion detection systems has often focused on testing the quality of an IDS. The most prominent effort to this end is the DARPA IDS evaluation carried out at MIT Lincoln Labs [9]. Reports on the design of the test traffic and the rational behind it provide a valuable resource for others attempting a similar effort. However, as the evaluation is geared towards comparing a wide variety of systems, it is unable to provide insights into the sources of performance bottlenecks. Industrial whitepapers can add valuable practical experience testing and evaluating intrusion detection systems, but are by their nature much more limited in scope [6][17].

Puketza et al. describe an integrated approach to NIDS evaluation that combines quality and performance metrics [16]. It is designed to compare different intrusion detection systems in terms of the number of alerts generated under a variety of loads, including overload situations intended to subvert the NIDS. As such, the approach takes the capabilities of the NIDS platform into account and can be used to compare a variety of platforms running the same NIDS software.

This work, in contrast, is mainly concerned with the throughput of a network IDS sensor platform and is designed to give insights into the sources of inadequacies. In addition, the experimental setup used here is intentionally kept simple to make the methodology widely applicable.

Several proposed network IDS approaches have been tested and evaluated with respect to their performance [12][14][20]. However, the experiments are usually restricted to test the peak performance of a system, without addressing sources of bottlenecks, their relationship to architectural parameters or their scalability across different platforms.

Previous work in high-performance networking has characterized the bottlenecks of various systems and proposed solutions either in the form of hardware support or protocol stack optimizations [1][3][8][23]. Conclusions largely agree with results presented here, emphasizing the cost of interrupt handling and data copying. However, since NIDS systems are not actively participating in network communications, many proposed optimizations such as larger frame sizes are not applicable to NIDS platforms. Furthermore, to remain general, previous studies usually do not consider the applications impact on overall performance, whereas this work studies the combined performance requirements of the device driver, operating system and network intrusion detection software.

5   Conclusions and Future Work

This paper presents a simple methodology to measure and characterize the performance of general-purpose systems when used as network intrusion detection sensors. The methodology constructs a performance profile by measuring the cost of the two main classes of NIDS processing for different packet sizes. By varying the number of rules applied to each packet, the peak performance of a given configuration can be established without the need to control the packet rate or bandwidth of the test traffic. The performance profile obtained in this way can be used to predict the performance of a computer system as network IDS sensor.

A comparative study of six distinct systems shows that general-purpose computers are generally inadequate to act as sensors even on moderate-speed networks. On a nearly saturated 100 Mbit per second network link, even the best-performing system can only support a maximum of 720 header rules without losing packets. For larger numbers of rules, a significant percentage of packets are dropped, thus degrading the NIDS effectiveness in detecting security breaches. For minimum-size packets, only two of the six systems are able to perform any significant processing. As a point of comparison, the default rule file supplied with the Snort 1.9 distribution contains over 1000 rules. These results highlight the need to understand the processing capabilities of network intrusion detection platforms and to consider the processing cost of NIDS algorithms in addition to their quality.

In addition, results indicate that no single architectural parameter alone determines network IDS capabilities, instead a combination of factors contributes to the sustained performance. In particular, processor speed is not a suitable predictor of NIDS performance, as demonstrated by a nominally slower Pentium-3 system outperforming a Pentium-4 system with higher clock frequency. Memory bandwidth and latency is the most significant contributor to the sustainable throughput [19]. Furthermore, a comparison between two popular operating systems reveals that the more efficient interrupt handling by the Linux kernel leads to non-negligible performance improvements. Multiprocessor architectures, on the other hand, offer a relatively small advantage for network intrusion detection. While an additional processor is able to offload the interrupt processing, the kernel synchronization and cache coherency traffic resulting from shared buffers limits the benefit. Current trends in processor, memory and network performance improvements show that main memory is becoming an increasingly important bottleneck for overall system performance. Since network intrusion detection systems are largely memory-bound, NIDS sensor performance will likely remain critical in the future.

Given these results, optimization of rule-based intrusion detection systems remains an important concern. Advances in pattern matching algorithms [4], decision-tree based clustering of rules [11] and compilation of rules into optimized detection engines [7] reduce the number of comparisons needed as well as the cost of individual comparisons, but may in the process increase the memory footprint of the signature matching engine. Given that NIDS performance is shown to be memory-bound, improving the cache behavior of pattern matching techniques is a promising approach. Minimizing the memory requirements, for instance through blocking or tiling of internal data structures may let processors keep a larger portion of frequently accessed data in the cache, thus improving overall performance. Other promising approaches to improve NIDS throughput include the distribution of network traffic over a number of sensors using a loadbalancer, pipelining the processing of packets through a series of NIDS processes and the distribution of different rules over multiple sensors. However, given the large percentage of CPU time spent inside the operating system kernel, optimizations of the NIDS software alone have limited benefit. Instead, effective optimizations should include the interface between the intrusion detection software the the operating system.

As the work presented here focuses on rule-based NIDS sensors using signature matching, future work involves extending the methodology to other network IDS approaches such as protocol-based filtering and analysis [15]. In addition, on high-speed networks, even highly effective sensors may produce alerts at a rate greater than the analysis backend can absorb. Consequently, it is important that the performance of the analysis components of network intrusion detection systems be accurately quantified as well.

The authors wish to thank Frank Irving and Matthew Liszewski for their contributions to carrying out the numerous experiments, and Aaron Striegel and the anonymous reviewers for the encouraging and helpful comments. This work was in part supported by a Faculty Research Grant from the University of Notre Dame Graduate School. This material is based upon work supported by the National Science Foundation under Grant No. 0231535. Any opinions, findings, and conclusions or recommendations expressed in this material are those of the authors and do not necessarily reflect the views of the National Science Foundation.

References

1. D. Banks and M. Prudence, "A High-performance Network Architecture for a PA-RISC Workstation", *IEEE Journal on Selected Areas in Communications*, vol. 11, no. 2, Feb. 1993, pp. 191-202.
2. S. Cheung, R. Crawford, M. Dilger, J. Frank, J. Hoagland, K. Levitt, S. Staniford-Chen, R. Yip, and D. Zerkle, *"The Design of GrIDS: A Graph-Based Intrusion Detection System"*, tech. report CSE-99-02, Computer Science Dept., Univ. of California Davis, Calif., 1999.
3. D. Clark, V. Jacobson, J, Romkey, and M. Salwen, "An Analysis of TCP Processing Overhead", *IEEE Communications Magazine*, vol. 27, June 1989, pp. 23-29.
4. J. Coit, S. Staniford, J. McAlerney, "Towards Faster String Matching for Intrusion Detection or Exceeding the Speed of Snort", *Proc. DARPA Information Survivability Conference and Exposition (DISCEX II '02)*, IEEE CS Press, Los Alamitos, Calif., 2001, pp. 367-373.
5. R. Danyliw, *"ACID: Analysis Console for Intrusion Databases"*, http://acidlab.sourceforge.net, 2001.
6. S. Edwards, *"Vulnerabilities of Network Intrusion Detection Systems: Realizing and Overcoming the Risks. The Case for Flow Mirroring"*, whitepaper, Top Layer Networks, Inc., 2002.
7. S. Egorov, G. Savchuk, *"SNORTRAN: An Optimizing Compiler for Snort Rules"*, whitepaper, Fidelis Security Systems, Inc.
8. A. Gallatin, J. Chase, and K. Yocum, "Trapeze/IP: TCP/IP at Near-Gigabit Speeds", *Proc. 1999 Usenix Technical Conference*, Usenix Assoc., Berkeley, Calif., 1999, pp. 109-120.
9. J. Haines, R. Lippmann, D. Fried, J. Korba, and K. Das, *"1999 DARPA Intrusion Detection System Evaluation: Design and Procedures"*, tech. report 1062, MIT Lincoln Laboratory Technical Report, Boston, Mass., 2001.
10. G. Hinton et al, *"The Microarchitecture of the Pentium 4 Processor,"* Intel Technology Journal, Q1 2001.

11. C. Kruegel and T. Toth, *"Automatic Rule Clustering for improved, signature-based Intrusion Detection,"* tech. report, Distributed Systems Group, Technical Univ. Vienna, Austria.
12. C. Kruegel, F. Valeur, G. Vigna and R. Kemmerer, "Stateful Intrusion Detection for High-Speed Networks," *Proc. IEEE Symposium Security and Privacy*, IEEE Computer Society Press, Calif., 2002.
13. D. Marr et al., "Hyper-Threading Technology Architecture and Microarchitecture", Intel Technology Journal, vol. 6, no. 1, February 2002, pp. 4-15.
14. V. Paxson, "Bro: A System for Detecting Network Intruders in Real-Time," *Computer Networks*, vol. 31, no. 23-24, 1999, pp. 2435-2463.
15. *"Protocol Analysis vs. Pattern Matching,"* whitepaper, Network ICE, 2000.
16. N. Puketza, K. Zhang, M. Chung, B. Mukherjee, R. Olsson, "A Methodology for Testing Intrusion Detection Systems," *IEEE Transactions Software Engineering*, vol. 22, no. 10, 1996, pp. 719-729.
17. *M. Ranum, "Experiences Benchmarking Intrusion Detection Systems,"* whitepaper, Network Flight Recorder Security, Inc. , http://www.snort.org/docs/Benchmarking-IDS-NFR.pdf
18. M. Roesch, "Snort – Lightweight Intrusion Detection for Networks," *Proc. Usenix LISA '99 Conf.*, November 1999. http://www.snort.org/docs/lisapaper.txt
19. M. Rosenblum, E. Bugnion, S. Herrod, E. Witchel, and A. Gupta, "The Impact of Architectural Trends on Operating System Performance," Proc. 15th ACM Symp. Operating System Principles, ACM Press, New York, N.Y, 1995.
20. R. Sekar, Y. Guang, S. Verma, T. Shanbhag, "A High-Performance Network Intrusion Detection System," *Proc. 6th ACM Symp. Computer and Communication Security*, ACM Press, New York, N.Y., 1999.
21. *"Snort 2.0 - Detection Revisited,"* whitepaper, Sourcefire Network Security Inc, 2002.
22. Snort Rules for Version 1.9.x as of March 25, 2003. http://www.snort.org/dl/rules/snortrules-stable.tar.gz
23. P. Steenkiste, "A Systematic Approach to Host Interface Design for High-Speed Networks", *IEEE Computer*, vol. 27, no. 3, March 1994, pp. 47-57.
24. L. McVoy, C. Staelin, "lmbench: Portable Tools for Performance Analysis," *Proc. USENIX Ann. Technical Conference*, Usenix Assoc., Berkeley, Calif., 1998, pp. 279-294.

Using Decision Trees
to Improve Signature-Based Intrusion Detection[*]

Christopher Kruegel[1] and Thomas Toth[2]

[1] Reliable Software Group
University of California, Santa Barbara
chris@cs.ucsb.edu
[2] Distributed Systems Group
Technical University Vienna
ttoth@infosys.tuwien.ac.at

Abstract. Most deployed intrusion detection systems (IDSs) follow a signature-based approach where attacks are identified by matching each input event against predefined signatures that model malicious activity. This matching process accounts for the most resource intensive task of an IDS. Many systems perform the matching by comparing each input event to all rules sequentially. This is far from being optimal. Although sometimes *ad-hoc* optimizations are utilized, no general solution to this problem has been proposed so far.

This paper describes an approach where machine learning clustering techniques are applied to improve the matching process. Given a set of signatures (each dictating a number of constraints the input data must fulfill to trigger it) an algorithm generates a decision tree that is used to find malicious events using as few redundant comparisons as possible.

This general idea has been applied to a network-based IDS. In particular, a system has been implemented that replaces the detection engine of Snort [14, 16]. Experimental evaluation shows that the speed of the detection process has been significantly improved, even compared to Snort's recently released, fully revised detection engine.

Keywords: Signature-based Intrusion Detection, Machine Learning, Network Security

1 Introduction

Intrusion detection systems (IDSs) are security tools that are used to detect evidence of malicious activity which is targeted against the network and its resources. IDSs are traditionally classified as anomaly-based or signature-based. Signature-based systems are similar to virus scanners and look for known, suspicious patterns in their input data. Anomaly-based systems watch for deviations

---

[*] This work has been supported by the FWF (Fonds zur Förderung der wissenschaftlichen Forschung), under contract number P13731-MAT. The views expressed in this article are those of the authors and do not necessarily reflect the opinions or positions of the FWF.

G. Vigna, E. Jonsson, and C. Kruegel (Eds.): RAID 2003, LNCS 2820, pp. 173–191, 2003.
© Springer-Verlag Berlin Heidelberg 2003

of actual behavior from established profiles and classify all 'abnormal' activities as malicious.

The advantage of signature-based designs is the fact that they can identify attacks with an acceptable accuracy and they tend to produce fewer false alarms (i.e., classifying an action as malicious when in fact it is not) than their anomaly-based cousins. The systems are easier to implement and simpler to configure, especially in large production networks. As a consequence, nearly all commercial systems and most deployed installations use signature-based detection. Although anomaly-based variants offer the advantage of being able to find prior unknown intrusions, the costs of dealing with a large number of false alarms is often prohibitive.

Depending on their source of input data, IDSs can be classified as either network- or host-based. Network-based systems collect data from network traffic (e.g., packets from network interfaces in promiscuous mode) while host-based systems collect events at the operating system level, such as system calls, or at the application level. Host-based designs can collect high quality data directly from the affected system and are not influenced by encrypted network traffic. Nevertheless, they often seriously impact performance of the machines they are running on. Network-based IDS, on the other hand, can be set up in a non-intrusive manner without interfering with the existing infrastructure. In many cases, these characteristics make network-based IDS the preferred choice.

Although some vendors claim to have incorporated anomaly-based detection techniques into their system, the core detection of most intrusion detection systems is signature-based. Commercial IDSs like ISS RealSecure [13], Symantec's Intruder Alert/Net Prowler [19] or Cisco's IDS [2] offer a wide variety of different signatures and regular updates. Unfortunately, their engines are mostly undocumented. Academic designs like STAT [20] or Bro [10] and open-source tools like Snort [14] also follow a signature-based approach. They differ significantly in the way a signature (or rule) can be defined, ranging from single-line descriptions in Snort to complex script languages such as Bro or STATL [4]. The latter allows one expressing complete scenarios that consist of a number of related basic alerts in a certain sequence and therefore require that state is kept. Nevertheless, all systems require a component that produces basic alerts as a result of comparing the properties of an input element to the values defined by their rules. These basic alerts can then be combined as building blocks to describe the more complex scenarios.

Most systems perform the detection of basic alerts by comparing each input event to all rules sequentially. Some of the aforementioned programs utilize ad-hoc optimizations, but they require domain specific knowledge and are not optimal for different rule sets. Therefore, a general solution to this problem is needed. Our paper describes an approach that improves the matching process by introducing a decision tree which is derived directly from and tailored to the installed intrusion detection signatures by means of a clustering algorithm. By using decision trees for the detection process, it is possible to quickly determine all firing rules (i.e., rules that match an input element) with a minimal number of comparisons.

The paper is organized as follows. Section 2 discusses related work and describes current rule matching techniques. Section 3 and Section 4 present the idea of applying rule clustering and the creation of decision trees in detail. Section 5 explains how the comparison between an input element and a single feature value is performed. Section 6 shows the experimental results obtained with the improved system. Finally, in Section 7, we briefly conclude.

2 Related Work

The simplest technique for determining whether an input element matches a rule is to sequentially compare it to the constraints specified by each element of the rule set. Such an approach is utilized by STAT [20] or by SWATCH [18], the simple log file watchdog.

Consider a STAT (state transition analysis) scenario that consists of three states, one start state and two terminal states. In addition, consider that a transition connects the start state to each of the two terminal states (yielding a total of two transitions). Every transition represents a rule such that it has associated constraints that determine whether the transition should be taken or not, given a certain input element. In our simple scenario with two transitions leading from the start node to each terminal node, none, one or both transitions could be taken, depending on the input element. To decide which transitions are made, every input element is compared sequentially to all corresponding constraints. In addition, as STAT sensors keep track of multiple scenarios in parallel, an input element has to be compared to all constraints of all currently active scenarios. No parallelism is exploited and even when multiple transitions have constraints that are identical or that are mutual exclusive, no optimization is performed and multiple comparisons are carried out. The same is true for the much simpler SWATCH system. All installed regular expressions (i.e., SWATCH rules) are applied to every log file entry to determine suspicious instances.

Some systems attempt to improve this process using *ad-hoc* techniques, but these optimizations are hard-wired into the detection engine and are not flexibly tailored to the set of rules which is actually used. A straightforward optimization approach is to divide the rule set into groups according to some criteria. The idea is that rules that specify a number of identical constraints can be put together into the same group. During detection, the common constraints of a rule group need only be checked once. When the input element matches these constraints, each rule in the group has to be processed sequentially. When the constraints are not satisfied by the input element, the whole group can be skipped.

This technique is utilized by the original version of Snort [14], arguably the most deployed signature-based network intrusion detection tool. Snort builds a two-dimensional list structure from the input rules. One list consists of Rule Tree Nodes (RTNs), the other one of Option Tree Nodes (OTNs). The RTNs represent rule groups and store the values of the group's common rule constraints (the source and destination IP addresses and ports in this case). A list of OTNs is attached to each RTN – these lists represent the individual rules of each group and hold the additional constraints that are not checked by the group constraints of the corresponding RTN.

In theory, Snort's two-dimensional list structure could allow the length of the lists, and therefore the number of required checks, to grow proportional to the square root of the total number of rules. However, the distribution of RTNs and OTNs is very uneven. The 1092 TCP and 82 UDP rules that are shipped with Snort-1.8.7 and enabled by default are divided into groups as shown below in Table 1. The Maximum, Minimum and Average columns show the maximum, the minimum and the average number of rules that are associated with each rule group.

Table 1. Statistics - Snort Data Structures.

Protocol	# Groups	# Rules	Maximum	Minimum	Average
UDP	31	82	23	1	2.6
TCP	88	1092	728	1	12.4

For UDP, 31 different groups are created from only 82 rules and each group has only three rules associated with it on average. This requires every input packet to be checked at least against the common constraints of all 31 groups. For TCP, more than half of the rules (i.e., 728 out of 1092) are in the single group that holds signatures for incoming HTTP traffic. Therefore, each legitimate packet sent to a web server needs to be compared to at least 728 rules, lots of them requiring expensive string matching operations. As can be seen easily, the ad-hoc selection of source and destination addresses as well as ports provides some clustering of the rules, but it is far from optimal. According to our experience, the destination port and address are two discriminating features, while the source port seems to be less important. However, valuable features such as ICMP code/type or TCP flags are not used and are checked sequentially within each group.

The division of rules into groups with common constraints is also used for packet filters and firewalls. Similar to Snort, the OpenBSD packet filter [6] combines rules with identical address and port parameters into skip-lists, moving on when the test for common constraints fails.

With the introduction of Snort-2.0 [17] and its improved detection engine, the two-dimensional list structure and the strict sequential search within groups have been abandoned. The idea is to introduce more parallelism when checking rules, especially when searching the content of network packets for matching character strings. A rule optimizer attempts to partition the set of rules into smaller subsets which can then be searched in parallel.

The goal of the revised detection engine is similar to our decision trees in the sense that both systems attempt to partition the set of rules in smaller subsets where only a single subset has to be analyzed for each input element. The differences to our approach are the mechanism to select rule subsets and the extent of parallelism that is introduced. In Snort-2.0, rules are partitioned only based on at most two statically chosen constraints (source and destination port for TCP and UDP, type for ICMP packets). Within each group, a parallel search is only performed for content strings, while all other feature constraints are still evaluated sequentially. Our decision trees, on the other hand, dynamically pick the most discriminating features for a rule set and allow to perform parallel evaluation of every feature. This yields superior performance (as shown in Section 6), despite the fact that the detection engine of Snort-2.0 is heavily tailored to the Snort rule set (which has many similar rules that only specify different content strings – and the content string is the only feature that can be evaluated in parallel).

Another system that uses decision trees and data mining techniques to extract features from audit data to perform signature-based intrusion detection is presented in [7]. In contrast to our approach, however, they derive the decision tree and the signatures from the audit data while we assume an existing set of signature rules as the basis for our decision model.

3   Rule Clustering

The idea of rule clustering allows a signature-based intrusion detection system to minimize the number of comparisons that are necessary to determine rules that are triggered by a certain input data element.

We assume that a signature rule specifies required values for a set of features (or properties) of the input data. Each of these features has a type (e.g., integer, string) and a value domain. There are a fixed number of features $f_1..f_n$ and each rule may define values drawn from the respective value domain for an arbitrary subset of these properties. Whenever an input data element is analyzed, the actual values for all n features can be extracted and compared to the ones specified by the rules. Whenever a data item fulfills all constraints set by a rule, the corresponding signature is considered to *match* it.

A rule defines a constraint for a feature when it requires the feature of the data item to meet a certain specification. Notice that it is neither required for a rule to specify values for all features, nor that the specification is an equality relationship. It is possible, for example, that a signature requires a feature of type integer to be less than a constant or inside a certain interval.

The basic technique utilized to compare a data item with a set of rules is to consecutively check every defined feature of a rule against the input element and then move to the next one, eventually determining every matching signature.

As described above, a popular *ad-hoc* optimization is implemented by considering certain features more important or discriminating than others and by checking on a combination of those first before considering the rest. This technique, which is, for example, used by the original Snort and the OpenBSD packet filter, bases on domain specific knowledge and still requires a number of comparisons that is about linear to the rule set size. Unfortunately, novel attacks are discovered nearly on a daily basis and the number of needed signatures is increasing steadily. This problem is exacerbated by the fact that network and processor speeds are also improving, thereby raising the pressure on intrusion detection systems. Although Snort has been recently released with an improved detection engine that addresses some of these issues, its parallelization efforts are limited to searching strings in packet payloads and the discriminating features are chosen based on domain knowledge. This limits the general applicability of the solution and forfeits potential gains by processing all features in parallel.

Similar to the revised detection engine of Snort, we attempt to mitigate the performance problem by changing the comparison mechanism from a rule-to-rule to a feature-to-feature approach. Instead of dealing with each rule individually, all rules are combined in a large set and partitioned (or clustered) based on their specifications for the different features. By considering a single feature at a time, we partition all rules of a set into subsets. In this clustering process, all rules that specify identical values for this feature are put into the same subset. The clustering process is then performed recursively on all subsets until each subset contains only a single rule or there are no more features left to split the remaining rules into further subsets. In contrast to the Snort engine, our solution is applicable to different kinds of signature-based systems and not limited to input from the network. It requires no domain specific feature selection and is capable of performing parallel checks for all features.

4   Decision Tree

The subset structure obtained by the partitioning of the rule set can also be represented as a *decision tree*. Given this representation, the set that initially contains all rules can be considered as the tree's root node while its children are the direct subsets created by partitioning the rule set according to the first feature. Each subset is associated with a node in the tree. When a node contains more than one rule, these rules are subsequently partitioned and the node is labeled with the feature that has been used for this partitioning step. An arrow that leads from a node to its child is annotated with the value of the feature that is specified by all the rules in this child node. Every leaf node of the tree contains only a single rule or a number of rules that can not be distinguished by any feature. Rules are indistinguishable when they are identically with respect to all the features used for the clustering process.

Consider the following example with four rules and three features. A rule specifies a network packet from a certain source address to a certain destination address and destination port. The source and destination address features have the type IPv4 address while the destination port feature is of type short integer.

```
(#) Source Address --> Destination Address : Destination Port

(1) 192.168.0.1 --> 192.168.0.2 : 23
(2) 192.168.0.1 --> 192.168.0.3 : 23
(3) 192.168.0.1 --> 192.168.0.3 : 25
(4) 192.168.0.4 --> 192.168.0.5 : 80
```

A possible decision tree is shown in Figure 1. In order to create this tree, the rules have been partitioned on the basis of the three features, from left to right, starting with the source address. When the IDS attempts to find the matching rules for an input data item, the detection process commences at the root of the tree. The label of the node determines the next feature that needs to be examined. Depending on the actual value of that feature, the appropriate child node is selected (using the annotations of the arrows leading to all children). As the rule set has been partitioned by the respective feature, it is only necessary to continue detection at a single child node.

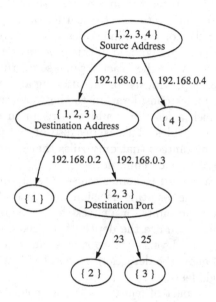

Fig. 1. Decision Tree.

When the detection process eventually terminates at a leaf node, all rules associated with this node are *potential matches*. However, it might still be necessary to check additional features. To be precise, all features that are specified by the potentially matching rules but that have not been previously used by the clustering process to partition any node on the path from the root to this leaf must be evaluated at this point. Consider Rule 1 in the leftmost leaf node in Figure 1. Both, source address and destination address have been used by the clustering process on the path between this node and the root, but not the destination port. When a packet which has been sent from 192.168.0.1 to 192.168.0.2 is evaluated as input element, the detection process eventually terminates at the leaf node with Rule 1. Although this rule becomes a potential match, it is still possible that the packet was directed to a different port than 23. Therefore, the destination port has to be checked additionally. Our implementation solves this problem by simply expanding the tree for all defined features that have not been used so far. This only requires the ability to further 'partition' a node with only one rule, a step that results in a single child node.

At any time, when the detection process cannot find a successor node with a specification that matches the actual value of the input element under consideration (i.e., an arrow with a proper annotation), there is no matching rule. This allows the matching process to exit immediately.

4.1 Decision Tree Construction

The decision tree is built in a top-down manner. At each non-leaf node, that is for every (sub)set of rules, one has to select a feature that is used for extending the tree (i.e., partitioning the corresponding rules). Obviously, features that are not defined by at least one rule are ignored in this process as a split would simply yield a single successor node with the exactly same set of rules. In addition, all features that have been used previously for partitioning at any node on the path from the node currently under consideration to the root are excluded as well. A split on the basis of such a feature would also result in only a single child node with exactly the same rules. This is because of the partitioning at the predecessor node, which guarantees that only rules that specify identical values for that feature are present at each child node.

The choice of the feature used to split a subset has an important impact on the shape and the depth of the resulting decision tree. As each node on the path from the root to a leaf node accounts for a check that is required for every input element, it is important to minimize the depth of the decision tree. An optimal tree would consist of only two levels - the root node and leaves, each with only a single rule. This would allow the detection process to identify a matching rule by examining only a single feature.

As an example of the impact of feature selection, consider the decision tree of Figure 2 which has been built from the same four rules introduced above. By using the destination port as the first selection feature, the resulting tree has a maximum depth of only two and consists of six nodes instead of seven.

In order to create an optimized decision tree, we utilize a variant of ID3 [11, 12], a well-known clustering algorithm applied in machine learning. This algorithm builds a decision tree from a classified set of data items with different features using the notion of information gain. The information gain of an attribute or feature is the expected reduction in entropy (i.e., disorder) caused by partitioning the set using this attribute. The entropy of the partitioned data is calculated by weighting the entropy of each partition by its size relative to the original set. The entropy E_S of a set S of rules is calculated by the following Formula 1.

$$E_S = \sum_{i=1}^{S_{max}} -p_i \log_2(p_i) \tag{1}$$

where p_i is the proportion of examples of category i in S. S_{max} denotes the total number of different categories. In our case, each rule itself is considered to be a

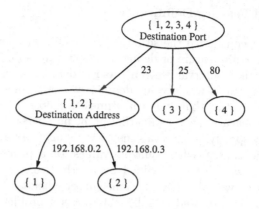

Fig. 2. Optimized Decision Tree.

category of its own, therefore S_{max} is the total number of rules. When S is a set of n rules, p_i is equal to $\frac{1}{n}$ and the equation above becomes

$$E_S = \sum_{i=1}^{n} -\frac{1}{n} \log_2(\frac{1}{n}) = -\log_2(\frac{1}{n}) = \log_2(n) \tag{2}$$

The notion of entropy could be easily extended to incorporate domain specific know-ledge. Instead of assigning the same weight to each rule (that is, $\frac{1}{n}$ for each one of the n rules), it is possible to give higher weights to rules that are more likely to trigger. This results in a tree that is optimized toward a certain, expected input.

Given the result about entropy in Formula 2 above, the information gain G for a rule set S and a feature F can be derived as shown in Formula 3.

$$G_{(S,F)} = E_S - \sum_{v=\text{Val}(F)} \frac{|S_v|}{|S|} E_{S_v} = \log_2(|S|) - \sum_{v=\text{Val}(F)} \frac{|S_v|}{|S|} \log_2(|S_v|) \tag{3}$$

In this equation, $\text{Val}(F)$ represents the set of different values of feature F that are specified by rules in S. Variable v iterates over this set. S_v are the subsets of S that contain all rules with an identical specification for feature F. $|S|$ and $|S_v|$ represent the number of elements in the rule sets S and S_v, respectively.

ID3 performs local optimization by choosing the most discriminating feature, i.e., the one with the highest information gain, for the rule sets at each node. Nevertheless, no optimal results are guaranteed as it might be necessary to choose a non-local optimum at some point to achieve the globally best outcome. Unfortunately, creating a minimal decision tree that is consistent with a set of data is NP-hard.

4.2   Non-trivial Feature Definitions

So far, we have not considered the situation of a rule that completely omits the specification of a certain feature or defines multiple values for it (e.g., instead of a single integer, a whole interval is given). As not defining a feature is equivalent to specifying the feature's whole value domain, we only consider the definition of multiple values. Notice that it is sometimes not possible to enumerate the value domain of a feature (such as floating point numbers) explicitly. This can be easily solved by specifying intervals instead of single values.

When a certain rule specifies multiple values for a property, there can be a potential overlap with a value defined by another rule. As the partitioning process can only put two rules into the same subset when both specify the exact same value for the feature used to split, this poses a problem. The solution is to put both rules into one set and annotate the arrow with the value that the two have in common **and** additionally put the rule which defines multiple values into another set, labeling the arrow leading to that node with the value(s) that only that rules specifies.

Obviously, this basic idea can be extended to multiple rules with many overlapping definitions. The value domain of the feature used for splitting is partitioned into distinct intersections of all the values which are specified by the rules. Then, for each rule, a copy is put into every intersection that is associated with a value defined by that rule. Consider the example rules that have been previously introduced and change the second rule to one that allows an arbitrary destination port as shown below.

(2) `192.168.0.1` --> `192.168.0.3` : **any**

The decision tree that results when the destination port feature is used to partition the root node is shown in Figure 3. The value domain $[0, 2^{16}-1]$ of destination port has been divided into the seven intersections represented by the following intervals $[0,22]$, 23, 24, 25, $[26,79]$, 80 and $[81, 2^{16}-1]$. Rules that define the appropriate values are put into the successor nodes with the corresponding arrow labels. Notice that a packet sent from `192.168.0.1` to `192.168.0.3` and port 25 satisfies the constraints of both rules, number 2 and 3. This fact is reflected by the leaf node in the center of the diagram that holds two rules but cannot be partitioned any further.

The total number of rules in all node's successors does not necessarily need to be equal to the number of rules in the ancestor node (as one might expect when a set is partitioned). This has effects on the size of the decision tree as well as on the function that chooses the optimal feature for tree construction. When many rules need to be processed and each only defines a few of all possible features, the size of the tree can become large. To keep the size manageable, one can trade execution speed during the detection process for a reduced size of the decision tree. This is achieved by dividing the rule set into several subsets and building separate trees for each set. During detection, every input element has then to be processed by all trees sequentially. For our detection engine implementation, we

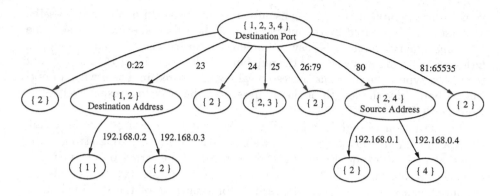

Fig. 3. Decision Tree with **any** Rule.

have used this technique to manage the large number of Snort rules (see Section 6 for details).

The number of checks that each input element requires while traversing the decision trees is bound by the number of features, which is independent of the number of rules. However, our system is not capable of checking input data with a constant overhead independent of the rule set size. The additional overhead, which depends on the number of rules, is now associated with the checks at every node. In contrast to a system that checks all rules in a linear fashion, the comparison of the value extracted from the input element with a rule specification is no longer a simple operation. In our approach, it is necessary to select the appropriate child node by choosing the arrow which matches the input data value. As the number of rules increases and the number of successor nodes grows, this check becomes more expensive. Nevertheless, the comparison can be made more efficient than an operation with a cost linear (i.e., $O(n)$) in the number of elements n.

5   Feature Comparison

This section discusses mechanisms to efficiently handle the processing of an input element at nodes of the decision tree. As mentioned above, each feature has a type and an associated value domain. When building the decision tree or evaluating input elements, features with different names but otherwise similar types and value domains can be treated identically. It is actually possible to reuse functionality for a certain type even when the value domains are different (e.g., 16 or 32 bit variations of the type integer). For our prototype, we have implemented functionality for the types integer, IPv4 address, bitfield and string. Bitfield is utilized to check for patterns of bits in a fixed length bit array and is needed to handle the flag fields of various network protocol headers.

The basic operation that has to be supported in order to be able to traverse the decision tree is to find the correct successor node when getting an actual value from the input item. This is usually a search procedure among all possible successor values created by the intersection of the values specified by each rule.

Using binary search, it is easy to implement this search with an overhead of $O(\log n)$ for `integer`, where n is the number of rules. For the IPv4 `address` and `bitfield` types, the different successor values are stored in a tree with a depth that is bound by the length of the addresses or the bitfields, respectively. This yields a $O(1)$ overhead.

The situation is slightly more complicated for the `string` type, especially when a data item can potentially contain a nearly arbitrary long string value. When attempting to determine the intersections of the string property specifications of a rule set during the partition process, it is necessary to assume that the input can contain any of all possible combinations of the specified string values. This yields a total of 2^n different intersections or subsets where n is the number of rules under consideration. This is clearly undesirable. We tackle this problem by requiring that the `string` type may only be used as the last attribute for splitting when creating the decision tree. In this setup, the nodes that partition a rule set according to a string attribute actually become leaf nodes. It is then possible to determine all matching rules (i.e., all rules which define a string value that is actually contained in the input element) during the detection process without having to enumerate all possible combinations and keep their corresponding nodes in memory.

Systems such as Snort, which compare input elements with a single rule at a time, often use the Boyer-Moore [9] or similar optimized pattern matching algorithms to search for string values in their input data. These functions are suitable to find a single keyword in an input text. But often, the same input string has to be scanned repeatedly because multiple rules all define different keywords.

As pointed out in [3], Snort's rule set contains clusters of nearly identical signatures that only differ by slightly different keywords with a common, identical prefix. As a result, the matching process generates a number of redundant comparisons that emerge where the Boyer-Moore algorithm is applied multiple times on the same input string trying to find nearly similar keywords. The authors propose to use a variation of the Aho-Corasick [1] tree to match several strings with a common prefix in parallel and reduce overhead. Unfortunately, the approach is only suitable when keywords share a common prefix. When creating the decision tree following our approach, it often occurs that several signatures that specify different strings end up in the same node. They do not necessarily have anything in common. Instead of invoking the Boyer-Moore algorithm for each string individually, we use an efficient, parallel string matching implementation introduced by Fisk and Varghese [5]. This algorithm has the advantage that it does not require common prefixes and delivers good performance for medium sized string sets (containing a few up to a few dozens elements).

In the Fisk-Varghese approach, hash tables are utilized to reduce the number of strings that need to be evaluated on an expensive character-by-character basis when a partial match between the rule strings and the input string is detected.

However, when a few hundred strings are compared in parallel, some hash table buckets can contain so many elements that the efficiency is negatively effected. This is solved by selectively replacing hash tables by tries when a hash table bucket contains a number of elements above a certain, definable threshold (the default value is 8).

A trie is a hierarchical, tree like data structure that operates like a dictionary. The elements stored in the trie are the individual characters of 'words' (which are, in our case, the string features of the individual rules). Each character of a word is stored at a different level in the trie. The first character of a word is stored at the root node (first level) of the trie, together with a pointer to a second-level trie node that stores the continuation of all the words starting with this first character. This mechanism is recursively applied to all trie levels. The number of characters of a word is equal to the levels needed to store it in a trie. A pointer to a leave node that might hold additional information marks the end of a word.

When a partial match is found by the detection process, the trie is utilized to perform the expensive character-by-character search for all string candidates in parallel. It is no longer necessary to sequentially match all words of a hash bucket against the input string (as with the Fisk-Varghese approach).

Although tries would be beneficial in all cases, we limit their use to the replacement of large hash tables only because of the significant increase in memory usage.

6   Experimental Data

This section presents the experimental data that we have obtained by utilizing decision trees to replace the detection engine of Snort. We have implemented patches named Snort NG (next-generation) for Snort-1.8.6 and Snort-1.8.7 that can be downloaded from [15]. The reader is referred to Appendix A for details about the integration of our patch into Snort and interesting findings about the current rule set. Our performance results are directly compared to the results obtained with the latest version of Snort and its improved detection engine, that is Snort-2.0rc1.

For our first experiment, we set up Snort-2.0 and our patched Snort NG with decision trees on a Pentium IV with 1.8 GHz running a RedHat Linux 2.4.18 kernel. Both programs read tcpdump log files from disk and attempted to process the data as fast as possible. When performing the measurements, most preprocessors have been disabled (except for HTTP-decoding and TCP stream reassembling) and only fast-logging was turned on to have our results reflect mostly the processing cost of the detection algorithms themselves. Obviously, the overhead of the operating system to read from the file and the parsing functionality of Snort still influences the numbers, but it does so for both approaches.

We measured the total time that both programs needed to complete the analysis of our test data sets. For each of these data sets, we performed ten runs and averaged the results. For the experiment, the maximum number of 1581

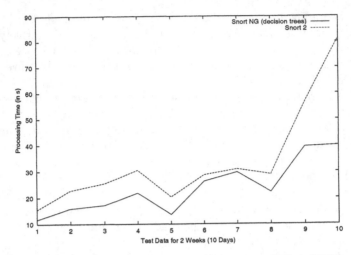

Fig. 4. Time Measurements for 1999 MIT Lincoln Lab Traffic.

Snort-2.0 rules that were available at the time of testing have been utilized. As Snort NG bases on Snort-1.8.7 that uses a rule language incompatible to Snort-2.0, all rules have been translated into a suitable format. Both programs were executed consecutively and did not influence each other while running.

We used the 'outside' tcpdump files of the ten days of test data produced by MIT Lincoln Labs for their 1999 DARPA intrusion detection evaluation [8]. These files have different sizes that range from 216 MB to 838 MB. The comparison of the results for the ten days of the MIT/LL traffic is shown in Figure 4. For each test set, both systems reported the same alerts. Although the actual performance gain varies considerably depending on the type of analyzed traffic (as Snort-2.0 is tuned to process HTTP traffic), the decision trees performed better for every test case and yielded an average speed up of 40.3%. The maximum speed up seen during the tests was 103%, and the minimum was 5%.

The second experiment used the same setup as the first one. This time, however, the number of rules were increased (starting from 150 up to the maximum of 1581) while the input file was left the same (we used the first day of the 1999 MIT Lincoln Labs data set). The rules were added in the order implied by the default rule set of Snort-2.0. All default rule files were sorted in alphabetical order and their rules were then concatenated. From this resulting list, rules were added in order. Similar to the previous test, both programs reported the same alerts for all test runs. Figure 5 depicts the time it took both programs to complete the analysis of the test file given the increasing number of input rules. The graph shows that the decision tree approach performs better, especially for large rule sets.

Building the decision tree requires some time during start up and increases the memory usage of the program. Depending on the number of rules and the features which are defined, the tree can contain several tens of thousands of nodes. A few Snort configuration options, such as being able to specify lists of source

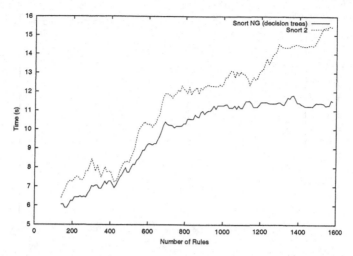

Fig. 5. Time Measurements for increasing Number of Rules.

or destination addresses for certain rules, cause our system to create several internal signature instances from that rule which are later treated independently during the building of the decision tree. When defining a network topology with different subnets and multiple web servers (as needed for the MIT/LL data), the complete rule set used for our evaluation is transformed into 2398 rule instances that need to be processed internally. As a single tree would be too large for this amount of rules, the detection engine splits the rule set for each supported protocol into two subsets and builds two separate trees.

Figure 6 shows the total memory consumption of the patched version of Snort for increasing amounts of rules. It indicates that even when the complete set of rules is loaded, the memory demands are reasonable given todays main memory sizes. The time to build the tree (including the case for the maximum number of rules) has never exceeded 12 seconds.

Notice the interesting irregularity that Figure 6 shows for the modified version of Snort around rule number 700. The reason is a change in the shape of the decision tree. Given the tree for the previous rules and adding a single additional one, the ID 3 algorithm creates a tree which has the same height but is much broader. It contains noticeable more nodes (mostly due to copied rule instances with unspecified feature values) and therefore consumes more memory. However, additional rules fit well into the resulting tree structure and the detection time does not increase significantly after that as more rules are added (as can be seen in Figure 5).

7   Conclusion

Signature-based intrusion detection systems face the challenge of an constantly increasing number of rules that need to be compared to input elements. Combined with the facts that the amount of data is constantly growing and that

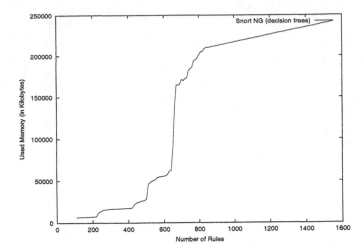

Fig. 6. Memory Consumption.

users expect results in real-time, current systems have already met their limits in coping with this challenge. Novel approaches to re-structure or cluster the signature rules are necessary in order to relieve the detection engines of as many redundant checks as possible.

This paper presents a clustering approach based on decision trees which utilizes machine learning principles to optimize the rules-to-input comparison process. We describe an application of our mechanism to Snort, the most popular open-source network intrusion detection system, and show that a significant improvement of its processing speed was possible. Decision trees, however, are a general solution that can be of benefit to other intrusion detection systems (host- and network-based), packet filters and firewalls as well.

Acknowledgments

This research was supported by the Army Research Office, under agreement DAAD19-01-1-0484. The U.S. Government is authorized to reproduce and distribute reprints for Governmental purposes notwithstanding any copyright annotation thereon. The views and conclusions contained herein are those of the author and should not be interpreted as necessarily representing the official policies or endorsements, either expressed or implied, of the Army Research Office, or the U.S. Government.

References

1. A. Aho and M. Corasick. Efficient string matching: An aid to bibliographic search. *Communications of the Association for Computing Machinery*, 18:333–340, 1975.
2. Cisco IDS - formerly NetRanger. `http://www.cisco.com/warp/public/cc/pd/sqsw/sqidsz/index.shtml`, 2002.

3. C. Jason Coit, Stuart Staniford, and Joseph McAlerney. Towards Faster String Matching for Intrusion Detection or Exceeding the Speed of Snort. In *Proceedings of DISCEX 2001*, 2001.

4. S.T. Eckmann, G. Vigna, and R.A. Kemmerer. STATL: An Attack Language for State-based Intrusion Detection. In *Proceedings of the ACM Workshop on Intrusion Detection Systems*, Athens, Greece, November 2000.

5. M. Fisk and G. G. Varghese. An analysis of fast string matching applied to content-based forwarding and intrusion detection. Technical Report UCSD TR CS2001-0670, UC San Diego, 2001.

6. Daniel Hartmeier. Design and Performance of the OpenBSD Stateful Packet Filter (pf). In *USENIX Annual Technical Conference – FREENIX Track*, 2002.

7. Wenke Lee, Sal Stolfo, and Kui Mok. A Data Mining Framework for Building Intrusion Detection Models. In *In Proceedings of the IEEE Symposium on Security and Privacy*, Oakland, CA, May 1999.

8. MIT Lincoln Labs. DARPA Intrusion Detection Evaluation. http://www.ll.mit.edu/IST/ideval, 1999.

9. J.S. Moore and R.S. Boyer. A Fast String Searching Algorithm. *Communications of the Association for Computing Machinery*, 20:762–772, 1977.

10. Vern Paxson. Bro: A system for detecting network intruders in real-time. In *7th USENIX Security Symposium*, San Antonio, TX, USA, January 1998.

11. J. R. Quinlan. Discovering rules by induction from large collections of examples. In *Expert Systems in the Micro-Electronic Age*. Edinburgh University Press, 1979.

12. J. R. Quinlan. Induction of decision trees. *Machine Learning*, 1(1):81–106, 1986.

13. RealSecure. http://www.iss.net/products_services/enterprise_protection.

14. Martin Roesch. Snort - Lightweight Intrusion Detection for Networks. In *USENIX Lisa 99*, 1999.

15. Snort-NG. Snort - Next Generation: Network Intrusion Detection System. http://www.infosys.tuwien.ac.at/snort-ng.

16. Snort. Open-source Network Intrusion Detection System. http://www.snort.org.

17. Sourcefire. Snort 2.0. http://www.sourcefire.com/technology/whitepapers.htm.

18. Swatch: Simple Watchdog. http://swatch.sourceforge.net.

19. Symantec - NetProwler and Intruder Alert. http://enterprisesecurity.symantec.com/products/products.cfm?ProductID=%50, 2002.

20. Giovanni Vigna, Steve Eckmann, and Richard A. Kemmerer. The STAT Tool Suite. In *Proceedings of DISCEX 2000*, Hilton Head, South Carolina, January 2000. IEEE Computer Society Press.

Appendix A

Integrating Decision Trees into Snort

When integrating our data structures and the detection process into Snort, we attempted to keep the changes to the original code as little as possible. This ensures that the modifications can be ported to new versions of Snort easily and enables us to test our components independently of the main program. The two major changes occurred in the parser and in the code that calls the original detection process with its two-dimensional lists.

The parser (i.e., the functions `ParseRule()` and `ParseRuleOptions()`) in `rules.c` had to be adapted to extract the relevant signature information from the rules. Snort translates the checks of properties into function pointers which are later called by the detection process and encapsulates their values in private data areas that have a feature dependent layout. Although possible, it seems undesirable to extract values required by our functions from function pointers and their corresponding private data structures, therefore they are directly gathered during parsing. Nevertheless, the original lists structure is still created and utilized by our code (e.g., for dynamic rule activation) whenever possible.

The second part of changes affected the detection function (`Detect()`) in `rules.c`. Instead of calling the original processing routine, it redirects to our decision trees. The modified detection procedure calls response and logging functions in a similar way than the old one. However, it is possible that they are called several times for a single packet as our engine determines all matching signatures for each input element. When this behavior is undesirable, our module can be put into a mode where only the first match per packet is reported (with the command line switch `-j`). In this mode, our system imitates the original reporting behavior of Snort.

All other changes were only minor modifications of function prototypes to accommodate additional arguments or the addition of variables to data structures such as `OptTreeNode`. Neither the preprocessing nor the response and logging functionality is affected in any way by our patch. It simply replaces the lists with decision trees. Therefore, it is further on possible to use and write new plug-in modules as desired. In addition, it is also possible to add new features (i.e., to introduce new keywords) to the signature language. Although this seems contradicting at first glance as our decision tree requires the knowledge of these features and their corresponding types, it can be done by excluding these properties from the decision tree and simply check them afterward for all signatures that have triggered for a certain packet. This obviously reduces the effectiveness of our approach but allows one to extend Snort and keep the ability of deploying the modified detection engine.

Discussion of Snort Rules

The rule set of Snort has evolved together with the program itself. Whenever a new threat has been discovered, rules that specify an appropriate signature to detect it have been added. The current version ships with 1581 rules that are stored in 47 files. When testing our implementation, we used Mucus to generate test data for a subset of 848 signatures. Mucus is a tool that reads a rule and creates a network packet with exactly the properties specified by that signature. When running our prototype on each test packet, we obviously expected to detect the corresponding rule used to create it. Sometimes however, not only the expected signature triggered on a single packet, but several others as well. This has three main reasons.

Rules are identical: A few rule pairs simply specify identical values for the same features.

```
alert tcp $EXTERNAL_NET any -> $HOME_NET any (msg:"SCAN SYN FIN";flags:SF;
    classtype:attempted-recon; sid:624; rev:1;)
alert tcp $EXTERNAL_NET any -> $HOME_NET any (msg:"SCAN synscan portscan";
    id: 39426; flags: SF; classtype:attempted-recon; sid:630; rev:1;)
```

Rules are nearly identical: Several rule pairs specify identical values for all but one feature. For this feature, one rule does not define a value at all, thereby matching all packets that trigger the other one. Notice that for the second rule pair, only the destination ports differ. The content string represented by the ASCII values |57 48 41 54 49 53 49 54| is identical to 'WHATISIT'.

```
alert tcp $HOME_NET 23 -> $EXTERNAL_NET any (msg:"TELNET Bad Login";
    content: "Login incorrect"; nocase; flags:A+; sid:1251; )
alert tcp $HOME_NET 23 -> $EXTERNAL_NET any (msg:"TELNET login incorrect";
    content:"Login incorrect"; flags:A+; sid:718; rev:5;)

alert tcp $HOME_NET 146 -> $EXTERNAL_NET 1024: (msg:"BACKDOOR Infector";
    content: "WHATISIT"; flags: A+; sid:117; )
alert tcp $HOME_NET 146 -> $EXTERNAL_NET 1000:1300 (msg:"BACKDOOR Infector
    to Client"; content:"|57 48 41 54 49 53 49 54|"; flags:A+; sid:120;)
```

Rules are imprecise: Certain rules specify feature values that can appear with a reasonable high probability in random, usually non-malicious packets as well. This affects many rules which define a very short content string that is searched for inside the packet payload.

```
alert tcp $EXTERNAL_NET any -> $HOME_NET 21 (msg:"FTP wu-ftp attempt [";
    flags:A+; content:"~"; content:"["; classtype:misc-attack; sid:1377;)
alert tcp $EXTERNAL_NET any -> $HOME_NET 21 (msg:"FTP wu-ftp attempt {";
    flags:A+; content:"~"; content:"{"; classtype:misc-attack; sid:1378;)
```

The problem with multiple matching rules is the fact that Snort only reports the first one. This might result in a packet that triggers a signature which indicates only a minor threat although it would also match one reporting a serious security problem. When using Snort, one has to make sure that signatures are specified as precise as possible and have only a negligible probability of matching benign traffic. We circumvent this limitation by reporting all rules that match a certain packet (when desired).

Ambiguity Resolution
via Passive OS Fingerprinting

Greg Taleck

NFR Security, Inc.,
5 Choke Cherry Rd, Suite 200,
Rockville, MD 20850
taleck@nfr.com
http://www.nfr.com/

Abstract. With more widespread use of tools (such as fragrouter and fragroute[11]) that exploit differences in common operating systems to evade IDS detection, it has become more important for IDS sensors to accurately represent the variety of end hosts' network stacks. The approach described in this paper uses the passively detected OS fingerprint of the end host in an attempt to correctly resolve ambiguities between different network stack implementations. Additionally, a new technique is described to increase the confidence level of a fingerprint match by looking more extensively at TCP connection negotiations.

1   Introduction

Ptacek and Newsham[3] describe "a fundamental problem for network intrusion detection systems (IDS) that passively monitor a network link is the ability of a skilled attacker to *evade* detection by exploiting ambiguities in the traffic stream as seen by the NIDS." [4] These ambiguites on the wire arise from the fact that ambiguities exist in common Internet protocols which led to differing protocol implementations by different operating system vendors.

This paper describes a new approach to the problem of passively providing a IDS sensor knowledge of an end host's network stack implementation to prevent the aforementioned attackers from evading detection or inserting false alerts. We also describe our implementation of this approach in version 4 of the NFR IDS Sensor.

1.1   Motivation

Correctly resolving network protocol ambiguities has long been a thorn in the side of network intrusion detection systems. Exploitable ambiguities show themselves in three scenarios[4]: incomplete analysis on the part of the IDS sensor; lack of detailed knowledge of the end host's protocol implementation; lack of detailed topology knowledge to determine whether a host sees any given packet. This solution mainly deals with the problem arising from the second scenario.

G. Vigna, E. Jonsson, and C. Kruegel (Eds.): RAID 2003, LNCS 2820, pp. 192–206, 2003.

That is, how can the IDS gain more detailed information about the end host in a passive environment?

The ambiguity of the Internet Protocol[16] with respect to fragmentation leads to numerous problems. The most serious of these is to accurately determine exactly what a given end host would see in the presence of overlapping fragments, to properly detect network intrusions, when, and only when they actually happen.

Implementations of the Transmission Control Protocol[17] also vary with respect to handling TCP segments with overlapping TCP data. The specfication states that segments should be trimmed to only contain new data, but in practice, network stacks handle this condition in different ways.

These two problems present two common exploitable conditions for current IDS sensors. We attempt to minimize these opportunities for attackers with the approach described in this paper.

The rest of the paper is organized as follows: Section 2 looks at related work and research in this area. Section 3 looks at existing, state-of-the-art fingerprinting technology. In Section 4, we describe how we build the fingerprint databases and show new techniques for accurately identifying host operating systems. Section 5 shows our current implementation and 6 expands on the resource consumption of our implementation, including methods to reduce it. Our results and measurements are presented in Section 7 and other areas of possible research and future work are described in Section 8.

2   Related Work

2.1   Active Mapping

Inspiration for this work is drawn mainly from the research done on Active Mapping[1]. This method relies on a separate system, the *Mapper*, to actively map hosts within a network to determine its *ambiguity resolution policies*. That is, how does a host interpret ambiguous packets. The Mapper builds a *Host Profile Table* by sending different combinations of overlapping, fragmented IP packets and overlapping TCP segments. It then feeds that host profile information, or ambiguity resolution policies, to an IDS sensor. When the IDS detects an ambiguity on the wire, it looks up the IP in the Host Profile Table for instruction on how to resolve it.

Unfortunately, there are drawbacks to this type of setup for many network installations. By definition, Active Mapping requires that the mapper *actively* send out anomalous traffic that may be rejected by firewalls or routers within the network. Clients that are dynamically assigned IP addresses via DHCP would fail to be mapped properly, and could potentially be mapped to a different profile of another machine. These handcrafted packets could also potentially harm hosts on a network.

2.2 Traffic Normalization

Traffic normalization[5] solves the problem of ambiguity by mostly (or completely) eliminating it. A *traffic normalizer* acts as a gateway for all ingress, and possibly egress, traffic and removes any ambiguities when it detects them. However, traffic normalization cannot always scale to large networks because of the process overhead per packet, and can also break connectivity between hosts when they rely on un-normalized traffic. Normalizers must also be extremely fault tolerant, as any traffic that is to enter the network must first pass the normalizer.

2.3 nmap, queso, ettercap, pOf, prelude-ids

Active and passive OS fingerprinting tools have been around for quite some time. These tools identify hosts by taking advantage of subtle variations in network stack implementations. Mainly ICMP and TCP packets are used to remotely deduce operating system type. Fyodor's nmap[7] tool, first released in 1997, makes extensive use of variations in reply packets from hosts when sent invalid, unusual, or non-conforming payloads, as does queso[12]. The pOf [13] tool uses the unique variations of TCP SYN Segments to *passively* identify hosts on a network. Similarly, ettercap [14], a multi-purpose network sniffer, attempts to identify hosts in the same fashion as pOf. Recently, a patch was submitted to the Prelude IDS Development [15] (prelude-devel) mailing list that can extract pertinent fingerprint information from a TCP SYN or SYNACK segment and save it to a database in the ettercap signature style. This allows Prelude-IDS users the ability to attempt to identify either an attacker's or victim's host operating system.

These tools implement valuable approaches to identifying hosts on a network that have not yet been widely integrated into available IDS solutions. However, the information they provide can only be used to forensically investigate an attack. In other words, these approaches collect data from TCP SYN/SYNACK segments that can then be used later to assess the host.

3 OS Fingerprinting

Two methods exist for remotely fingerprinting hosts on a network: active and passive.

3.1 Active Fingerprinting

Active fingerprinting requires one to send interesting, malformed, and unique payloads to a remote host and examine the values returned by the host. Both the nmap and queso tools do this. The common tests send special combinations of TCP flags, such as FIN—PSH—URG, with a NULL TCP payload to both open and closed ports on the host.

3.2   Passive Fingerprinting

Passive fingerprinting attempts to determine the host type by *passively* monitoring a network link, and not sending any traffic onto the wire. Existing passive OS fingerprinting tools examine the values of fields in the IP and TCP headers of initial TCP SYN segments sent from clients. Common fields used are:

- Initial Window Size (WS)
- Time To Live (TTL)
- Maximum Segment Size (MSS)
- Don't Fragment (DF) Bit
- Window Scale Value
- SackOK option presence
- Nop option presence

This technique also relies on requiring an exact match of all the fields used in the fingerprint[1].

Other techniques[20] look at how to detect network stack implementations by examining TCP segments *throughout* the connection, or by examining the timing of TCP segments traveling back and forth[24].

3.3   Defeating OS Fingerprinting

As accurate as both active and passive OS fingerprinting may be, there are methods to prevent a potential attacker from guessing a host's operating system[9]. For example, a host can fool pOf, in the simplest case, by changing any one of the values enumerated above. Fooling nmap or queso requires a little more effort, since these tools send multiple tests. In order to avoid detection, one must ensure that a majority of the tests sent fail to provide enough intelligence to make a guess.

3.4   Exploitation of the TCP Three-Way Handshake

Existing passive fingerprinting tools work by looking at the first SYN segment of a TCP connection. However, the replying SYNACK from the server can also yield pertinent information that can be used to identify the host. Since the servers are typically within the same network as the deployed IDS, this information is much more important. Most attacks are initiated by the *client side* of the connection. Additionally, if a person or program were to try to evade an IDS, they would do so in order to push an attack through without the IDS detecting it. Since the *server side* that will be accepting the ambiguous traffic, it is this side we are more interested in fingerprinting.

During the three-way handshake to initialize the TCP connection, a client connects to a server within the network by sending a TCP SYN segment, and

---

[1] Exceptions to this are the pOf tool, which will incrementally alter the TTL field to obtain a match since a packet in flight can have a variable TTL value depending on the network path taken, and Xprobe, which can use a best-match algorithm.

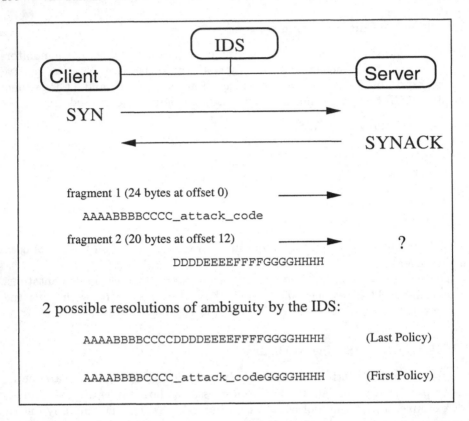

Fig. 1. Network packets from a potential attacker and its victim as seen by an IDS.

the server replies with a SYNACK segment. Consider the example shown in Figure 1, where packets are sent between a client (potential attacker) and server (potential victim) as seen by an IDS sensor.

In this scenario, the only information seen on the wire that can be used to identify the server is the SYN from the client and the corresponding SYNACK reply from the server to open the connection. However, depending on the values within the TCP header and the options present within the SYN from the attacker and how the server negotiates those options, it is possible to make a guess at the operating system of *both* the client and the server. If an accurate guess is made for the operating system type of the server, then we can attempt to resolve the ambiguity in the subsequent fragmented packets sent by the client to the server and have a better chance of determining whether an attack occurred.

Another example can be an attack from a server to a client, where we can lookup the client via its TCP SYN segment and possibly determine the operating system type. Consider the case where a web browser within the network connects to a malicious server outside of the network in an attempt to gain control of the client.

It should be noted the the ettercap tool mentioned in Section 2 *does* have an entry for the ACK bit in its signature database. However, it does not correlate the formation of the SYNACK response to the SYN request.

The next section describes how we can build a collection of fingerprints and their corresponding ambiguity resolution policies.

4   Building TCP SYN/SYNACK Fingerprint Tables

In order to passively map hosts on a network to a particular operating system, we need to deploy IDS sensors with a pre-built table containing mappings of TCP SYN/SYNACK fingerprints to ambiguity resolution policies. Two tables are necessary: one table for identifying TCP SYN segments and another, more important, table for identifying TCP SYNACK segments. We use the existing active fingerprinting techniques, as well as some new ones, to build these policy tables.

4.1   Eliciting TCP SYNs

The pOf tool contains a reasonably robust table of fingerprints to map TCP SYN segments, but it requires human intervention to keep it up-to-date. To automate this task, one simply needs to be able to automatically elicit TCP SYN segments from a variety of hosts, keep track of the values set in the SYN segment, and then use an active OS fingerprinting tool, such as nmap, to identify the operating system. We do this with a tool that scans the Internet at large for hosts running FTP servers that accept anonymous connections[2]. Luckily, there are many of these. The tool connects to the FTP server, attempts to negotiate and verify active transfer mode (since most FTP servers default to passive), and invokes the LIST command to obtain a directory file listing. This results in a TCP SYN segment sent from the FTP server to the listening port sent by the FTP client, as shown in Figure 2.

The tool uses libpcap[23] to catch all initial SYN segments with a TCP destination port equal to the port number sent in the FTP LIST command, and gathers the fields and values present in the SYN segment. It then detects its fragment reassembly policy and overlapping TCP segment policy using the same methods described in [1]. This is done by sending specially crafted IP fragments and TCP segments across the same TCP connection and observing how the host responds. The tool then attempts to identify the host OS type by forking off an nmap process. If nmap fails to identify the host operating system, we will still know how that stack resolves network protocol ambiguities. Having knowledge of the host operating system is really only useful as eye candy to an administrator.

---

[2] It is also possible to exploit the gnutella protocol by creating a lightweight client to connect to the network and both accept connections and send PUSH descriptors to elicit TCP SYN segments. This would nicely complement the set of SYNs from FTP servers, which are primarily high-end OS's.

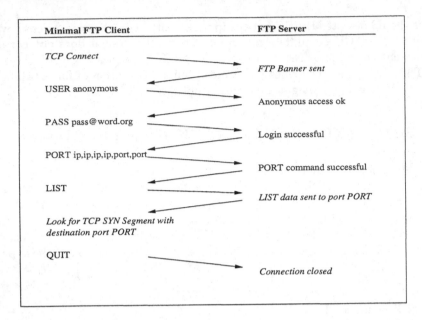

Fig. 2. Sample network dialogue between a minimal FTP client and an FTP server to elicit a TCP SYN segment from the server.

By polling many hosts, we can also weed out bogus entries where administrators have set up the host to fool nmap by using methods described in Section 3.3. Since this tool really requires no human interaction, it can continuously poll new IP's and re-poll old ones.

4.2   Eliciting TCP SYNACKs

The process of eliciting TCP SYNACK segments from a host is much simpler. This only requires that the host have at least one unfiltered port open. Existing active OS fingerprinting tools, such as nmap and queso, utilize a number of TCP tests against open ports to evaluate the network stack behavior. We also utilize these tests, and additionally, make more extensive use of TCP options.

The most prevalent TCP options used in common, modern operating systems are the Maximum Segment Size (mss), Selective Acknowledgment (sackok), Timestamping (timestamp), and the Window Scaling (wscale) options. nmap first exploited the use of these options as the default set to actively examine stack implementations in nmap. Fyodor mentions that TCP options are "truly a gold mine in terms of leaking information" [7]. However, nmap fails to fully mine the information available via these options.

TCP Options Tests. Using these four most common TCP options, 16 new nmap-like tests are created. Once a host is found with at least one open port, 16

Table 1. Enumeration of the possible combinations of TCP options, padded appropriately with `nop` options .

#	Possible combinations of TCP options
1	`mss 1460`
2	`timestamp nop nop`
3	`sackok nop nop`
4	`wscale 0 nop`
5	`wscale 0 nop sackok nop nop`
6	`wscale 0 nop mss 1460`
7	`wscale 0 nop timestamp nop nop`
8	`sackok nop nop mss 1460`
9	`sackok nop nop timestamp nop nop`
10	`mss 1460 timestamp nop nop`
11	`timestamp nop nop sackok nop nop wscale 0 nop`
12	`mss 1460 sackok nop nop wscale 0 nop`
13	`mss 1460 timestamp nop nop wscale 0 nop`
14	`mss 1460 timestamp nop nop sackok nop nop`
15	`mss 1460 timestamp nop nop sackok nop nop wscale 0 nop`

TCP SYN segments are sent with the 2^4 different possible combinations of TCP options, as shown in Table 1.

We can encode options ordering to simplify a later lookup to an `int` comparison. A bit-field can be used to identify the options present in the client's SYN segment. Since we use the most prevalent options, (timestamp, mss, wscale, sackok), we only need bits bits, and can encode them as shown in Table 2.

These tests allow us to build 16 sub-tables for SYNACK lookups. When a lookup is requested for a SYNACK, we take the encoded value of the TCP options present in the SYN segment, as shown in Table 2, for which the SYNACK corresponds, and hash into one of the 16 sub-tables to match the SYNACK TCP and IP values.

The TCP Timestamp. Another ambiguous bit of behavior was discovered during testing. This has to do with network stack implementations of the TCP Timestamp option.

RFC 1323 specifies the requirement for using TCP timestamps as a method to calculate "reliable round-trip time estimates"[18] between two connected hosts. Specifically, section 3.2 states:

"The Timestamp Echo Reply field (TSecr) is only valid if the ACK bit is set in the TCP header; if it is valid, it echos a timestamp value that was sent by the remote TCP in the TSval field of a Timestamps option. When TSecr is not valid, its value must be zero."

However, some operating systems do *not* set the *TSecr* field to the TSval given in the sent TCP SYN segment of a SYNACK reply, where the sent SYN

Table 2. Encoding of TCP options present in TCP SYN segments: bit 3: timestamp, 2: wscale, 1: sackok, 0: mss.

TCP options	Bits	Value
no options	0000	0
mss	0001	1
sackok	0010	2
sackok mss	0011	3
wscale	0100	4
wscale mss	0101	5
wscale sackok	0110	6
wscale sackok mss	0111	7
timestamp	1000	8
timestamp mss	1001	9
timestamp sackok	1010	10
timestamp sackok mss	1011	11
timestamp wscale	1100	12
timestamp wscale mss	1101	13
timestamp wscale sackok	1110	14
timestamp wscale sackok mss	1111	15

segment contained a non-zero *TSval* field. This is not necessarily a violation of the specification, but it does provide useful information that can be used to differentiate operating systems when monitored passively.

Window Sizes. Additionally, some stacks will adjust their initial window size depending on whether the timestamp or other options were requested by the client. Table 3 illustrates some differences and similarities between operating systems and the initial window size.

Table 3. Initial Window Sizes (WS) of various operating systems with and without the TCP timestamp (TS) option requested.

Operating System	WS without TS	WS with TS
Linux 2.4.0	5840	5792
Microsoft Windows NT4.0	64240	65160
MacOS 10.1	32768	33000
OpenBSD 3.3	64240	65160
FreeBSD 2.2	16384	17520
FreeBSD 4.6	57344	57344

5 Implementation

The current version of the NFR IDS sensor implements both IP fragment and TCP overlapping segment ambiguity resolution. Concerning IP fragmentation, five common variations exist [1]:

- BSD: left-trim incoming fragments to existing fragments with a lower or equal offset; discard if they overlap completely
- BSD-Right: Same as BSD, except right-trim existing fragments when a new fragment overlaps
- Linux: Same as BSD, except only fragments with a lower offset are trimmed
- First: always accept the first value received
- Last: always accept the last value received.

The IP fragment reassembly engine implements all five of the observed policies described in [1]. The TCP Re-sequencing engine emulates the BSD and Last policies also described in [1]. The rest of this section describes how the sensor utilizes the fingerprint tables at runtime.

5.1 Performing a Lookup Operation

During runtime, TCP SYN and SYNACK values for TCP traffic seen by the IDS are kept in a cache. The cache is keyed by IP address, so if an entry already exists its values are overwritten.

Once it is deemed necessary to perform a lookup of a particular IP address to determine its operating system type (this event is triggered by an ambiguity on the wire), we first need to see if any cached SYN or SYNACK information is available in the cache. If SYN information is available, we can perform a lookup of the SYN values in the SYN table containing the mappings. If SYNACK information is available for that particular IP (corresponding to a server process), then we take the encoded value of the TCP options present in the SYN segment, as shown in Table 2, corresponding to the SYNACK, and hash into one of 16 fingerprint sub-tables to match the SYNACK TCP/IP values.

A successful lookup will give the sensor access to its ambiguity resolution policies. Whether the ambiguity is with overlapping IP fragments or overlapping TCP segments, the sensor can perform the proper correction and push the correctly sequenced data up the protocol stack.

5.2 *Best-Match* Fingerprinting

Xprobe2[10] utilizes a "fuzzy" approach to actively fingerprinting remote hosts. In a similar fashion, we employ a *best-match* algorithm to obtain a best guess of the host's operating system type in the situation where no exact match is found.

When a lookup is attempted, as described in section 5.1, and fails to find an entry in the SYN or SYNACK fingerprint tables, we invoke the best-match algorithm. Upon failure, then we iterate over every entry in the particular table that failed (either the SYN table or one of the 16 SYNACK sub-tables) and tally a score for each field. Once all fingerprint scores have been calculated, the highest score wins.

6   Resource Consumption

With ever-increasing network speeds, it is important for the network analysis of packets by an IDS to be as fast as possible. To this end, a number of optimizations have been made to satisfy the constraints placed on the IDS sensor.

6.1   On-demand Resolution

Since detecting the OS type can be an $O(n)$ operation, the SYN and SYNACK data from an IP are cached in a tree based upon the IP address of the host. To prevent dubious SYN/SYNACK entries from flooding the cache, the insertion is only done once the three-way handshake is complete and we understand a complete connection has been made. There is little sense in occupying resources for some port scan or even a flood.

When an ambiguity arises in future traffic received by the IDS, a lookup is performed on the IP address of the host receiving the ambiguous packets, and a decision is made as to how to resolve the ambiguity. With this approach, only costly operations are performed when necessitated by the network traffic.

6.2   Fingerprint Caching

As described in the previous section, when an ambiguity arises, a lookup is made into the IP SYN/SYNACK cache. If an entry is found that matches the destination IP address of the packet(s) containing the ambiguity, the values of the SYN/SYNACK entry are used to look up the OS type in a fingerprint *cache*.

Since the IDS does not perform any computationally intensive operations *until* an ambiguity arises, the average runtime cost is merely the cost of caching SYN and SYNACK information. The resulting computational overhead is negligible.

At cold start, this cache is initialized to contain all the fingerprints of the database, built as described in Section 4. During runtime, if the lookup of the OS type in the fingerprint cache fails, the best-match algorithm is invoked to make a best guess. This resulting value is then *inserted* as a new entry into the fingerprint cache, such that any following lookup will result in a cache hit.

6.3   Memory Utilization

The two caches used for the SYN/SYNACK lookup tree and the OS fingerprint tree can grow to very large sizes. Even though the amount of memory per entry may be small, an IDS monitoring a large network can quickly expand the size of these caches. Our implementation does not limit the size of these caches; rather, when all available memory resources are consumed, the memory manager calls back into these cache routines to free memory, effectively wiping out as much of the cache as needed for the system to continue monitoring. When memory resources become available again, the cache can be rebuilt.

7   Experiments and Results

Using the mapping tool described in Section 4, we were able to map almost 1,200 hosts and identify 42 different operating systems.

The TCP options tests gathered 223 unique responses from different operating systems[3], which is a wealth of information that can be used to identify hosts.

Further examination of TCP traffic, as shown in Table 4, yielded several common TCP SYN segments, that show the dispersion of SYNs to cover just over 50% (9 of 16) of the 16 SYNACK sub-tables.

Table 4. Common options and variations of a TCP SYN Segment and the corresponding encoded options for the SYNACK sub-table lookup.

#	TCP options	Encoding
1)	`<mss 1460>`	1
2)	`<mss 1460,nop,nop,sackOK>`	2
3)	`<mss 1460,wscale 0,nop>`	5
4)	`<mss 1380,wscale 0,eol>`	5
5)	`<mss 536,nop,wscale 1>`	5
6)	`<mss 512,nop,wscale 0,nop,nop,timestamp 0>`	13
7)	`<mss 1360,nop,wscale 0,nop,nop,sackOK>`	7
8)	`<mss 1460,sackOK,timestsamp 0,nop,wscale 0>`	15
9)	`<mss 1380,nop,nop,sackOK,nop,wscale 0,nop,nop,timestsamp 0>`	15
10)	`<mss 536,nop,wscale 0,nop,nop,timestamp 0,nop,nop,sackOK>`	15
11)	`<wscale 10,nop,mss 265,timestamp 0,eol>`	14
12)	`<nop,nop,sackOK,mss 1380>`	2
13)	`<timestamp nop nop mss>`	9

7.1   Drawbacks

This solution suffers from the cold start dilemma: If no traffic has been seen by the IDS for a particular host that can be used to identify its ambiguity resolution policies, then nothing can be done if the first packets the IDS sees contain ambiguities.

---

[3] This number does not consider the TTL value since the TTL varies depending on the path taken from the scanner to the host.

The "freshness" of the fingerprint database existing on the IDS is also another potential source of failure. While we do actively maintain our internal fingerprint database as described in Section 4, our current solution does not *automatically* fetch the latest copy on its own. We rely on the IDS administrators to occasionally refresh the packages .

7.2   Implications

Because there does not exist a one-to-one mapping of operating system ambiguity resolution to TCP SYN/SYNACK negotiation behavior, this solution is prone to resolving ambiguities incorrectly. For example, a false negative would result if an administrator changes the default TCP behavior of his or her Windows 2000 server to match that of FreeBSD 5.0, which is then hit with an ambiguity attack for Windows 2000. Since the IDS identified the server as FreeBSD, which has a different ambiguity resolution policy than Windows 2000, the attack would be missed by the IDS. Similarly, false positives can also be generated in this scenario if the attacking IP fragments or TCP segments formatted for FreeBSD.

However, note that an attacker is not able to change the IDS's view of a server the IDS is trying to protect. They will only be able to change the identity of the system from they are connecting.

7.3   Comparison to Related Work

8   Future Work

The approach described in this paper can be extended in many other directions, both to increase the accuracy of identifying end host network stacks and in resolving protocol ambiguities.

Current passive OS fingerprinting works only with the IP and TCP headers, and even then not to their full extent. Research [21] has shown how web servers operate differently under congestion. The tcpanoly[20] tool uses many passive methods that could be integrated into the detection engine by noting gratuitous ACKing, Reno implementations, and other variations throughout a TCP conversation.

The sensor has the ability to use temporal knowledge of a particular IPs passively detected OS fingerprint to statistically guess the OS type in a NATed environment.

Passive fingerprinting can also be used to detect NATed hosts. Since NAT typically only rewrites IP addresses, and possibly TCP or UDP ports, and leaves other fields and options unscathed, the IDS can identify a NAT by counting the number of unique fingerprints for the same IP. If a fingerprint radically changes repeatedly in a given amount of time, a NAT can be detected and used more intelligently by the engine.

We can increase the confidence level of SYNACK fingerprint lookups by paying closer attention when we cache values. When a SYNACK is cached, its corresponding SYN options encoded value is also cached. However, this value may change from client to client. If we can cache a SYNACK for *each* encoded SYN, then when a lookup happens, we could potentially have 16 entries to match against each sub-table. The best-match algorithm could then find the closest operating system type for the given host.

9   Summary

In this paper, we describe a new method and implementation for emulating end host network stacks by using new passive OS fingerprinting techniques.

Compared to previous approaches, this method requires no work on the part of administrators and still allows the stealth operation of the IDS sensor. Additionally, the mapping occurs in real-time. That is, traffic from a host that was just brought up via DHCP can be mapped as soon as the sensor sees traffic from or to it.

Passive detection does not rely on cooperation of firewalls or some given network topology to operate effectively. While knowing the network topology is useful in detecting TTL evasions, it is not necessary for passive fingerprinting.

This approach, while not perfect, attempts to remove some of the exploits available to attackers trying to evade detection.

Finally, passive detection allows us to deploy IDS sensors on a read-only cable and in a passive tap configuration, and still reap the benefits of Active Mapping.

Acknowledgments

Thanks to Mike Frantzen, Kevin Smith, and Jim Bauer for assistance with this work and reviews of this paper.

References

1. Shankar, Umesh.: Active Mapping: Resisting NIDS Evasion Without Altering Traffic http://www.cs.berkeley.edu/~ushankar/research/active/activemap.pdf (2003)
2. Spitzner, L.: Know Your Enemy: Passive Fingerprinting, Identifying remote hosts, without them knowing. http://project.honeynet.org/papers/finger/
3. Ptacek, T. H., Newsham, T.N.: Insertion, Evasion and Denial of Service: Eluding Network Intrusion Detection. Secure Networks, Inc. 1998.
   http://www.aciri.org/vern/Ptacek-Newsham-Evasion-98.ps
4. Handley, M. and Paxson, V.: Network Intrusion Detection: Evasion, Traffic Normalization, and End-to-End Protocol Semantics. Proc. 10th USENIX Security Symposium, 2001.
   http://www.icir.org/vern/papers/norm-usenix-sec-01-html/norm.html
5. Paxson, V.: Bro: A System for Detecting Network Intruders in Real-Time. Computer Networks, 1999.
6. Fyodor: The Art of Port Scanning.

7. Fyodor: Remote OS detection via TCP/IP Stack FingerPrinting
   http://www.insecure.org/nmap/nmap-fingerprinting-article.html
8. Smart, M., Malan, G., Jahanian, F,: Defeating TCP/IP Stack Fingerprinting. Proc. 9th USENIX Security Symposium. 2000.
9. Berrueta, D.B.: A practical approach for defeating Nmap OS-Fingerprinting
   http://voodoo.somoslopeor.com/papers/nmap.html
10. Arkin O., Yarochkin, F.: Xprobe v2.0, A Fuzzy Approach to Remote Active Operating System Fingerprinting.
    http://www.sys-security.com/archive/papers/Xprobe2.pdf
11. Song, D.: fragroute. http://www.monkey.org/~dugsong/fragroute/
12. Savage. queso. http://www.apostols.org/projects.html
13. Michal Zalewski, M., Stearns, W.: pOf. http://www.stearns.org/pOf/
14. Alberto Ornaghi, Marco Valleri.: ettercap. http://ettercap.sourceforge.net/
15. Yoann Vandoorselaere, et. al.: prelude-ids. http://www.prelude-ids.org/
16. Postel, J.: Internet Protocol, RFC 791. September 1981.
17. Postel, J.: Transmission Control Protocol, RFC 793. September 1981.
18. Jacobson, V., Braden, R., Borman, D.: TCP Extensions for High Performance, RFC 1323. May 1992
19. Griffin, J.L.: Testing Protocol Implementation Robustness. 29th Annual International Symposium on Fault-Tolerant Computing, 15-18 June 1999.
20. Paxson, V.: Automated Packet Trace Analysis of TCP Implementations SIGCOMM, 1997.
21. Padhye, J., Floyd, S: Identifying the TCP Behavior of Web Servers. ICSI Technical Report 01-002, 2000.
22. Comer, D.E.: Probing TCP Implementations. Usenix Summer, 1994.
23. McCanne, S., Leres, C., Jacobson, V.: libpcap http://www.tcpdump.org/, 1994.
24. Veysset, F., Courtay, O., Heen, O,: New Tool and Technique For Remote Operating System Fingerprinting Intranode Research Team. 2002.

Two Sophisticated Techniques to Improve HMM-Based Intrusion Detection Systems

Sung-Bae Cho and Sang-Jun Han

Dept. of Computer Science, Yonsei University,
134 Shinchon-dong, Sudaemoon-ku, Seoul 120-749, Korea
{sbcho,sjhan}@cs.yonsei.ac.kr

Abstract. Hidden Markov model (HMM) has been successfully applied to anomlay detection as a technique to model normal behavior. Despite its good performance, there are some problems in applying it to real intrusion detection systems: it requires large amount of time to model normal behaviors and the false-positive error rate is relatively high. To remedy these problems, we have proposed two techniques: extracting privilege flows to reduce the normal behaviors and combining multiple models to reduce the false-positive error rate. Experimental results with real audit data show that the proposed method requires significantly shorter time to train HMM without loss of detection rate and significantly reduces the false-positive error rate.

Keywords: anomaly detection, hidden Markov model, privilege flow, combining multiple models

1 Introduction

Due to worldwide proliferation and rapid progress in networking, faster and more diversified services have become in reality. Because the reliance on computers gets extremely high, security of critical computers is very important. Especially, since important network infrastructures on finance, defense, and electric power are being intruded, intrusions should be detected to minimize the damage. While the demand and interest in intrusion detection have increased, the most active effort in this area was mainly on the development of system security mechanisms like firewalls. However, recently many intrusion detection systems (IDSs) have been developed.

An IDS detects unauthorized usage and misuses by a local user as well as modification of important data by analyzing system calls, system logs, activation time, and network packets [1]. Most server computer systems support C2 security auditing that allows an IDS to obtain detailed information on events generated within the system [2].

The rationale is that human-computer interaction has a cause and effect relation as mentioned by Lane and Brodley [3]. Causal relationship or usage pattern can be captured as temporal sequence of events. Various techniques

G. Vigna, E. Jonsson, and C. Kruegel (Eds.): RAID 2003, LNCS 2820, pp. 207–219, 2003.
© Springer-Verlag Berlin Heidelberg 2003

have been employed to determine how far a temporal sequence of events deviates from the normal model. In [4], after normal behavior model is built based on user activities, event sequence vector similarity is evaluated using pattern matching techniques. [5] and [6] model each program's usage pattern. There are several works that evaluate collections of modeling and matching techniques. [5] compares pattern matching, BP neural network and Elman neural network. [6] compares frequency, data mining, and HMM. Results in [5] and [6] show that exploiting temporal sequence information of events leads to better performance and hidden Markov model (HMM) is a good technique for modeling sequence information.

IDS based on HMM was originally designed by S. Forrest at New Mexico University for modeling and evaluating invisible events based on system calls. HMM-based intrusion detection systems proposed by Arizona State University, RAID at New Mexico University, and Hong Kong University of Science and Technology showed substantial reduction of false-positive errors and increase in detection rate compared to other anomaly detection techniques [14]. Furthermore, desirable results have been produced in modeling normal behavioral events generated from BSM data with HMM when using system call related measures [7].

In spite of good performance of HMM-based IDS, the amount of time required to model normal behaviors and determine intrusions is huge and error rate is higher than that of misuse detection techniques. Thus, it is difficult to detect intrusions in real-time. Therefore, to improve the system performance, an efficient way of refining data for modeling normal behaviors is required.

In this paper, we propose two sophisticated techniques to overcome the drawbacks of conventional HMM-based IDS: modeling privilege flows and combining multiple models. The technique that models privilege flows reduces the time required for training HMM. By combining multiple HMMs, the false positive error rate can be reduced.

The rest of this paper is organized as follows. In Section 2, we give a brief overview of the related works. The overall design and detailed description of the proposed methods are presented in Section 3. Experimental results are shown in Section 4.

2   Hidden Markov Model

An HMM is a doubly stochastic process with an underlying stochastic process that is not observable, and can only be observed through another set of stochastic processes that produce the sequence of observed symbols [8]. HMM is a useful tool to model sequence information. This model can be thought of as a graph with N nodes called 'state' and edges representing transitions between those states. Each state node contains initial state distribution and observation probabilities at which a given symbol is to be observed. An edge maintains a transition probability with which a state transition from one state to another state is made. Fig. 1 shows a left-to-right HMM with 3 states.

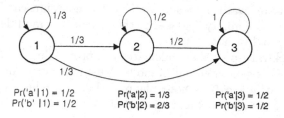

Fig. 1. An example of left-to-right HMM.

Given an input sequence $O = O_1, O_2, ..., O_T$, HMM can model this sequence with its own probability parameters using Markov process though state transition process cannot be seen outside. Once a model is built, the probability with which a given sequence is generated from the model can be evaluated. A model λ is described as $\lambda = (A, B, \pi)$ using its characteristic parameters. The parameters used in HMM are as follows:

T = length of the observation sequence

N = number of states in the model

M = number of observation symbols

$Q = \{q_1, q_2, ..., q_N\}$, states

$V = \{v_1, v_2, ..., v_M\}$, discrete set of possible symbol observations

$A = \{a_{ij}|a_{ij} = \Pr(q_j \text{ at } t+1|q_i \text{ at } t)\}$, state transition probability distribution

$B = \{b_j(k)|b_j(k) = \Pr(v_k \text{ at } t|q_j \text{ at } t)\}$, observation probability distribution

$\pi = \{\pi_i|\pi_i = \Pr(q_i \text{ at } t = 1)\}$, initial state distribution

Suppose, for example, a sequence *aba* is observed in a model λ in Fig. 1 and initial state is 1, then the probability with which the given sequence is generated via state sequence 1-2-3 is calculated as follows:

$$\begin{aligned}
\Pr(O &= aba, q_1 = 1, q_2 = 2, q_3 = 3|\lambda) \\
&= \pi_1 \cdot b_1(a) \cdot a_{12} \cdot b_2(b) \cdot a_{23} \cdot b_3(a) \\
&= 1 \cdot 1/2 \cdot 1/3 \cdot 1/2 \cdot 1/2 \cdot 1/2 \\
&= 1/48
\end{aligned}$$

The probability with which the sequence is generated from the model can be calculated by summing the probabilities for all the possible state sequences. In practice, a more efficient method, known as forward-backward procedure, is used. Recognition can be done with sequences of measures of events as its input using well-established HMM procedures.

2.1   Anomaly Recognition

Anomaly recognition matches current behavior against the normal behavior models and calculates the probability with which it is generated out of each model. Forward-backward procedure or Viterbi algorithm can be used for this purpose [9]. Each probability is passed to the recognition module for determining whether it is normal or not.

Forward-backward procedure calculates the probability $\Pr(O|\lambda)$ with which input sequence O is generated out of model λ using forward and backward variables. Forward variable $\alpha_t(i)$ denotes the probability at which a partial sequence $O = O_1, O_2, ..., O_t$ is observed and stays at state q_i.

$$\alpha_t(i) = \Pr(O = O_1, O_2, ..., O_t, q_t = S_i|\lambda)$$

According to the above definition, $\alpha_t(i)$ is the probability with which all the symbols in input sequence are observed in order and the current state is i. Summing up $\alpha_t(i)$ for all i yields the value $\Pr(O|\lambda)$. $\alpha_t(i)$ can be calculated by the following procedure.

- Initialization:
$$\alpha_1(i) = \pi_i b_i(O_1)$$
- Induction:
  for $t = 1$ to $T - 1$
$$\alpha_{t+1}(j) = \left[\sum_{i=1}^{N} \alpha_t(i) a_{ij}\right] b_j(O_{t+1})$$
- Termination:
$$\Pr(O|\lambda) = \sum_{i=1}^{N} \alpha_T(i)$$

Backward variable $\beta_t(i)$ is defined as follows:
$$\beta_t(i) = \Pr(O = O_{t+1}, O_{t+2}, ..., O_T, q_t = S_i|\lambda)$$
It can be calculated by the similar process to calculate α.

- Initialization:
$$\beta_T(i) = 1$$
- Induction:
  for $t = T - 1$ to 1
$$\beta_t(i) = \sum_{j=1}^{N} a_{ij} b_j(O_{t+1}) \beta_{t+1}(j)$$

2.2   Normal Behavior Modeling

The determination of HMM parameters is to adjust $\lambda = (A, B, \pi)$ to maximize the probability $\Pr(O|\lambda)$. Because no analytic solution is known to do it, an iterative method called Baum-Welch reestimation is used [9]. This requires two more variables: $\xi_t(i, j)$ is defined as the probability with which it stays at state q_i at time t and stays at state q_j at time $t + 1$.

$$\xi_t(i, j) = \Pr(i_t = q_i, i_{t+1} = q_j|O, \lambda)$$
$$= \frac{\alpha_t(i) a_{ij} b_j(O_{t+1}) \beta_{t+1}(j)}{\Pr(O|\lambda)}$$

$\gamma_t(i)$ is the probability with which it stays at state q_i at time t.

$$\gamma_t(i) = \sum_{j=1}^{N} \xi_t(i, j)$$

Summing up the two variables over time t respectively, we can get the expectation that state i will transit to state j and the expectation that it will stay at state i. Given the above variables calculated, a new model $\bar{\lambda} = (\bar{A}, \bar{B}, \bar{\pi})$ can be adjusted using the following equations:

$$\bar{\pi}_i = \text{expected frequency (number of times) in state } S_i \text{ at time } t = 1$$
$$= \gamma_1(i)$$

$$\bar{a}_{ij} = \frac{\text{expected number of transitions from state } S_i \text{ to state } S_j}{\text{expected number of transitions from state } S_i}$$
$$= \frac{\sum_{t=1}^{T-1} \xi_t(i,j)}{\sum_{t=1}^{T-1} \gamma_t(i)}$$

$$\bar{b}_j(k) = \frac{\text{expected number of times in state } S_j \text{ and observing symbol } v_k}{\text{expected number of times in state } j}$$
$$= \frac{\sum_{\substack{t=1 \\ s.t. O_t = v_k}}^{T} \gamma_t(j)}{\sum_{t=1}^{T} \gamma_t(j)}$$

After $\bar{\lambda}$ is adjusted from sequence O, $\Pr(O|\bar{\lambda})$ is compared against $\Pr(O|\lambda)$. If $\Pr(O|\lambda)$ is greater than $\Pr(O|\bar{\lambda})$, it implies that a critical point in likelihood has been reached, thus finishing the reestimation. Otherwise, $\Pr(O|\lambda)$ is replaced by $\Pr(O|\bar{\lambda})$ and reestimation continues.

3   Improvement of HMM-Based IDS

The intrusion detection system developed in this paper is composed of a pre-processing module and an anomaly detection module (Fig. 2). The former is in charge of data reduction using self-organizing map (SOM) and privilege flow detection. The latter is responsible for the normal behavior modeling and anomaly detection. The normal behavior modeling module generates HMM-based normal behavior models from collected normal audit data. The intrusion detection module determines whether an intrusion has occurred by comparing accumulated target audit data with the normal behavior model. The core technology in this proposed IDS lies in filtering of audit data from abstracted information around the change of privilege flows to reduce the required time to build normal behavior model and combining multiple HMM to reduce false-positive errors.

3.1   Extracting Privilege Flow

The ultimate way of an intrusion is to acquire root privilege and the most prevalent attack is known as buffer overflow. This attack breaks into the system with unused user account or an account without any password and acquires root privilege with advanced attack techniques. Here, we analyze host-based attack types that aim to acquire root privilege. Most of user-to-root intrusions attack the files which have SETUID privilege that gives the attacker the opportunity to execute

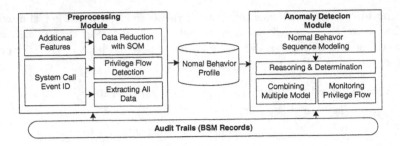

Fig. 2. The overview of intrusion detection system.

arbitrary program with the root privilege. Typical buffer overflow attacks acquire root privilege by attacking SETUID files that does not thoroughly examine the length of inputted parameter. The core difference between a normal SETUID file and an exploited SETUID file in execution is in the process of transition of EUID privilege. Generally after the privilege flow, EUID changes to local user with the call to exit event, but an exploited file executes root shell with execve call and maintains root privilege.

Thus, we can realize that the majority of host-based attacks exploit system bugs or misuse of a local user to acquire root privilege. Therefore, if we model information on the acquisition of normal root privilege to detect any indication of an attack, we can monitor more than 90% of illegal privilege flow attacks excluding denial of service attacks and this indicates that majority of host-based attacks can be detected. In addition, if we effectively minimize the number of targets of intrusion detection, we can also minimize the consumption of system resources which makes it possible for practical operation in real world.

In UNIX system, several users share fixed amount of disk and memory in a single system so that each user must have its own privilege. However, the problem of acquiring super user privilege caused by program error or misuse of a system is always possible. A normal privilege flow happens when an administrator logs in through local user account and acquires root privilege using SU command or by the local user who executes temporarily a file whose SETUID is set to super user. SETUID is a rule applied to the file that temporarily changes the privilege of the user, and anyone who executes that file will execute the file with the SETUID of the file [10].

Most host attacks exploit vulnerabilities described above. Fig. 3 is an example of privilege flow when buffer overflow attack is in action. Normally if a user executes fdformat command from a normal state (Q0), the command is executed temporarily with super user privilege (Q1), and on termination of the task, it returns to its original state (Q0). However if buffer overflow attack occurs during the transaction, it does not return to its original state (Q0) but retains super user privilege (Q2) and ultimately the user can access the system with super user privilege. But if security module knows the sequence of normal privilege flow related to fdformat command, it can identify the transition to an abnormal

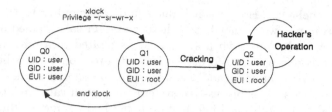

Fig. 3. An example of privilege change by buffer overflow attack.

state (Q2) caused by buffer overflow. The learning model for user privilege flows collects the sequence of normal system calls that happen before the occurrence of normal privilege change. Then, it models normal behaviors and detects intrusion by comparing each user's state of privilege flow.

The filtering subsystem imports the reformatted audit data from the preprocessor and determines which system calls are eligible and which audit data fields are sufficiently available to conduct our experiments. From this preliminary study, we analyze the data to detect privilege change from a regular user to root. By examining the result, we can assure that many events are not in use, but only 25% of the events have been used. In training an HMM, running time is roughly proportional to the number of system calls. For this reason, among the 267 different events audited by BSM, only 80 were used. It could be a good reduction technique that extracts the events around privilege change. Although abundant training data using system calls require significantly longer training time, these reduction techniques can reduce computational cost. Proposed privilege change model evaluated with taking fixed data sequence based on the situation where transitions between UID and EUID occur, which are derived from BSM data. However, during the detailed analysis of theses attacks, acquiring root privilege not only can be from user's change but also from group's change. For the sake of this case, this system detects privilege flows of both user and group.

Table 1. Events related with privilege flows.

Event ID	System Call	Event ID	System Call	Event ID	System Call
2	fork	27	setpgrp	200	setuid
11	chown	38	fchroot	214	setegid
16	stat	39	fchown	215	seteuid
21	symlink	40	setreuid	237	lchown
23	execve	41	setrgid	6158	rsh
24	chroot	69	fchroot	6159	su

3.2 Combining Multiple Models

Conventional HMM-based intrusion detection technique have used only system call ID as the measure of user's behavior. System call ID is useful measure to monitor user's behavior. However, it is inadequate for monitoring the whole be-havior. For example, we cannot know whether system call is failed or executed successfully. It is also unknown if system call is related to a critical file or an ordinary file. Therefore more information is needed to model user's behavior ac-curately. Solaris BSM provides additional information on user's behavior besides the system call ID: such as process ID, system call return value, related file, etc. We also model these additional information using HMMs and combine them to improve the performance.

Because additional system-call-related information is too large and various to apply to HMM directly, some data reduction technique is needed. We use self-organizing map (SOM) to reduce these additional information. System call-related information and process-related information and file access-related infor-mation are extracted from each BSM event and reduced using SOM as shown in Table 2.

Table 2. Measures extracted from the BSM to detect intrusion.

Group	Measures
System call	ID, return value, return status
Process	ID, IPC ID, IPC permission
	exit value, exit status
File access	access mode, path, file system
	file name, argument length

SOM is an unsupervised learning neural network, using Euclidean distance to compute distance between input vector and reference vector [11]. Algorithm of SOM is as follows. Here, $i(x)$ is the best matching neuron to input vector, λ_i means neighborhood function and η is learning rate.

1. Initialize the reference vectors $(w_j(n))$ $(n = 0)$
2. Compute distance and select the minimum value
   $i(x) = argmin\|x(n) - w_j(n)\|$
3. Update the reference vectors
   $w_j(n + 1) = w_j(n) + \eta(n)\lambda_{i(x)}(n, j)(x(n) - w_j(n))$
4. repeat from 2 to 3 until the stop condition satisfies.

Several measures can be extracted from one audit record of BSM which includes an event and the information is normalized for the input of SOM. As an output of SOM, we can get one representative instead of many measures, that is, one record is converted into one representative.

Fig. 4 shows the flow of reducing audit data. In this paper, we reduce the measure size based on the locality of user action: We observe the range of the measures and save actual ones used in the system as table where we find the value of measure of current action. As a result of mapping of measures, we can obtain reduced data.

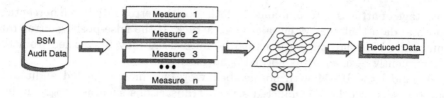

Fig. 4. Overall flow of reducing BSM audit data.

When one event is evaluated through each model, a vector of evaluation values are generated. A method to combine multiple models are required to finally decide whether current sequence is an anomaly. Combining multiple detectors is good for improving the performace of detection systems. [12] and [13] combines detectors using ensemble learning. They have applied machine learning tehniques such as artificial neural networks and support vector machine to intrusion detection and showed that combining different detectors is superior to individual approches. In this paper, we have combined HMM-based detectors that determines if current sequence is abnormal according to the measure it is responsible for:system call-related, process-related and file access-related measure. Each detector participates in the final anomaly decision.

Each detector is given a weight W_m according to their confidence. Voting method is determined. Typical voting methods include unanimity, majority and OR voting. In OR voting, anomaly is determined if at least one member votes positively. Voting is to determine whether or not the total result R is greater than or equal to the T dependent on the voting method.

$$R = \sum W_m * V_m \quad \left(\begin{matrix} W_m & : & \text{model weight} \\ V_m & : & \text{model voting value} \end{matrix} \right)$$

$$\text{anomalous if} \begin{cases} R = 1 & \text{(unanimity)}, \\ R \geq 0.5 & \text{(majority)}, \\ R > 0 & \text{(OR voting)} \end{cases}$$

Generally, OR voting enhances a detection rate but it increases an error rate. Unanimity improves an error rate but a detection rate also decreases.

4   Experimental Results

At first, we have checked whether the method that models privilege flow can produce a better performance. To show the usefulness of the proposed method, we compare the performance of modeling method with partial sequence data only around the privilege transition and that with all sequence data. We have conducted experiments to decide the optimal HMM parameters for effective intrusion detection. A desirable intrusion detection system would show high intrusion detection rate with low false-positive error rate. The detection rate is the percentage of attacks detected, and the false-positive error rate is the percentage of normal data that the system alarms as attack. If the false-positive error rate is high, the IDS may not be practical because users may be warned from the IDS frequently even with the normal behaviors.

To model the HMM with normal behaviors, we have collected audit data from 10 users who have conducted several transactions such as programming, navigating Web pages, and transferring FTP data for one month. Because it is crucial to define normal traffic for IDS based on anomaly detection,we have attempted to balance the data with every-day usage of computer systems. The number of users and period of collection time should be extended at the future work.

In this paper, the BSM auditing tool of Sun Solaris operating environment is used and a total of 767,237 system calls have been collected. The performance of IDS is measured against 19 times u2r (user-to-root) intrusions with the observation of the variation of the Receiver Operating Characteristic (ROC) curve. Most attacks are attempted to acquire root privilege by exploiting a subtle temporary file creation and race condition bug.

Standard HMM has a fixed number of states, so that one must decide the size of the model before training. Preliminary study indicates that the number of optimal states roughly equals to that of distinct system calls used by the program [14]. A range of 5-15 states are examined in HMM.

To measure the runtime-performance, the program is executed 10 times in UltraSparc 10 and the results of the shell are recorded using time command. Table 3 summarizes the results of time for modeling the HMMs with different settings. As mentioned previously, training an HMM requires very expensive computation, but the model with privilege transition flows has obtained approximately 250 times faster than that with all data. We can expect to reduce the time consumption substantially with privilege transition flows.

Table 3. A comparison of performance in running time.

Modeling	State/sequence	Number of sequence	Timestamp
All data	5/20	767218	5 hours 07 min
All data	15/30	767208	6 hours 29 min
Privilege change data	5/20	5950	26.3 sec
Privilege change data	15/30	5792	57.5 sec

In addition to the running time, we have compared the detection rates and the false-positive error rates for two cases in ROC curve as shown in Fig. 5 and 6. The model with privilege transition flows yield higher performance than that with all data. There exists a clear gap between the minimum and maximum detection rates for the model with all data.

We have compared the result at same detection rate as shown in Table 4. The results indicate that privilege flows data are useful to detect intrusions when we have modeled normal behaviors by HMM. The model with 10 states and 30

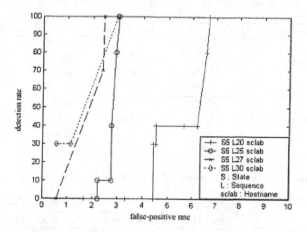

Fig. 5. ROC for privilege change data.

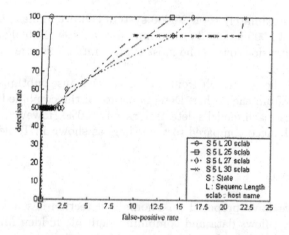

Fig. 6. ROC for all train data.

sequences in privilege transition flows data is seen to be the most effective in this experiment, while the model with 10 states and 30 sequences in all train data is not good enough. The lowest false-positive error has been obtained when the number of states is 10 and the number of sequences is 20 in all data.

Next, we have conducted the experiments to compare the detection methods based on system call ID and that on additional measures reduced by SOM and the combined method. Two models have combined by unanimity voting, majority voting and OR voting methods are tested. Each models is given the same voting weight.

For this experiment, we have used data obtained from one graduate student for one week. He has mainly used text editor, compiler and programs of their

Table 4. The anomaly detection rate for each modeling method.

Modeling	State/sequence	Threshold	Detection rate	F-P error
All data	5/20	-92.4	100%	4.234%
	10/25	-102.1	100%	3.237%
	10/20	-93.7	100%	1.6165%
	15/30	-118.3	100%	12.426%
Privilege change data	5/20	-53.8	100%	6.707%
	15/25	-65.2	100%	2.367%
	10/27	-73.1	100%	2.439%
	10/30	-81.2	100%	0.602%

Table 5. The performance of combining multiple models.

	only system call ID	SOM reduced	Voting method		
			unanimity	majority	OR voting
detection rate	100	100	100	100	100
false-positive error rate	5.33%	23.53%	1.18%	25.75%	25.75%

own writing. Approximately total 20,000 system call events have been collected and among them 10,000 are used for training and another 10,000 are for testing. 17 cases of u2r intrusion, one of the most typical intrusions, are included in the user's test data set.

We have used the best result from each model because subthreshold for each model may differ from each other. Detection rate of the combined method does not change because each model's detection rate is 100%. However, False-positive error rate has enhanced compared to the others as shown in Table 5.

5   Conclusions

In this paper, we have proposed an anomaly detection-based IDS using the privilege transition flows data and combining multiple hidden Markov models. Experimental results show that the training of the privilege transition flows is substantially faster than that of conventional data without any loss of detection rate. Moreover, modeling privilege change data has less error than conventional modeling. This method can open a new way of utilizing computation-intensive anomaly detection technique in the real world, based on behavioral constraints imposed by security policies and on models of typical behavior for users. We can also reduce false positive error rate by combining multiple hidden Markov models, thereby improving the reliability of the HMM-based intrusion detection system. It is because some attacks cannot be detected by reflecting single aspect of user events.

Currently, the ROC curve that shows the change of the error rate as the threshold changes is adopted to demonstrate the detection capability of the system. For the deployment of the system in the real world, an automatic mechanism to adjust the threshold appropriately is needed. In the future, studies on the discriminative event extraction and modeling among user behaviors must be followed.

Acknowledgments

This research was supported by University IT Research Center Project.

References

1. H. S. Vaccaro and G.E. Liepins, "Detection of anomalous computer session activity," *In Proceedings of IEEE Symposium on Research in Security and Privacy*, pp. 280-289, 1989.
2. K. E. Price, "Host-based misuse detection and conventional operating system's audit data collection," *M.S. Dissertaion*, Purdue University, Purdue, IN, December 1997.
3. T. Lane and C. E. Brodley, "An application of machine learning to anomaly detection," *In Proceedings of the National Information Systems Security Conference*, pp. 366-380, Washington, DC, October 1997.
4. T. Lane and C. E. Brodley, "Temporal sequence learning and data reduction for anomaly detection," *In Proceedings of the Fifth ACM Conference on Computer and Communications Security*, pp. 150-158, 1997.
5. A. K. Ghosh, A. Schwartzbard and M. Schatz, "Learning program behavior profiles for intrusion detection," *In Proceedings of Workshop on Intrusion Detection and Network Monitoring*, pp. 51-62, Santa Clara, USA, April 1999.
6. C. Warrender, S. Forrest and B. Pearlmutter, "Detecting intrusion using calls: Alternative data models," *In Proceedings of IEEE Symposium on Security and Privacy*, pp. 133-145, May 1999.
7. D. Y. Yeung and Y. Ding. "Host-based intrusion detection using dynamic and static behavioral models," *The Journal of the Pattern Recognition society*, December 2001.
8. L. R. Rabiner, "A tutorial on hidden Markov models and selected applications in speech recognition," *Proceedings of the IEEE*, vol. 77, no. 2, pp. 257-286, 1989.
9. L. R. Rabiner and B.H. Juang, "An introduction to hidden Markov models," *IEEE ASSP Magazine*, pp. 4-16, January 1986.
10. B. A. Kuperman and Eugene H. Spafford. "Generation of application level audit data via library interposition", *CERIAS TR 99-11*, COAST Laboratory, Purdue University, West Lafaytte, IN, October 1998.
11. Kohonen, T., *Self-Organizing Maps*, Springer press, 1995.
12. S. Mukkamala, A. H. Sung and A. Abraham, "Intrusion Detection Using Ensemble of Soft Computing Paradigms," *Third International Conference on Intelligent Systems Design and Applications, Intelligent Systems Design and Applications, Advances in Soft Computing*, Springer Verlag, Germany, pp. 239-248, 2003.
13. L. Didaci, G. Giacinto and F. Roli, "Ensemble Learning for Intrusion Detection in Computer Networks," *In Proceedings of the Workshop on Machine Learning, Methods and Applications, held in the context of the 8th Meeting of the Italian Association of Artificial Intelligence (AI*IA)*, pp. 10-13, September, 2002.
14. J. H. Choy and S. B. Cho, "Anomaly detection of computer usage using artificial intelligence techniques, " *Lecture Notes in Computer Scinece 2112* , pp. 31-43, Springer 2001.

An Analysis of the 1999 DARPA/Lincoln Laboratory Evaluation Data for Network Anomaly Detection

Matthew V. Mahoney and Philip K. Chan

Computer Science Department, Florida Institute of Technology
150 W. University Dr., Melbourne, Florida 32901
{mmahoney,pkc}@cs.fit.edu

Abstract. The DARPA/MIT Lincoln Laboratory off-line intrusion detection evaluation data set is the most widely used public benchmark for testing intrusion detection systems. Our investigation of the 1999 background network traffic suggests the presence of simulation artifacts that would lead to overoptimistic evaluation of network anomaly detection systems. The effect can be mitigated without knowledge of specific artifacts by mixing real traffic into the simulation, although the method requires that both the system and the real traffic be analyzed and possibly modified to ensure that the system does not model the simulated traffic independently of the real traffic.

1 Introduction

One of the most important data sets for testing intrusion detection systems (IDS) is the DARPA/Lincoln Laboratory off-line evaluation data set, or IDEVAL [1-3]. Since the two evaluations in 1998 and 1999, at least 17 papers have been written on intrusion detection systems tested on this benchmark [4-20]. The network traffic from the 1998 data set was also used to develop the 1999 KDD cup machine learning competition [21], which had 25 participants, and which continues to be used to test intrusion detection methods [22-23].

IDEVAL is the most comprehensive test set available today. The 1999 evaluation data allows testing of 244 labeled instances of 58 different attacks on four operating systems (SunOS, Solaris, Linux, and Windows NT). It supports both host based methods, using audit logs, file system dumps, and system call traces, and network based methods using captured traffic. Attack-free data is available for training anomaly detection systems.

Prior to IDEVAL, researchers usually had to test their systems using data collected from a live environment in which they simulated attacks. In order to protect users' privacy, this data would typically not be released, making it impossible for other researchers to independently confirm published results or to evaluate competing intrusion detection systems in any meaningful way. When live data is released, it is often limited in scope to protect user privacy. For example, the Internet Traffic Archive [24] traces are stripped of application payload data. Forrest's *s-tide* data set [25] would only be useful for testing the detection of UNIX based attacks by analyzing system call sequences without arguments.

G. Vigna, E. Jonsson, and C. Kruegel (Eds.): RAID 2003, LNCS 2820, pp. 220–237, 2003.

IDEVAL solved the user privacy problem by using custom software to synthesize typical user behavior and network traffic to make a small, isolated network (four "victim" machines on an Ethernet) appear as if it were part of a large Air Force network with hundreds of hosts, thousands of users, and an Internet gateway. This was a significant undertaking, considering the complexity of such a system. McHugh [26] criticized many aspects of IDEVAL, including questionable collected traffic data, attack taxonomy, distribution of attacks, and evaluation criteria. With respect to the collected traffic data, he criticized the lack of statistical evidence of similarity to typical Air Force network traffic (especially with respect to false alarms), and low traffic rates. His critique is based on the procedure to generate the data set, rather than on an analysis of the data. To our knowledge, our analysis of the IDEVAL background network traffic is the first of its kind. We do not address issues related to the host based data.

We also do not address attack simulation. Most of the attacks used in IDEVAL are derived from published sources such as the Bugtraq mailing list. We believe that these were simulated correctly. Rather, we question the accuracy of the network traffic portion of the background data. If this is the case, then any simulation errors should affect anomaly detection systems, which model normal behavior to detect novel attacks, and not signature detection systems, which model previously known attacks.

In this paper, we analyze the IDEVAL background network traffic and find evidence of simulation artifacts that could result in an overestimation of the performance of some anomaly detection algorithms, including some trivial ones. Fortunately, all is not lost. We propose that the artifacts can be removed by mixing IDEVAL with real network traffic, in effect simulating the labeled IDEVAL attacks in a real environment. The method does not require any specific knowledge of simulation artifacts, but does require that the real data and the IDS be analyzed and possibly modified to prevent the simulated traffic from being modeled independently of the real traffic.

This paper is organized as follows. In Section 2, we describe related work in anomaly detection and previously known artifacts in IDEVAL. In Section 3, we compare traffic in IDEVAL to real traffic and identify attributes that meet two of three preconditions for simulation artifacts. In Section 4, we propose a method of mixing IDEVAL and real traffic to remove those preconditions wherever they exist. In Sections 5 we find that many attacks can be non-legitimately or trivially detected by some of the attributes that met our preconditions, but that these detections are removed when IDEVAL is mixed with real traffic. In Section 6, we conclude.

2   Related Work

An anomaly detection system builds a model of "normal" behavior (e.g. network client behavior) in order to flag deviations as possible novel attacks. We briefly describe several network based systems.

SPADE [27] models IP addresses and ports of inbound TCP SYN packets, the first packet from a client to a local server. Depending on its configuration, it models the joint probability of the destination address (DA) and port number (DP), and possibly the source address (SA) and source port number (SP), e.g. $p = P(DA, DP, SA)$. The probability is estimated by counting all TCP SYN packets from the time it was turned on until the current packet. It assigns an anomaly score of $1/p$, and outputs an alarm if this score is above a threshold. SPADE can detect port scans if they probe rarely used ports (i.e. $P(DA, DP)$ is low). If SA is included, then SPADE can detect novel (possibly unauthorized) users on restricted ports. For example, if DP = 22 (*ssh*), then $P(DA, DP, SA)$ will be low whenever SA is not the IP address of a regular user on server DA.

ADAM [4], like SPADE, monitors client TCP addresses and ports, in addition to address subnets, weekday and hour. It uses market basket analysis to find rules among these attributes with high support and confidence. ADAM combines signature and anomaly detection by passing low probability events to a classifier (a decision tree) trained on labeled attacks. It classifies each session as normal, known attack or unknown attack. Unlike SPADE, ADAM has specific training and test phases.

eBayes [5] models aggregate attributes over a short time window, such as number of open connections, ICMP error rate, number of ports accessed, and so on. It maintains a set of conditional probabilities of the form $P(\text{attribute} = \text{value} \mid \text{category})$ and uses naive Bayesian inference to classify events as normal, known attack or unknown attack. It includes mechanisms to adjust probabilities to reinforce existing categories and to add new categories when an event does not easily fit the existing categories.

Our prior work includes four systems, PHAD [6], ALAD [7], LERAD [8], and NETAD [9]. These systems have distinct training and test phases, and output an alarm only when a test attribute has a value *never* seen in training. The alarm score is not based on training frequency. Rather it is highest when the time since the previous anomaly is large, the training support is large, and the size of the set of allowed values is small. PHAD and NETAD model network packets including the complete headers, allowing them to detect exploits of low level protocols, such as IP fragmentation vulnerabilities. ALAD and LERAD model TCP streams including words in the application payload, allowing them to detect attacks on open servers (e.g. HTTP or SMTP) that address/port analysis would miss. LERAD uses a market basket approach to finding associations between attributes to synthesize rules. The others use fixed rule sets. All of the systems except PHAD model only inbound client traffic.

Our systems perform competitively on IDEVAL by our own evaluation. In [8] we identify five types of anomalies leading to attack detection.

- Address and port anomalies (traditional firewall model), such as scanning closed ports, or unauthorized users attempting to connect to password protected services identified by previously unseen client IP addresses.
- Use of legal but seldom used protocol features, for example, IP fragmentation. These features are more likely to contain vulnerabilities because they are poorly field tested during ordinary usage.
- Idiosyncratic (but legal) differences in protocol implementations, such as using lower case SMTP mail commands when upper case is usual.
- Manipulation of low-level protocols to hide attack signatures in higher level protocols, for example, FIN scanning to prevent TCP sessions from being logged.
- Anomalies in the victim's output in response to a compromise, for example, a root shell prompt emitted by an SMTP server compromised by a buffer overflow.

However, analysis of the attacks that we detect reveals that many do not fit into any of these categories. We believe these are simulation artifacts. In particular:

- Our published results for PHAD exclude the TTL (time to live) field because over half of the attacks it detects would otherwise be due to anomalies in this field. TTL is an 8 bit field which is decremented after each router hop to prevent infinite loops. In IDEVAL, the values 126 and 253 appear only in hostile traffic, whereas in most background traffic the value is 127 or 254. Most of those attacks exploit application protocols and would have no reason to manipulate TTL. This is also not an attempt to conceal the attacks because the values are too large [28]. We believe these anomalies are due to the underlying configuration of the simulation, in which attacking traffic and background traffic (even with the same IP address) were synthesized on different physical machines [3].

- ALAD, LERAD, and NETAD detect a large number of attacks (about half) by anomalous source addresses, including attacks on DNS, web and mail servers, where previously unseen addresses should be the norm.

- NETAD detects several attacks that exploit application protocols by anomalies in the TCP window size field.

3 IDEVAL Background Traffic Analysis

All of the suspected simulation artifacts we observed occur in well behaved attributes. We say that an attribute is *well behaved* if the set of observed values is small and if any two samples collected over different, short time intervals result in the same set of observed values. A well behaved attribute modeled in an anomaly detection system ordinarily will not generate false alarms after a short training period. On the other hand, the set of values observed in a poorly behaved attribute would grow over time. Often, the values have a power law distribution: a few values might appear frequently, while a large number of values would occur only once or a few times.

In IDEVAL, the TTL, client IP address and TCP window size attributes are well behaved. However, this alone does not establish the presence of a simulation artifact. Three preconditions must exist:

1. The attribute is well behaved in simulated traffic without attacks.
2. The attribute is not well behaved in real traffic without attacks.
3. The attribute is not well behaved in traffic containing simulated attacks.

The first condition is required because otherwise the attribute would generate false alarms and not be useful for anomaly detection. (Our systems detect this case and either assign lower anomaly scores or discard the attribute). The second condition is necessary or else the simulation is accurate. The third condition is necessary or else there would be no anomaly. We have not established the second condition, that the attribute is not well behaved in real traffic.

In this section we compare the IDEVAL background traffic with one source of real traffic to test the first two preconditions for simulation artifacts. We test whether an attribute is well behaved in IDEVAL but not in real traffic. We analyze the attributes that are most commonly modeled by network anomaly detection systems: addresses, ports, other packet header fields, and words (delimited by white space) in application protocols (e.g. SMTP, HTTP) in attack-free inbound client traffic.

Lacking published sources of real traffic, we collect our own. We caution that our comparison is based on just once source. However it represents samples from over 24,000 sources on the Internet over most of the protocols used by IDEVAL.

3.1 FIT Data Set

We compare the 256 hours of IDEVAL attack-free training data from inside sniffer weeks 1 and 3 with 623 hours of traffic which we denote as FIT. FIT was collected on a university Solaris machine which is the main server for our CS department (cs.fit.edu). It has several faculty user accounts and serves several thousand web pages. We collected 50 traces of 2,000,000 packets each on weekdays (Monday through Friday) over 10 weeks from September through December 2002. Each trace was started at midnight and lasted 10 to 15 hours. Packets were truncated to 200 bytes. FIT differs from IDEVAL in the following respects:

- The Ethernet traffic is switched, so only traffic originating from or addressed to the host (or multicast) is visible.
- Some hosts on the local network use dynamic IP addresses which can change daily.
- FIT is protected by a firewall.
- There is no *telnet* traffic and very little FTP traffic. The real host instead supports secure shell and secure FTP. Non secure FTP data is not transported on the standard port (20) normally used for this purpose.

However, most of the other protocols found in the IDEVAL background data are found in FIT. These include Ethernet, ARP, IP, TCP, UDP, ICMP, HTTP, SMTP, POP3, IMAP, *nbname, nbdatagram*, DNS, NTP, *auth* and *printer*. The FIT traffic also has many protocols not found in IDEVAL: IGMP, OSPFIGP, PIM, NFS, RMI, *portmap*, and some obscure and undocumented protocols.

Although FIT is protected by a firewall, it is not free of attacks. We examined the traffic manually and with SNORT [29] and we are aware of at least four attacks from 17 sources: a port/security scan from a host inside the firewall similar to *mscan* or *satan* (although we did not identify the tool used), and multiple probes from three HTTP worms: *Code Red II, Nimda*, and *Scalper*. In addition, we are aware of a large number of lower risk probes on open ports: an HTTP proxy scan, a DNS version probe, and numerous ICMP echo probes from scanning tools identified by SNORT as *L3-retriever, CyberKit, Speedera, SuperScan*, and *nmap*.

We filtered both IDEVAL and FIT using TF [30], which passes only inbound client IP traffic prior to analysis. TF also truncates TCP streams by passing only packets containing the first 100 payload bytes. Filtering reduces IDEVAL to 3% of its original number of packets, and FIT to 1.6%.

3.2 Findings

We compared filtered attack-free inbound client traffic from IDEVAL inside sniffer traffic from weeks 1 and 3 with FIT. To test whether an attribute is well behaved, we used the size of the set of the allowed values and its rate of growth. If an attribute is well behaved, then the set will be the same size in the first half of the data as in the full set. If the attribute is poorly behaved, then the first half will contain about half as many values.

TCP SYN Regularity. In all 50,650 inbound TCP SYN packets in IDEVAL weeks 1 and 3 (the initial packet to the server), there are always exactly 4 option bytes (MSS = 1500). In FIT (210,297 inbound TCP SYN packets, not including 6 TCP checksum errors), we found 103 different values for the first 4 option bytes alone. The number of option bytes varies from 0 to 28. Also the IDEVAL window size field always has one of 7 values (from 512 to 32,120), but we found 523 different values in FIT, covering the full range from 0 to 65,535.

Source Address Predictability. There are only 29 distinct remote TCP client source addresses in IDEVAL weeks 1 and 3. Half of these are seen in the first 0.1% of the traffic. FIT has 24,924 unique addresses, of which 53% are seen only in the second half of the data, suggesting that the number increases at a steady rate with no upper bound. Furthermore, 45% of these appear in only a single TCP session, compared to none in IDEVAL. These statistics are consistent with the power law distribution normally found in Internet addresses [31-32] in FIT only.

Checksum Errors. About 0.02% of non-truncated FIT TCP and ICMP packets have checksum errors. This estimate is probably low because we could not compute checksums for larger packets due to truncation. We did not find any FIT UDP or IP checksum errors. The 12 million unfiltered packets of IDEVAL traffic from inside week 3 have no IP, TCP, UDP, or ICMP checksum errors. (We did not test week 1).

Packet Header Fields. Only 9 of the possible 256 TTL values were observed in IDEVAL. We observed 177 different values in FIT. For TOS, we observed 4 values in IDEVAL and 44 values in FIT.

IP Fragmentation. Fragments were found only in FIT (0.45% of packets). The DF (don't fragment) flag was set in all of these packets.

"Crud". The following events were observed FIT (in packets with good checksums), but not in IDEVAL.
- Nonzero values in the TCP ACK field when the ACK flag is not set (0.02%).
- Nonzero values in the urgent pointer field when the URG flag is not set (0.02%).
- Nonzero values in the two TCP reserved flags (0.09%).
- Nonzero values in the 4 reserved bits of the TCP header size field (0.006%).

HTTP Requests. In IDEVAL, the 16,089 HTTP requests are highly regular, and have the form "GET *url* HTTP/1.0" followed by optional commands of the form "*Keyword: values*". There are 6 possible keywords (within the first 200 bytes of the first data packet, which is all we can compare). The keywords are always capitalized with a space after the colon and not before. In the "User-Agent" field, there are 5 possible values, all versions of *Mozilla* (Netscape or Internet Explorer).

In the 82,013 FIT HTTP requests, the version may be 1.0 or 1.1. (The data is newer). There are 8 commands: GET (99% of requests), HEAD, POST, OPTIONS, PROPFIND, LINK, and two malformed commands "No" and "tcp_close". There are 72 different keywords. Keywords are usually but not always capitalized, and the spacing around the colon is occasionally inconsistent. Some keywords are misspelled (*Connnection* with 3 n's, or the correctly spelled *Referrer* instead of the usual *Referer*). Some keywords are malformed ("XXXXXXX:" or "~~~~~~~:"). A few request lines are missing a carriage return before the linefeed. There are 807 user agents, of which 44% appear only once. The top five are:

- *Scooter/3.2*
- *googlebot/2.1*
- *ia_archiver*
- *Mozilla/3.01*
- *http://www.almaden.ibm.com/cs/crawler.*

SMTP Requests. In IDEVAL, the 18,241 SMTP mail requests are always initiated with a HELO or EHLO (echo hello) command. There are 3 different HELO arguments (identifying the local sender host name) and 24 different EHLO arguments (identifying the remote sender host name), all but one of which appear at least twice. In the 12,911 FIT SMTP requests there are 1839 different HELO arguments, of which 69% appear only once, and 1461 different EHLO arguments (58% appearing only once). In addition, 3% of FIT SMTP requests do not start with a HELO/EHLO handshake. (SMTP does not require it). Instead, they start with RSET, QUIT, EXPN, NOOP, or CONNECT. In none of the IDEVAL requests but 0.05% of the FIT requests, the SMTP command is lower case. Also, 0.1% of the FIT requests are malformed with binary data in the argument.

SSH Requests. An SSH request initiates with a string identifying the client version. In the 214 IDEVAL requests, the string is always "SSH-1.5-1.2.22". In the 666 FIT requests, there are 32 versions, of which 36% appear only once.

We are aware that a few unusual values are due to attacks, in particular, the unusual *Connnection* appears only in the *Nimda* worm, and *EXPN* appears in the security scan (*EXPN root*). However, the great majority of these values appear in what we believe is non-hostile traffic. Also, we do not claim that FIT statistics generalize to all sites. Nevertheless, the FIT traffic contains packets from tens of thousands of Internet sources with a plausible distribution. It would be difficult to suggest that the wide differences between FIT and IDEVAL are due to unsolicited inbound FIT traffic being atypical at the protocol levels we examined.

4   Evaluation with Mixed Traffic

We stated that two of the three preconditions for a simulation artifact are that the attribute must be well behaved in simulation, but poorly behaved in real traffic. Note that if we take the union of a well behaved and poorly behaved attribute, that the result is poorly behaved, i.e., the set of values is large and growing. This suggests that if we mix the IDEVAL traffic with real traffic, then simulation artifacts (if there are any) would be removed. This result is independent of whether the third precondition is met (that simulated attacks make the attribute poorly behaved). Also, if either the first or second precondition is not met, then we are not changing the statistics of the attribute (since they are the same in both traffic sources). This allows us to remove simulation artifacts even if we don't know where they are.

One difficulty with this approach is ensuring that the IDS cannot model the two traffic sources independently. For example, IDEVAL and FIT can be distinguished by the destination IP address, timestamp, the presence of some protocols, and probably many other attributes. If an IDS models the two sources independently, as in $P(\text{TTL} \mid \text{destination address})$, then we have two independent attributes, TTL | IDEVAL (which is well behaved and detects attacks), and TTL | FIT (which is poorly behaved and has no effect). We must analyze the IDS for such dependencies and then remove them either by modifying the IDS or the input data. For example, we could modify the IDS to model TTL unconditionally by ignoring the destination address, or we could map FIT addresses to IDEVAL before input to the IDS.

A second difficulty is that some attributes present in IDEVAL may be missing in the real traffic. For example, FIT has no *telnet* traffic, so any *telnet* model will be unaffected by mixing. We did not identify any simulation artifacts in *telnet*, but we cannot assume that none exist. To be sure, we must either modify IDEVAL to remove *telnet* traffic or modify the IDS to ignore it.

A third difficulty is that both traffic sources will generate false alarms, resulting in a higher rate than either source by itself. This is important because an IDS may be evaluated at a fixed false alarm rate.

A fourth difficulty is that mixed traffic has all of the problems of real traffic with regard to privacy, reproducibility, and independent comparison. Essentially we are testing an IDS on live traffic into which the labeled IDEVAL attacks have been injected. Although we are no longer testing on a standard benchmark, we are spared the effort of having to simulate and/or label the hostile traffic.

With these caveats, we propose to add real traffic to the IDEVAL data to make it appear as if it were being sent and received during the simulation. We do this by setting back the packet timestamps of the real traffic to correspond to the collection periods used in IDEVAL. We use this method rather than setting forward the IDEVAL timestamps because it simplifies the evaluation procedure. We do not have to adjust the timestamps of the IDEVAL alarms during evaluation.

Both the IDEVAL and real traffic sources may contain gaps in collection. The mixing procedure is to adjust the timestamps of the real traffic to remove the gaps, resulting in a contiguous trace, then adjust them again to insert gaps where they occur in IDEVAL (e.g. nights and weekends). Then the two traces are interleaved to create a single trace maintaining the chronological order of the new timestamps. The procedure is illustrated in Figure 1. It would also be possible to stretch or compress the real data to match the packet rate or duration of IDEVAL, although in our experiments the rates are already similar so we just discard any leftover real traffic.

5   Experimental Procedure

We wish to test whether the mixing procedure we propose actually removes unexplained detections, i.e. possible simulation artifacts. To do this, we test six anomaly detection systems on IDEVAL and on mixed data sets at fixed false alarm rates. When necessary, we modify the IDS or input data to avoid modeling attributes whose values originate solely from IDEVAL. We establish a criteria for detection legitimacy, essentially asking whether the IDS detects a feature of the attack. If mixing removes artifacts, then the fraction of detections judged legitimate should be higher when tested on mixed traffic.

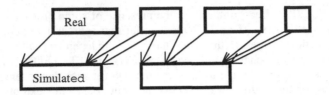

Fig. 1. Mapping real time into simulation time when there are gaps in collection in both data sets. Time reads from left to right

We test six anomaly detection systems: SAD, SPADE, PHAD, ALAD, LERAD, and NETAD. SAD is a trivially simple anomaly detector that exploits the artifacts described in Section 2 to achieve results competitive with the 1999 blind evaluation. The others are "real" systems as described previously. Space limitations prevent us from describing all of the experiments in detail, so we describe SAD, SPADE, and LERAD, then summarize the results for the others.

5.1 Mixed Data Preparation

We prepare three mixed data sets by mixing the 146 hours of filtered IDEVAL inside sniffer traffic from training week 3 and 197 hours of test weeks 4-5 with different portions of the 623 hours of filtered FIT traffic described in Section 3. We denote the filtered IDEVAL traffic as set S, and the three mixed sets as A, B, and C (Table 1). Each mixed set is constructed by mixing three of the ten weeks of FIT traffic into week 3, and 4 weeks into weeks 4-5. The traces are not compressed or stretched. Rather, leftover FIT traffic from the end of the 3 or 4 week period is discarded.

The traffic rates for IDEVAL and FIT are similar. After filtering, there are 1,101,653 IDEVAL packets from inside weeks 3-5 (about 3% of original, 0.9 packets per second), and 1,663,608 FIT packets (1.6% of original, 0.8 packets per second). The mixing program, TM, is available at [30].

Table 1. Mixed data sets used for evaluation. All data is filtered

Set	Training data	Test data
S	IDEVAL inside week 3	IDEVAL inside weeks 4-5
A	S + FIT weeks 1-3	S + FIT weeks 4-7
B	S + FIT weeks 4-6	S + FIT weeks 7-10
C	S + FIT weeks 7-9	S + FIT weeks 1-4

5.2 Evaluation Procedure

We evaluate each IDS by training on week 3 and testing on weeks 4 and 5 for sets S, A, B, and C. We use EVAL [30], our implementation of the 1999 IDEVAL detection criteria. IDEVAL requires that the IDS identify the victim IP address (or at least one if there are multiple targets) and the time of any portion of the attack with 60 seconds leeway, and assign a score for ranking alarms. Only attacks identified as "in-spec" are counted. Alarms identifying out of spec attacks are counted neither as detections nor false alarms.

An attack is in-spec if there is evidence for it in the data examined, and it is in one of the categories appropriate for the technique used. In the inside sniffer traffic, there is evidence for 177 attacks according to the IDEVAL truth labels. The most appropriate categories for network based systems are probes, denial of service (DOS) and remote to local (R2L). However we will consider all 177 attacks as in-spec, including user to root (U2R) and data (secrecy policy violation) attacks because they might be detectable due to artifacts. Normally such attacks would be difficult to detect because they are launched from a shell, which could be hidden from the IDS by encryption, e.g. *ssh*.

We usually set EVAL to report attacks detected at a threshold allowing 100 false alarms (10 per day), consistent with the 1999 evaluation.

In order to reduce alarm floods, we evaluate all systems after consolidating duplicate alarms (using AFIL [30]) that identify the same target within a 60 second window prior to evaluation. After consolidation, the group of alarms is replaced with the single alarm with the highest anomaly score.

5.3 Criteria for Legitimate Detection

Most of the systems we examine identify the anomaly that is responsible (or most responsible) for each alarm. To answer the question of whether mixed traffic removes simulation artifacts, we must decide whether the anomaly was a "legitimate" feature of the attack, or of the IDEVAL simulation. Because this is a subjective judgment, we establish the following criteria:

- Source address is legitimate for denial of service (DOS) attacks that spoof it, or if the attack is on an authenticated service (e.g. telnet, auth, SSH, POP3, IMAP, SNMP, syslog, etc), and the system makes such distinctions. FTP is anonymous in IDEVAL, so we consider it public.

- Destination address is legitimate for probes that scan addresses, e.g. *ipsweep*.

- Destination port is legitimate for probes that scan or access unused ports, e.g. *portsweep, mscan, satan*. It is debatable whether it is legitimate for attacks on a single port, but we will allow them.

- TCP state anomalies (flags, duration) are legitimate for DOS attacks that disrupt traffic (*arppoison, tcpreset*), or crash the target (*ntfsdos, dosnuke*).

- IP fragmentation is legitimate in attacks that generate fragments (*teardrop, pod*).

- Packet header anomalies other than addresses and ports are legitimate if a probe or DOS attack requires raw socket programming, where the attacker must put arbitrary values in these fields.

- Application payload anomalies are legitimate in attacks on servers (usually R2L attacks, but may be probes or DOS).

- TCP stream length is legitimate for buffer overflows.

- No network feature should legitimately detect a U2R or Data attack.

5.4 Experimental Results

5.4.1 SAD

SAD [30] is a trivially Simple Anomaly Detector which we developed for this paper to illustrate how simulation artifacts can be exploited in IDEVAL. SAD examines one byte at a fixed offset (specified as a parameter, e.g. TTL) of inbound TCP SYN packets. During training, SAD records which of the 256 possible values are observed at least once. During testing, it detects an anomaly if the value was never observed in training. If there have been no other anomalies in the last 60 seconds, it outputs an alarm with a score of 1. (The alarms are not ranked).

To find good parameters to SAD, we evaluate it on IDEVAL weeks 1 and 2, which was available in advance to the original 1999 participants for development. Week 1 is attack-free training data, and week 2 contains 43 labeled instances of 18 of the 58 attacks from the test set. We identify good parameters to SAD, defined as any that detect at least 2 attacks with no more than 50 false alarms (10 per day). We find 16 parameters that meet this requirement and submit them for testing.

Before any system can be tested on mixed traffic, we must answer the two questions posed in Section 4: are there any IDEVAL attributes missing from the FIT data, and can SAD model any aspect of the two traffic sources independently? The answer to both questions is no, so no modifications to SAD or the input data are needed. To answer the first question, there are 154,057 IDEVAL and 125,834 FIT inbound TCP SYN packets in set C, regardless of the parameter used, with similar numbers for sets A and B. To answer the second question, the model makes no distinction between the two traffic sources. We focus on set C throughout this paper because in most of the systems we test, the number of detections is intermediate between A and B.

The results for the 16 SAD parameters is shown in Table 2 for weeks 1-2 and for sets S and C. (Results for A and B are similar to C). The results for S are competitive with the top four systems in the 1999 evaluation, which detected 40% to 55% in-spec attacks at 100 false alarms [1]. We make two important observations. First, results from the development set (weeks 1-2) are a good predictor of results in the test set (weeks 3-5). Second, results from IDEVAL are a poor predictor of performance when FIT background traffic is mixed in.

We will not discuss the attacks detected in set S in detail except to say that most fail the criteria for legitimacy described in Section 5.3. For example, SAD detects many attacks on public services such as HTTP, SMTP, and DNS by source address anomalies. On set C, SAD detects only *neptune* (excluding coincidental detections) by an anomaly (10 or 11) in the high byte. This attack (a SYN flood) forges the source address with random values, including invalid addresses such as 10.x.x.x. The TTL detections in C (*land, portsweep, queso*) are all for attacks that manipulate low level protocols through raw socket programming, which again passes our legitimacy criteria.

5.4.2 SPADE

SPADE [27] models various joint probabilities of address/port combinations in inbound TCP SYN packets based on their observed frequency. It assigns an anomaly score of $1/p$, where p is the probability of the current values, calculated by n_i/n, where the current combination of values was observed n_v times out of n total packets (including the current packet to avoid division by 0). There is no specific training period. All packets are added to the training model after evaluation.

Table 2. Number and percentage of attacks detected (Det) and number of false alarms (FA) by SAD in weeks 1-2 (out of 43 attacks) and in sets S and C (out of 177 attacks)

SAD Byte	Weeks 1-2		Weeks 3-5 (S)		Mixed Set C	
	Det/43	FA	Det/177	FA	Det/177	FA
IP packet size, 2nd byte	4 (9%)	0	15 (8%)	2	0	1
TTL	25 (58%)	36	24 (14%)	4	5 (3%)	43
Source address, 1st byte	13 (30%)	7	64 (36%)	41	4 (2%)	0
Source address, 2nd byte	13 (30%)	7	67 (38%)	43	0	0
Source address, 3rd byte	16 (37%)	15	79 (45%)	43	0	0
Source address, 4th byte	17 (40%)	14	71 (40%)	16	0	0
Source port, 1st byte	2 (5%)	0	13 (7%)	0	0	0
Dest. port, 1st byte	4 (9%)	24	4 (2%)	0	4 (2%)	1664
Dest. port, 2nd byte	5 (12%)	6	0	0	0	0
TCP header size	4 (9%)	0	15 (8%)	2	0	5
TCP window size, 1st	5 (12%)	1	15 (8%)	2	7 (4%)	112
TCP window size, 2nd	3 (7%)	1	7 (4%)	1	4 (2%)	29
TCP options, 1st-3rd	4 (9%)	4	15 (8%)	2	0	1
TCP options, 4th byte	4 (9%)	4	15 (8%)	2	0	255

There are four user selectable probability modes, as shown in Table 3. The default mode is P(DA, DP) (destination address and port). However, DA is untestable with our data (since there is only one new destination address), and we did not find any evidence that DP is less well behaved in FIT than in IDEVAL. However, in mode P(DA, DP, SA) (destination address and port, and source address), the addition of FIT traffic should mask detections if SA is unrealistic, as we suspect. Two other modes include the source port (SP), which does not normally contain useful information.

Because DA carries information that can distinguish FIT and IDEVAL traffic, we modify the FIT traffic so that SPADE cannot make this distinction directly. SPADE monitors only TCP SYN packets, so our input to SPADE consists solely of TCP SYN packets from the two data sets. For each packet from the time-shifted FIT data, we randomly and independently replace the destination IP address with the IP address of one of the four IDEVAL victims (pascal, zeno, marx, or hume). This makes it appear to SPADE as if there are four copies of each FIT server on the four victims, each receiving one fourth of the FIT inbound traffic. IDEVAL addresses were not modified.

We tested SPADE version v092200.1, which is built into SNORT 1.7 Win32 [29]. We used sets S, A, B, and C. All SPADE options were set to their default values, and all SNORT rules other than SPADE were turned off. SPADE does not have separate training and test modes, so we ran it on weeks 3 through 5 continuously, discarding all alarms in week 3. SPADE uses an adaptive threshold with various parameters to control alarm reporting. However we used the raw score reported by SPADE instead. The default threshold allows thousands of false alarms so we do not believe that any were lost.

Results are shown in Table 3 for each of the four probability modes. We used a threshold of 200 false alarms rather than 100 because the numbers are low. SPADE detects about half as many attacks at 100 false alarms.

Table 3. Attacks detected by SPADE at 200 false alarms according to EVAL on filtered inside sniffer weeks 3-5 (S) and when mixed with FIT traffic (A, B, C) in each probability mode

SPADE detections at 200 false alarms	S	A, B, C
0: P(SA, SP, DA)P(SA, SP, DP)/P(SA, SP)	6	6, 6, 7
1: P(DA, DP, SA, SP)	1	0, 0, 0
2: P(DA, DP, SA)	6	2, 1, 1
3: P(DA, DP) (default)	8	9, 8, 7

Probability modes 0 and 1 include the source port (SP), which is normally picked randomly by the client and would not be expected to yield useful information. The six attacks detected in mode 0 on set S are *insidesniffer, syslogd, mscan, tcpreset, arppoison,* and *smurf.* All but *mscan* are probably coincidental because the others generate no TCP SYN packets. However, all but *syslogd* target multiple hosts, increasing the likelihood of a coincidental alarm for one of the targets.

However modes 2 and 3 show the effects of mixing clearly. We have previously identified source address (SA) as an artifact. We now find that adding FIT data removes most of the detections from mode 2, which uses SA, but not from mode 3, which does not. On S, mode 2 detects *guest, syslogd, insidesniffer, perl, mscan,* and *crashiis.* By our previously mentioned criteria, *guest* (telnet password guessing) could legitimately be detected by SA, and *mscan* (a probe for multiple vulnerabilities on a range of hosts) by destination address or port (DA or DP). We do not count *syslogd* or *insidesniffer* (no TCP traffic), *perl* (a U2R attack), or *crashiis* (an HTTP attack) as legitimate.

SPADE in mode 2 detects only *mscan* on all three mixed sets. On A, it also detects *portsweep,* which also can legitimately be detected by DP. Thus, our results are consistent with the claim that SA (but not DP) is an artifact and that the artifact is removed in mixed traffic. When FIT traffic is added, the fraction of legitimate detections goes from 2/6 to 1/1 (or 2/2 on set A).

5.4.3   LERAD

LERAD [8] models inbound client TCP streams. It learns conditional rules of the form "if $A_1 = v_1$ and $A_2 = v_2$ and ... and $A_k = v_k$ then $A \in V = \{v_{k+1}, ... v_{k+r}\}$", where the A_i are nominal attributes and the v_i are values. If LERAD observes a test stream which satisfies a rule antecedent but the value is not in V, then it assigns an anomaly score of tn/r where t is the time since the last anomaly for that rule, n is the number of training streams satisfying the antecedent, and $r = |V|$, the size of the set of values observed at least once in training. The attributes are the individual bytes of the source and destination address, the source and destination ports, stream length and duration (quantized log base 2), the TCP flags of the first and last two packets (as 3 attributes), and the first 8 words (separated by white space) in the application payload. LERAD uses a randomized learning algorithm to generate candidate rules with high n/r. It then discards rules likely to generate false alarms by using the last 10% of the training data as a validation set, discarding any rule that generates an alarm (known to be false) during this time. A typical run results in 60-80 rules after discarding 10-20% of them during validation.

To make sure that the rules generated by LERAD do not distinguish between the IDEVAL and FIT data, we modified LERAD to weight rules by the fraction of FIT traffic (identified by destination address) satisfying the antecedent in training. However, we find in practice that this weighting has very little effect. Almost all of the rules are satisfied by a significant fraction of FIT traffic. The effect of weighting is to decrease the number of detections in mixed traffic by less than 3%.

We also modified the TCP stream reassembly algorithm to handle truncated and filtered traffic. The IDEVAL data contains complete packets, allowing streams to be reassembled completely. However, truncated TCP packets would leave gaps. Thus, we truncate the stream after the first 134 bytes of the first payload packet to match the maximum payload size of the filtered traffic. The TF filter also removes closing TCP flags. Therefore we also modify the TCP flag attributes to be the flags of the last three packets up through the payload, instead of the first and last two packets in the completely reassembled stream. The modified reassembly is applied to both the IDEVAL and FIT traffic.

In 5 runs on set S, EVAL detects 87, 88, 80, 85, and 91 attacks. (The loss of detections, compared to about 114 on unfiltered traffic, is due mostly to the loss of TCP flags and some of the payload). On one run each on sets A, B, and C, the modified LERAD detects 29, 30, and 30 in-spec attacks. A typical run on these data sets now results in 30-40 rules after removing 50% of the rules in the validation phase.

In Table 4, we list attacks detected in sets S and C categorized by the attribute that contributes the most to the anomaly score. In each category we list the legitimate detections first, separated from the non-legitimate detections by a slash. By our criteria in Section 5.2, 56% of the attack instances detected in S are legitimate, compared to 83% in set C. All of the non-legitimate detections in C are due to destination address anomalies, which we cannot remove because the FIT traffic introduces only one new address. Sets A and B give results similar to C.

Table 4. Legitimate and total number of attacks detected by LERAD at 100 false alarms on sets S and C. The notation l/d: l_1, l_2.../n_1, n_2... means that l attack instances were legitimately detected out of d total detections. The legitimate attack types are l_1, l_2... and the non-legitimate attack types are n_1, n_2, ...

Attribute	Legitimate/Detected in S	Legitimate/Detected in C
Source address	8/26: dict, guesstelnet, guest, sshprocesstable, sshtrojan / casesen, crashiis, fdformat, ffbconfig, guessftp, netbus, netcat_setup, perl, ps, sechole, sqlattack, xterm, warezclient, warezmaster	0/0
Destination address	1/6: mscan / ncftp, guesstelnet	1/6: mscan / ncftp, guesstelnet
Destination port	14/14: ftpwrite, guesspop, imap, ls_domain, satan, named, neptune, netcat, netcat_breakin	11/11: ftpwrite, ls_domain, satan, named, netcat, netcat_breakin,
Payload	22/29: apache2, back, crashiis, imap, mailbomb, ntinfoscan, phf, satan, sendmail / guesstelnet, portsweep, yaga	8/8: back, imap, ntinfoscan, phf, satan, sendmail
Duration	0/1: insidesniffer	0/0
Length	0/2: netbus, ppmacro	1/1: sendmail
TCP flags	4/9: dosnuke / back, loadmodule, sendmail	4/4: dosnuke
Total	49/87 (56%)	25/30 (83%)

5.5 Results Summary

We tested SAD, SPADE and LERAD on mixed data, and found by an analysis of the detected attacks that suspected simulation artifacts in IDEVAL were removed. These are primarily source address anomalies, but also include some application payload and TCP flag anomalies in LERAD. Destination address anomalies could not be removed in either system.

We also reached similar conclusions in tests on three of our other systems, PHAD, ALAD and NETAD. We modified all programs so that no rule depends exclusively on simulated data. We present only a summary of the results here. Details are given in [33].

PHAD models Ethernet, IP, TCP, UDP, and ICMP packet header fields without regard to direction (inbound or outbound). No modification was needed because all of these packet types occur in the real traffic. In the results presented in Table 5, most of the non-legitimate detections are due to destination address. PHAD does not include the TTL field, because it is a known artifact, but in another experiment when we added it back in, we found that mixing real traffic removed the artifact.

ALAD models TCP streams like LERAD, but uses fixed rather than learned rules. We modified these rules to remove dependencies on the destination address, which would distinguish the real traffic. We also removed rules for application payloads other than HTTP, SMTP, and SSH. We used LERAD's modified TCP stream reassembly algorithm to handle truncated and filtered packets. The result of injecting FIT traffic was to increase the fraction of legitimate detections, mostly by removing detections by source address.

NETAD models packets, like PHAD, but for several types such as inbound TCP, inbound TCP SYN, HTTP, SMTP, telnet, and FTP. We removed the telnet and FTP rules. Again, the fraction of legitimate detections was increased, mostly by removing source address and TCP window size anomalies, which were the dominant means of detecting attacks in IDEVAL.

The results are summarized in Table 5. The original number of detections is the number reported in the literature at 100 false alarms when trained on inside week 3 and tested on weeks 4-5 before the data is filtered or the algorithm is modified. For sets S and C we show the number of legitimate and total detections, and the percentage legitimate. Set C generally resulted in a number of detections between those of sets A and B, and is therefore the most representative of the mixed results. In every case, the fraction of legitimate detections increases when mixed data is used.

Table 5. Legitimate and total detections at 100 false alarms on sets S and C. The original results are the published results based on the unmodified algorithm on unfiltered data (inside weeks 3-5). The notation l/d means that l detections are legitimate out of d total detections.

System	Original	Legit/S (pct)	Legit/C (pct)
SPADE, mode 2		2/6 (33%)	1/1 (100%)
PHAD	54	31/51 (61%)	19/23 (83%)
ALAD	59	16/47 (34%)	10/12 (83%)
LERAD (avg.)	114	49/87 (56%)	25/30 (83%)
NETAD	132	61/128 (48%)	27/41 (67%)

6 Concluding Remarks

We analyzed attack-free inbound client background traffic in the DARPA/Lincoln Laboratory IDS evaluation and compared it with Internet traffic from thousands of clients collected in one environment. Based on this comparison, we concluded that many attributes meet two of the three conditions required for simulation artifacts: they are well behaved in simulation but poorly behaved in our sample of real traffic. Some of these attributes meet the third condition by differing systematically in the simulated attacks, as demonstrated by a trivially simple network anomaly detector that competes with the top systems in the 1999 evaluation. The suspected artifacts are the client source IP address, TTL, TCP window size, and TCP options. We also suspect that most of the application protocols contain artifacts, as they satisfy the first two conditions and many attacks exploit these protocols. We have enough data to test only HTTP, SMTP, and *ssh*, and found that all three protocols meet the first two requirements.

We propose that mixing real traffic into the DARPA set will remove artifacts because it turns well behaved attributes into poorly behaved ones, so that the first condition is no longer satisfied whenever the second one is. This procedure does not require that we know where the artifacts are. However, it will fail if the IDS is able to model any attribute in the two traffic sources independently or if any attributes modeled by the IDS are missing in the real traffic. We must analyze and possibly modify both the IDS and the real traffic to ensure that this does not happen. We also lose the advantage of independent testing and comparison due to privacy issues inherent with real traffic. These costs must be weighed against the advantage of using the rich set of labeled attacks available in the DARPA set.

Our work is based on comparison and mixing with real traffic collected from only one environment. However, as we used unsolicited inbound traffic from tens of thousands of sources on the Internet, we believe it is representative with regard to one important characteristic: that poorly behaved attributes with power law distributions are prevalent in real traffic and are underrepresented in the DARPA set. Furthermore, our finding of non-legitimate detections in the DARPA set (e.g. source address anomalies in web server attacks) is independent of our source of real traffic.

We do not make any claims about how the six anomaly detection systems we tested would perform on real traffic. Any results we presented on mixed traffic would apply only to the one real source of traffic that we used, are not reproducible, and would have to be adjusted to account for the two sources of false alarms. The important result is that the fraction of legitimate detection is higher on (our) mixed traffic in all six cases.

We analyzed only the inside sniffer traffic in the 1999 evaluation. It is likely that simulation artifacts exist in the outside sniffer traffic, and also in the 1998 evaluation (from which the 1999 KDD cup data was generated), because the same methodology was used to generate this data. We did not address whether the attacks were simulated correctly, although we have no reason to believe that they were not, as they were taken mostly from published sources. Also, we did not address issues related to any host based data. We indicated a problem (and a solution) with regard to the evaluation of network anomaly detection systems using the DARPA set, but we cannot make any claims with regard to network signature detection or any type of host based detection.

Acknowledgments

This research is partially supported by DARPA (F30602-00-1-0603).

References

1. R. Lippmann, et al., "The 1999 DARPA Off-Line Intrusion Detection Evaluation", Computer Networks 34(4) 579-595, 2000. Data is available at
http://www.ll.mit.edu/IST/ideval/
2. Lippmann, R.P. and J. Haines, Analysis and Results of the 1999 DARPA Off-Line Intrusion Detection Evaluation, in Recent Advances in Intrusion Detection, Third International Workshop, Proc. RAID 2000, 162-182.
3. J. W. Haines, R.P. Lippmann, D.J. Fried, M.A. Zissman, E. Tran, and S.B. Boswell, "1999 DARPA Intrusion Detection Evaluation: Design and Procedures", Lexington MA: MIT Lincoln Laboratory, 2001.
4. D. Barbara, Wu, S. Jajodia, "Detecting Novel Network Attacks using Bayes Estimators", Proc. SIAM Intl. Data Mining Conference, 2001.
5. A.Valdes, K. Skinner, "Adaptive, Model-based Monitoring for Cyber Attack Detection", Proc. RAID 2000, 80-92.
6. M. Mahoney, P. K. Chan, "PHAD: Packet Header Anomaly Detection for Identifying Hostile Network Traffic", Florida Tech. technical report CS-2001-04, http://cs.fit.edu/~tr/
7. M. Mahoney, P. K. Chan, "Learning Nonstationary Models of Normal Network Traffic for Detecting Novel Attacks ", Proc. SIGKDD 2002, 376-385.
8. M. Mahoney, P. K. Chan, "Learning Models of Network Traffic for Detecting Novel Attacks", Florida Tech. technical report CS-2002-08, http://cs.fit.edu/~tr/
9. M. Mahoney, "Network Traffic Anomaly Detection Based on Packet Bytes", Proc. ACM-SAC 2003.
10. E. Eskin, "Anomaly Detection over Noisy Data using Learned Probability Distributions", Proc. Intl. Conf. Machine Learning, 2000.
11. E. Eskin, A. Arnold, M, Prerau, L. Portnoy & S. Stolfo. "A Geometric Framework for Unsupervised Anomaly Detection: Detecting Intrusions in Unlabeled Data", In D. Barbara and S. Jajodia (editors), *Applications of Data Mining in Computer Security*, Kluwer, 2002.
12. A.K. Ghosh, A. Schwartzbard, "A Study in Using Neural Networks for Anomaly and Misuse Detection", Proc. 8'th USENIX Security Symposium 1999.
13. Y. Liao and V. R. Vemuri, "Use of Text Categorization Techniques for Intrusion Detection", Proc. 11th USENIX Security Symposium 2002, 51-59.
14. P. G. Neumann, P. A. Porras, "Experience with EMERALD to DATE", Proc. 1st USENIX Workshop on Intrusion Detection and Network Monitoring 1999, 73-80.
15. A. Schwartzbard and A.K. Ghosh, "A Study in the Feasibility of Performing Host-based Anomaly Detection on Windows NT", Proc. RAID 1999.
16. R. Sekar, A. Gupta, J. Frullo, T. Shanbhag, S. Zhou, A. Tiwari and H. Yang, "Specification Based Anomaly Detection: A New Approach for Detecting Network Intrusions", Proc. ACM CCS, 2002.
17. R. Sekar and P. Uppuluri, "Synthesizing Fast Intrusion Prevention/Detection Systems from High-Level Specifications", Proc. 8th USENIX Security Symposium 1999.
18. M. Tyson, P. Berry, N. Williams, D. Moran, D. Blei, "DERBI: Diagnosis, Explanation and Recovery from computer Break-Ins",
http://www.ai.sri.com/~derbi/, 2000.
19. G. Vigna, S.T. Eckmann, and R.A. Kemmerer, "The STAT Tool Suite", Proc. 2000 DARPA Information Survivability Conference and Exposition (DISCEX), IEEE Press, 2000.
20. G. Vigna and R. Kemmerer, "NetSTAT: A Network-based Intrusion Detection System", Journal of Computer Security, 7(1), IOS Press, 1999.

21. C. Elkan, "Results of the KDD'99 Classifier Learning Contest",
    http://www.cs.ucsd.edu/users/elkan/clresults.html (1999)
22. L. Portnoy, "Intrusion Detection with Unlabeled Data Using Clustering", Undergraduate
    Thesis, Columbia University, 2000
23. K. Yamanishi, J. Takeuchi & G. Williams, "On-line Unsupervised Outlier Detection Using
    Finite Mixtures with Discounting Learning Algorithms", Proc. KDD 2000, 320-324.
24. V. Paxson, The Internet Traffic Archive, http://ita.ee.lbl.gov/ (2002).
25. S. Forrest, Computer Immune Systems, Data Sets and Software,
    http://www.cs.unm.edu/~immsec/data-sets.htm (2002).
26. J. McHugh, "Testing Intrusion Detection Systems: A Critique of the 1998 and 1999
    DARPA Intrusion Detection System Evaluations as Performed by Lincoln Laboratory",
    Proc. ACM TISSEC 3(4) 2000, 262-294.
27. J. Hoagland, SPADE, Silicon Defense,
    http://www.silicondefense.com/software/spice/ (2000).
28. T. H. Ptacek & T. N. Newsham (1998), Insertion, Evasion, and Denial of Service: Eluding
    Network Intrusion Detection,
    http://www.robertgraham.com/mirror/Ptacek-Newsham-Evasion-98.html
29. M. Roesch, "Snort - Lightweight Intrusion Detection for Networks", Proc. USENIX Lisa
    1999.
30. M. Mahoney, Source code for PHAD, ALAD, LERAD, NETAD, SAD, EVAL, TF, TM,
    and AFIL is available at http://cs.fit.edu/~mmahoney/dist/
31. L. A. Adamic, "Zipf, Power-laws, and Pareto - A Ranking Tutorial",
    http://ginger.hpl.hp.com/shl/papers/ranking/ranking.html (2002).
32. B. A. Huberman, L. A. Adamic, "The Nature of Markets in the World Wide Web",
    http://ideas.uqam.ca/ideas/data/Papers/scescecf9521.html (1999).
33. M. Mahoney, "A Machine Learning Approach to Detecting Attacks by Identifying
    Anomalies in Network Traffic", Ph.D. dissertation, Florida Institute of Technology, 2003.

Author Index

Lecture Notes in Computer Science

For information about Vols. 1–2721
please contact your bookseller or Springer-Verlag

Vol. 2758: D. Basin, B. Wolff (Eds.), Theorem Proving in Higher Order Logics. Proceedings, 2003. X, 367 pages. 2003.

Vol. 2759: O.H. Ibarra, Z. Dang (Eds.), Implementation and Application of Automata. Proceedings, 2003. XI, 312 pages. 2003.

Vol. 2761: R. Amadio, D. Lugiez (Eds.), CONCUR 2003 - Concurrency Theory. Proceedings, 2003. XI, 524 pages. 2003.

Vol. 2762: G. Dong, C. Tang, W. Wang (Eds.), Advances in Web-Age Information Management. Proceedings, 2003. XIII, 512 pages. 2003.

Vol. 2763: V. Malyshkin (Ed.), Parallel Computing Technologies. Proceedings, 2003. XIII, 570 pages. 2003.

Vol. 2764: S. Arora, K. Jansen, J.D.P. Rolim, A. Sahai (Eds.), Approximation, Randomization, and Combinatorial Optimization. Proceedings, 2003. IX, 409 pages. 2003.

Vol. 2765: R. Conradi, A.I. Wang (Eds.), Empirical Methods and Studies in Software Engineering. VIII, 279 pages. 2003.

Vol. 2766: S. Behnke, Hierarchical Neural Networks for Image Interpretation. XII, 224 pages. 2003.

Vol. 2768: M.J. Wilson, R.R. Martin (Eds.), Mathematics of Surfaces. Proceedings, 2003. VIII, 393 pages. 2003.

Vol. 2769: T. Koch, I. T. Sølvberg (Eds.), Research and Advanced Technology for Digital Libraries. Proceedings, 2003. XV, 536 pages. 2003.

Vol. 2773: V. Palade, R.J. Howlett, L. Jain (Eds.), Knowledge-Based Intelligent Information and Engineering Systems. Proceedings, Part I, 2003. LI, 1473 pages. 2003. (Subseries LNAI).

Vol. 2774: V. Palade, R.J. Howlett, L. Jain (Eds.), Knowledge-Based Intelligent Information and Engineering Systems. Proceedings, Part II, 2003. LI, 1443 pages. 2003. (Subseries LNAI).

Vol. 2776: V. Gorodetsky, L. Popyack, V. Skormin (Eds.), Computer Network Security. Proceedings, 2003. XIV, 470 pages. 2003.

Vol. 2777: B. Schölkopf, M.K. Warmuth (Eds.), Learning Theory and Kernel Machines. Proceedings, 2003. XIV, 746 pages. 2003. (Subseries LNAI).

Vol. 2778: P.Y.K. Cheung, G.A. Constantinides, J.T. de Sousa (Eds.), Field-Programmable Logic and Applications. Proceedings, 2003. XXVI, 1179 pages. 2003.

Vol. 2779: C.D. Walter, Ç.K. Koç, C. Paar (Eds.), Cryptographic Hardware and Embedded Systems – CHES 2003. Proceedings, 2003. XIII, 441 pages. 2003.

Vol. 2781: B. Michaelis, G. Krell (Eds.), Pattern Recognition. Proceedings, 2003. XVII, 621 pages. 2003.

Vol. 2782: M. Klusch, A. Omicini, S. Ossowski, H. Laamanen (Eds.), Cooperative Information Agents VII. Proceedings, 2003. XI, 345 pages. 2003. (Subseries LNAI).

Vol. 2783: W. Zhou, P. Nicholson, B. Corbitt, J. Fong (Eds.), Advances in Web-Based Learning – ICWL 2003. Proceedings, 2003. XV, 552 pages. 2003.

Vol. 2786: F. Oquendo (Ed.), Software Process Technology. Proceedings, 2003. X, 173 pages. 2003.

Vol. 2787: J. Timmis, P. Bentley, E. Hart (Eds.), Artificial Immune Systems. Proceedings, 2003. XI, 299 pages. 2003.

Vol. 2789: L. Böszörményi, P. Schojer (Eds.), Modular Programming Languages. Proceedings, 2003. XIII, 271 pages. 2003.

Vol. 2790: H. Kosch, L. Böszörményi, H. Hellwagner (Eds.), Euro-Par 2003 Parallel Processing. Proceedings, 2003. XXXV, 1320 pages. 2003.

Vol. 2792: T. Rist, R. Aylett, D. Ballin, J. Rickel (Eds.), Intelligent Virtual Agents. Proceedings, 2003. XV, 364 pages. 2003. (Subseries LNAI).

Vol. 2794: P. Kemper, W. H. Sanders (Eds.), Computer Performance Evaluation. Proceedings, 2003. X, 309 pages. 2003.

Vol. 2795: L. Chittaro (Ed.), Human-Computer Interaction with Mobile Devices and Services. Proceedings, 2003. XV, 494 pages. 2003.

Vol. 2796: M. Cialdea Mayer, F. Pirri (Eds.), Automated Reasoning with Analytic Tableaux and Related Methods. Proceedings, 2003. X, 271 pages. 2003. (Subseries LNAI).

Vol. 2798: L. Kalinichenko, R. Manthey, B. Thalheim, U. Wloka (Eds.), Advances in Databases and Information Systems. Proceedings, 2003. XIII, 431 pages. 2003.

Vol. 2799: J.J. Chico, E. Macii (Eds.), Integrated Circuit and System Design. Proceedings, 2003. XVII, 631 pages. 2003.

Vol. 2801: W. Banzhaf, T. Christaller, P. Dittrich, J.T. Kim, J. Ziegler (Eds.), Advances in Artificial Life. Proceedings, 2003. XVI, 905 pages. 2003. (Subseries LNAI).

Vol. 2803: M. Baaz, J.A. Makowsky (Eds.), Computer Science Logic. Proceedings, 2003. XII, 589 pages. 2003.

Vol. 2805: K. Araki, S. Gnesi, D. Mandrioli (Eds.), FME 2003: Formal Methods. Proceedings, 2003. XVII, 942 pages. 2003.

Vol. 2807: V. Matoušek, P. Mautner (Eds.), Text, Speech and Dialogue. Proceedings, 2003. XIII, 426 pages. 2003. (Subseries LNAI).

Vol. 2810: M.R. Berthold, H.-J. Lenz, E. Bradley, R. Kruse, C. Borgelt (Eds.), Advances in Intelligent Data Analysis V. Proceedings, 2003. XV, 624 pages. 2003.

Vol. 2812: G. Benson, R. Page (Eds.), Algorithms in Bioinformatics. Proceedings, 2003. X, 528 pages. 2003. (Subseries LNBI).

Vol. 2817: D. Konstantas, M. Leonard, Y. Pigneur, S. Patel (Eds.), Object-Oriented Information Systems. Proceedings, 2003. XII, 426 pages. 2003.

Vol. 2818: H. Blanken, T. Grabs, H.-J. Schek, R. Schenkel, G. Weikum (Eds.), Intelligent Search on XML Data. XVII, 319 pages. 2003.

Vol. 2820: G. Vigna, E. Jonsson, C. Kruegel (Eds.), Recent Advances in Intrusion Detection. Proceedings, 2003. X, 239 pages. 2003.

Vol. 2821: A. Günter, R. Kruse, B. Neumann (Eds.), KI 2003: Advances in Artificial Intelligence. Proceedings, 2003. XII, 662 pages. 2003. (Subseries LNAI).

Vol. 2832: G. Di Battista, U. Zwick (Eds.), Algorithms – ESA 2003. Proceedings, 2003. XIV, 790 pages. 2003.

Vol. 2834: X. Zhou, S. Jähnichen, M. Xu, J. Cao (Eds.), Advanced Parallel Processing Technologies. Proceedings, 2003. XIV, 679 pages. 2003.

Vol. 2839: A. Marshall, N. Agoulmine (Eds.), Management of Multimedia Networks and Services. Proceedings, 2003. XIV, 532 pages. 2003.